Service

ZIMBABWE

PHILIP BARCLAY is a British diplomat who lived and worked in Zimbabwe between 2006 and 2009. He has written several articles about Zimbabwe for the *Sunday Times* and the *Guardian Online*. *Zimbabwe* is Philip Barclay's first book. He lives in London and Ankara, Turkey.

ZIMBABWE
YEARS OF HOPE AND DESPAIR

PHILIP BARCLAY

B L O O M S B U R Y

LONDON · BERLIN · NEW YORK · SYDNEY

First published in Great Britain 2010
This paperback edition published 2011

Bloomsbury Publishing Plc
36 Soho Square
London W1D 3QY

www.bloomsbury.com

Bloomsbury Publishing, London, New York, Berlin and Sydney
A CIP catalogue record for this book is available from the British Library

ISBN 978 1 4088 0978 5
10 9 8 7 6 5 4 3 2 1

Typeset by Hewer Text UK Ltd, Edinburgh
Printed in Great Britain by Clays Limited, St Ives plc

MIX
Paper from
responsible sources
FSC
www.fsc.org
FSC® C018072

Contents

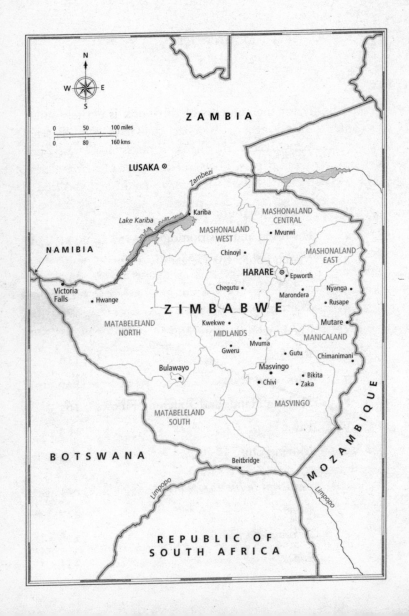

PREFACE

Responsibility for the contents of this book is entirely mine. Its contents do not necessarily reflect the views of the Foreign Office. While I worked at the British Embassy in Harare I had access to classified papers. I have made no use of that material, as it is not mine to share. There may be authors who find it profitable to betray confidence placed in them only because of their diplomatic position, but I am not one of them.

But this does not make my story wilfully incomplete. I have felt free to use material which was readily available to any well-connected person on the ground. Zimbabweans are remarkably indiscreet and are happy to gossip and leak to just about anyone. Communications supposedly secret at 10 a.m. were invariably common currency on the Chitungwiza combi* by the evening. So this book betrays no genuine confidence, but tells what I believe to be the full story.

While I have been happy to repeat what politicians told me, I have of course concealed the identities of most of the ordinary people who gave me stories and information, particularly when they were working at great personal risk for human rights groups, trade unions or other civil society organisations.

It would not be right to name any of my colleagues at the Embassy in Harare, but I am very grateful to them all for their

---

* 'Combi' is a contraction of 'commuter omnibus'. Combis are typically minibuses packed with seated and standing passengers.

friendship and collegiality. Many of the experiences I had were shared with others. My time in Zimbabwe would simply not have been possible without the help and work of others whom I have not named.

Introduction

I was sitting on the grass in Harare Gardens. The city was dark about me, without electricity as usual, but for once I didn't mind. The lack of light pollution allowed the stars and the thick smudge of the Milky Way to stand out vividly. The darkness was embracing, not frightening. I was waiting with my wife and my friends and 3,000 excited Zimbabweans for the show to begin.

One hundred kilometres away in Mvurwi, a young political activist getting ready for bed was disturbed by a knock on the door. Deceived by the quietness of the knock and by the peaceful atmosphere that had prevailed in the town for the last few months he opened the door readily. Outside were six teenagers from another village, armed with sticks, pangas* and knobkerries. The young men grabbed the activist and began to beat him right outside his house.

In my dark imagining of that beating, I see an older man with a bristling black beard, stocky in a tight-fitting t-shirt which carries the face of Robert Mugabe and the slogan '100% empowerment'. The older man is directing the beating and calls a halt after about forty minutes. They leave the activist, who works for a rival party, unconscious and bleeding, but not yet dead.

The young activist might perhaps have lived if his friends had found a way to get him to a medical centre away from Mvurwi. But they had no vehicle and instead tried to take him to the local mission hospital the next morning. As they wheeled him along in a handcart, they came across more young men in Mugabe t-shirts

* A panga is a broad-bladed machete.

– these groups were suddenly everywhere. These new attackers dragged the activist out of his makeshift stretcher and loaded him like a sack of mealie on to their new Chinese-made pick-up truck. His body, beaten again and now crushed and gaping, was found by the side of the road the next day.

In Harare Gardens, the lights of the main stage at the International Arts Festival, powered by a generator on the other side of the park, came on. Performers started to sing traditional songs of love and freedom. Riot police – theatrical but frightening – suddenly charged on to the stage. The singers were bound and tied, their songs not just silenced but stolen.

The Arts Festival was just a charade of course, albeit a brave and brilliant one. But the performance was apt. Out in the country, away from the lights, Zimbabweans had shown they wanted their country to change. But that desire, like the young life of the activist from Mvurwi, was about to be stifled.

I arrived in Zimbabwe in January 2006 and left in April 2009. This book is about my experiences there. For the first two and a half years I worked in the British Embassy in Harare as a second secretary in the political section. My role was to support civil society groups – a fashionably opaque piece of British Government-speak referring to a wide range of campaign and lobby groups, community and professional associations, trade unions and other sectional-interest organisations.

I became close to hundreds of gifted and brave individuals working in small ways to resist the predations of Robert Mugabe and his regime. I met people campaigning for media freedom, for fair elections, against local Government corruption and torture, women trying to dismantle the traditional tolerance of rape, farmers clinging desperately on to their land, conservationists trying to stop state-sanctioned rhino-poaching, lawyers defiantly representing clients while riot police ground their truncheons at the back of the court, people infected with HIV trying to create a livelihood. The breadth of resistance to Mugabe was always inspiring, though its lack of depth could be frightening. I sometimes felt that just a handful of people were standing up to the cruelties of the regime, though the reality was that tens of thousands were working unseen. I have never felt better about representing the British Government than when granting a small but invaluable sum of money to one of these courageous groups.

After my tour at the Embassy ended, I stayed in Harare while my wife finished her own tour. I wrote occasionally for newspapers and the Foreign Office's website, where my blogs hopefully gave an off-message account of the British Government's unwelcome presence in Robert Mugabe's country.

I had joined the Diplomatic Service as a humble third secretary in 1999. I had previously spent ten enjoyable years working for London Transport, as a temp in Sydney and as a market researcher in Bangkok; but when I turned thirty I felt it was time to get a proper job. Using a series of sharp-elbowed and duplicitous manoeuvres I was able to become a first secretary by 2001. I worked at that level in London and then from 2002 for three years in Poland.

Being a second secretary in Zimbabwe was therefore a demotion, but a semi-voluntary one. My wife joined the Foreign Office with me and secured an excellent posting in Zimbabwe, beginning in 2006. I was planning to move there without a job, but at the last minute a new slot came up and I decided to apply despite the fact that the seniority of my duties – and my pay – would be reduced. With hindsight, I am glad that I made that decision as I would otherwise not have been a part, albeit a small one, of Zimbabwe's 2008 – the year in which Zimbabweans made an inspiring effort to pull themselves out of the pit. Their efforts were brutally resisted and, it seemed, nullified. But ultimately the will for change was so clear that it has led to some positive developments, principally the elevation of Morgan Tsvangirai to the position of prime minister.

Zimbabwe's story started in 1980 – the year of independence. Mugabe's early messages to his people were of reconciliation and continuity with the apartheid-lite regime presided over by

Ian Smith. The fact that white power in Rhodesia ended fifteen years before it did in South Africa, and the appalling failings of Mugabe, have somehow obscured the fact that Rhodesia* was a society run entirely for white pleasure and convenience on the back of the labours of the black majority. To the side of the automatic doors of Harare's light, airy (if sometimes empty) supermarkets remain the wooden counters where blacks had to queue in the sun, waiting to be served, excluded from the whites-only retail palaces. Employment was fully segregated – professionals, landowners, businessmen, all those making money – were white. Farm labourers, factory workers, domestic servants were black. In Harare, whites lived in large villas with pools and leafy gardens to the north of the city, protected by the central business district from contact with the close-packed breezeblock houses to the south where the blacks lived.

Mugabe therefore enjoyed respect and credit in the 1980s – as Mandela did in the 1990s – for forgoing revenge and allowing the show to go on. Of course formal segregation ended, demeaning racist laws were repealed and a new black political elite emerged, but gross racial inequality remained in place. There was no revolutionary transformation of the traditional economic roles of black and white – a stability which reassured business and allowed Zimbabwe's economy to perform strongly right through the 1980s and 1990s, but which created resentments that grew beneath the country's apparent success.

Throughout the 1980s Mugabe was collecting, centralising and concentrating power. He adjusted the constitution at will, transforming himself from a prime minister, constrained by law, Parliament and collective government, into an executive president, with substantial personal power, troubled by no meaningful legislative or judicial oversight. Mugabe also showed a capacity, which he was to develop further, for savage social engineering,

* Named after Cecil Rhodes, who used a combination of colonial expansion, military force, bluff and diplomacy to create a British protectorate in the 1890s, made up of the land that is now Zimbabwe.

shifting the power balance in his favour at the cost of great loss of life. Mugabe is part of the Shona ethnic group but came to power in partnership with Joshua Nkomo, a member of the Ndebele* tribe, which violently dominated the Shona in the pre-colonial era. Between 1983 and 1985, Mugabe broke the Ndebele as a rival political force by means of a militarised programme of terror, 'Gukurahundi',† in which at least 20,000 people were killed.

The Western world averted its gaze from the death pits of Matabeleland. Governments wilfully ignored emerging evidence of the massacres and, once eventually assured that the horrible reports were true, declined to prevent Mugabe or even to criticise him as he eradicated his opponents in their thousands. He appeared to be an impressive and moderate leader, so the West calculated that intervention or criticism would bring much risk and little benefit. Mugabe learned a vital lesson that still serves him well – he can kill to retain power and the world will do no more than watch.

Needless to say, African states and the wider non-aligned movement ignored the death cries of the Ndebele too. The Cold War was still hot. The main battle in Southern Africa was to smash apartheid, not to protect the rights of minorities already liberated from white domination. Nobody was going to criticise a powerful Marxist pin-up like Mugabe.

We will never know if Mugabe would have continued on this course of business-friendly, albeit increasingly dictatorial, rule. A number of events coincided in the late 1990s the combined effect of which was to blow him irretrievably off whatever course he had set.

Externally, the election of Tony Blair in 1997 changed the cosy relationship that Mugabe had enjoyed with the Thatcher and Major Governments. New Labour placed great emphasis on development and on Africa. A new ministry, the Department for International Development (DFID), was created to deliver

* Known also as the Matabele, the Ndebele are Zimbabwe's Zulus and live mostly in its Southern provinces around Bulawayo.
† A Shona word meaning 'the early rain that washes away the chaff'.

aid at much increased levels. But this greater volume of assistance brought with it a matching greater emphasis on good government in Africa. Agreement by both sides to this quid pro quo was the big win of Blair's 2005 Gleneagles G8 summit, but it was bad news for Mugabe, whose power was based on corrupt patronage and the restriction of democracy.

Even before these trends in British policy became apparent, relations between Mugabe and the Blair administration were altered by a letter that the first DFID Secretary of State, Clare Short, wrote to Mugabe's Minister of Agriculture, Kumbirai Kangai, in 1997. Short claimed that New Labour was 'without links to former colonial interests' and that her Irish roots gave her affinity with the colonised rather than the colonisers. She concluded, 'It follows from this that a programme of rapid land acquisition as you now seem to envisage would be impossible for us to support. I know that many of Zimbabwe's friends share our concern about the damage which this might do to Zimbabwe's agricultural output and its prospects of attracting investment.'

Mugabe believed that the UK was bound by the terms of the 1979 Lancaster House Constitution, agreed by the then Foreign Secretary Lord Carrington, to fund a programme of land reform. He was infuriated by what he saw as the incoming British Government's attempt to shirk these historical duties. Beyond the promises Carrington had made, the UK had broader obligations because it had – in Mugabe's eyes – exploited indigenous Zimbabweans and bled the country for a century. Now, after less than twenty years of independence, the UK wanted to deny responsibility for its colonial past and cut off the aid which was the very least assistance it should offer to the country. Mugabe started to develop a public narrative of external disruption in his country; at the heart of his new account was the assertion that the UK had abandoned its interest in land reform and, by implication, its moral authority to comment on how Zimbabwe chose to drive that process.

Relations with the UK went from bad to worse. While visiting

London in 1999, Mugabe was the object of an attempted citizen's arrest by Peter Tatchell, who was protesting about Zimbabwe's illiberal sexuality laws. Foreign Office Minister Peter Hain attempted to assure Mugabe that the Government knew nothing about Tatchell's stunt, but Mugabe felt set up and began to rail in his public speeches against Blair and his 'gay gangsters'. This animosity was institutionalised when Mugabe was excluded from the UK – as well as from other European Union and like-minded countries – following his violent and arithmetically dubious re-election as president in 2002.

The second crisis for Mugabe in the late 1990s was a revolt by veterans of the liberation war. Two decades after defeating the Rhodesian armed forces, these 'war vets' were aggrieved that they had not received what they saw as a fair share of the spoils. Some no doubt wondered why they had fought for a country in which most black people remained poor, while for most whites the good times rolled on. But they were particularly incensed that able-bodied senior members of Mugabe's party were extracting resources from a fund supposedly set up to support injured combatants. Mugabe was in danger of becoming the target of this resentment.

Always astute at managing his internal politics, Mugabe moved quickly to secure the loyalty of this key group of supporters by gifting each veteran $50,000 – an astonishingly large amount. The war vets were, however, only briefly satisfied with these payments and correctly concluded that they could make further demands. From that point on, Mugabe needed to find ever more booty to satisfy them, at great cost to the country. Even the first huge outlay pushed inflation from normal levels up to 26 per cent overnight, caused a public deficit amounting to 8.3 per cent of gross domestic product and reduced foreign-exchange reserves to a point where Zimbabwe could not afford to pay for a single month's imports.

This economic damage could have been repaired and some work to restore public finances by raising taxes was done. But Mugabe learned a wrong-headed lesson, that he could address any problem by throwing money at it, whether the country could afford the outlay or not. He soon authorised the central bank to print money as necessary for desirable short-term political ends. Huge, then astronomical, inflation rates, which rapidly transformed Zimbabwe's robust currency into a worthless joke, were the inevitable consequence.

Another internal development, which destabilised Mugabe, was the formation of a new opposition party, the Movement for Democratic Change (MDC), in 1999. The MDC fused dissatisfied Zimbabweans from several traditions: participants in the liberation struggle who felt the revolution was being betrayed, the labour movement, which was starting to feel the pain of economic decline, and disgruntled members of Robert Mugabe's ZANU-PF party, of which MDC leader Morgan Tsvangirai himself had been a member. Many white commercial farmers also joined the MDC, alienated by Mugabe's newly hostile tone on land-reform issues. The new party had a strong organisational network principally because Tsvangirai was a grass-roots labour-movement activist – a miner who had risen to become general secretary of the Zimbabwe Confederation of Trade Unions.

Mugabe had not faced a credible opposition for more than a decade. But he had demonstrated few tolerant or pluralist instincts in the 1980s. The Matabeleland massacres had liquidated Joshua Nkomo's minority Ndebele party, and the rights of Zimbabwe's whites to a ring-fenced allocation of Parliamentary seats were abolished in 1987. However, Mugabe did not immediately react to the formation of the MDC, for example by proscribing the new party.

Indeed Mugabe underestimated the MDC dramatically and – but for some bad timing – his party might have been reduced to a minority position in Parliament a year after the new party's creation. Elections were due in June 2000, but before going to the people Mugabe wanted to push through a new constitution which would legitimise uncompensated nationalisation of agricultural land. A referendum on this new constitution took place in February, four months before the general election. Mugabe had felt confident of a yes vote, but was defeated by a coalition of the new MDC and civil society groups that favoured an alternative text. Although Mugabe was shocked by his defeat, he was ironically strengthened by the information which it gave him. He understood that he could lose the imminent Parliamentary elections unless he took special measures.

Mugabe's responses to the three challenges to his rule – external, internal and within his own party – were extreme by any measure. He developed a narrative that linked his opponents. He began to call the MDC a front for the UK. He claimed that the party was funded by the British and was an agent for the interests of white commercial farmers. It was impossible that black Africans could voluntarily support such a puppet party, hence Mugabe argued that commercial farmers were compelling farm workers to vote MDC.

All Mugabe's policy dilemmas could be addressed by targeting the commercial farms. By doing so, he could disrupt an MDC power base, generate a stream of 'liberated' property with which to reward supporters and punish the British. (Mugabe continues to this day to label all white farmers as British, even though most are Zimbabweans, not entitled to any foreign citizenship.) That the farms supported over a million Zimbabweans, generated more than two billion dollars of foreign exchange annually and grew much of the maize that fed the country were inconvenient facts and were ignored.

Violence was also the obvious approach to the June 2000 election. The electorate had shown an uppity ingratitude when it rejected Mugabe's constitution in February and needed a bloody reminder of its duties and of the acceptable limits of pluralism. Mugabe did not trouble to code his message; he used an election rally to 'declare war' on the MDC. His lieutenants took up this message. Border Gezi, Governor of Mashonaland Central, told a rally in Bindura on 26 March, 'You must warn supporters of opposition parties that ZANU-PF is well known for spilling blood.' Immediately after hearing this message, ZANU-PF supporters stoned to death Edwin Gomo, who had been attending an MDC rally in the town. Altogether about fifty people died in the run-up to polling day. Observers of the election, including Africans within the Southern African Development Community (SADC) and Commonwealth monitoring teams, condemned the violence, the hate speech and the pro-Mugabe bias of the state-owned media. But they noted, accurately, that the violence tailed off in the days before the election – once the election monitors were in place – and that the administration of voting was efficient.

June 2000 established a pattern for Zimbabwean elections in the twenty-first century. Subsequent polls in 2002 and 2005 were characterised by several months of intolerant language, abuse of state resources to favour the ruling party and widespread violence including substantial numbers of murders, rapes and serious beatings. But the conduct of the election days themselves was good. Malpractice re-emerged after election day in 2002 and 2005 – independent observers reported that the results were amended artificially to sustain flagging support for Mugabe.

Despite the violence, the MDC did extraordinarily well in its debut election in 2000, taking 57 of 120 seats contested. However Mugabe had awarded himself the right to add thirty placemen to his sixty-two elected MPs, giving him a healthy position in Parliament. He was irritated, however, to have lost the two-thirds majority which had allowed him to amend the constitution at will in the 1980s and 1990s.

The year 2000 was a transformational one for Mugabe. He understood that if his rule was to last into the new century, he would have to adapt to sustained opposition from critics at home and abroad. He adopted a literal carrot-and-stick approach: looted crops for his supporters and liberal use of the panga and the knobkerrie on his opponents. Those tactics were sufficient to secure further bloodstained and arithmetically questionable electoral victories in 2002 and 2005 and to sustain him in office until 2006, the year that I arrived.

I

The Battleground

I felt a passion for Zimbabwe from the moment I arrived at the British Embassy in Harare in January 2006. I had read everything I could about the country. According to some of the livelier newspaper stories, I was going into a war zone – something like the Congo or Sierra Leone. I was braced for violence, the chaos of hyperinflation and food shortages.

What I found was a temperate paradise of green hills and waterfalls, orderly and organised, filled with happy people. The rainy fertility of January made the grass grow a metre high. I saw some empty fields, but others filled with sunflower-like plants I soon learned were maize. The roads were smooth and wide, despite the warnings of expat Zimbabwean friends that they would be cratered with deep potholes.

I was ready to see homeless people and piles of rubble – the remnants of Mugabe's notorious Operation Murambatsvina* in 2005. But on the road from the airport into town I saw blocks of good-looking brick-built houses, each standing in its own garden, supplied with electricity and water. I asked the Embassy driver if the ruling ZANU-PF people lived in these good-looking houses. He laughed: 'These are for the ordinary people.' It was early afternoon and the number of children walking home

---

* During Murambatsvina (a Shona word sometimes translated as 'clearing away the shit'), security forces wholly or partially demolished 300,000 homes, making 700,000 people homeless. Supposedly a slum clearance exercise, Murambatsvina was actually an effort to punish and disrupt opposition mobilisation in urban areas.

from school astonished me. They were smartly dressed, clean and well behaved. It was immediately obvious that most children, even from Harare's poorer areas, went to school.

I could not believe it. Where was the blood on the streets? I stayed for my first few nights in the colonial-style comfort of the Meikles Hotel right in the centre of town. I was tense, ready for shooting to break out, but there was none. One morning at six o'clock I heard the stirring sound of dozens of male voices from the streets. They were singing a marching song. Was it the war veterans come to murder white tourists in their hotel beds? No, it was a squad of trainee policemen jogging through the streets, vigorous and ebullient, but rather comic in their green vests and shorts.

Sometimes I would walk to the Embassy. Initially I felt vulnerable and conspicuous in my white skin. But I soon came to see there was no threat from Harare's smartly dressed people heading for their offices. Anybody whose eye I caught would smile and ask how I was. When I started chatting to people, I found them usually to be open, good-natured and fluent in English. I had to keep reminding myself that English is a second language for black Zimbabweans.

These favourable first impressions made it hard to see immediately that there was something terribly wrong happening in Zimbabwe. But I soon worked out why the country's story is so grim and tragic despite all the excellent things I saw in early 2006. It is because everything is going backwards. Life expectancy is falling. National income declines every year. Roads get worse. Businesses fail. Unemployment grows. School attendance shrinks. Expectations and hopes contract. The deterioration and disappearance of good things eat into the spirit as well as taking happiness and ending life.

Premature death and desperate migration have almost halved the population in a decade. It has fallen sharply from fourteen million; today there may be as few as eight million Zimbabweans living in their homeland. Incredibly, the Government has welcomed this devastating depopulation. As Didymus Mutasa, Mugabe's Minister of Lands, put it, 'We would be better off with only six million people [if they were] our own people who supported the liberation struggle. We don't want all these people.'

During my three years in Harare I saw so many failings and endings. Hospitals no longer admit patients, as they have no doctors. Poor parents have given up trying to afford newly imposed school fees, particularly as the schools have hardly any teachers. Like most people, I soon had no working phone. The superb Delta drinks company, which used to supply the country with affordable Coca-Cola and beer in reusable bottles, has been largely supplanted by importers of expensive canned drinks from South Africa. The sight of piles of cans, which will never be collected, as Harare's dustcarts have no fuel, is new and nasty. So much that seemed excellent and clever when I arrived is no more.

But my three-year experience of decline is only the latest episode in a longer, sadder story. Old hands remember days when the postal service worked overnight, when the trains were swift and comfortable, when a ferry operated along Lake Kariba, when the farms were the envy of the world, when every rural school would have a full complement of inspired teachers, supplemented by young volunteers from the UK, keen to be part of the progressive African miracle that used to be Zimbabwe. These are not rose-tinted 'Rhodie' recollections of Ian Smith's days; rather, they are things which were taken for granted in the first two decades of Mugabe's rule, but which had already expired by the time I arrived.

Other lawless, failed African states – Somalia or the Democratic Republic of the Congo – have never had first-world infrastructure, a well-educated and skilled workforce or law-abiding stability. But Zimbabwe was an African statement – that the continent was not made up of people who could not govern themselves or their countries, but was capable of great and fine achievements. So the failure and destruction of so much that was good in Zimbabwe is symbolic as well as tragic.

It kills people, kills hope but also kills the belief – to which many try to hold – that Africa can do well.

My first trip out of Harare was to the Eastern Highlands, an area of hilly country which some people reckon resembles Yorkshire. The local economy is more British than African too, consisting of trout farms, fruit sellers, jam makers and twee coffee shops. I spent several weekends at beautiful lodges around Nyanga, such as the Inn on Rupurara, where I first tried riding up to a herd of zebras on horseback. Recognising a horse-cousin, albeit one with a strange deformity on its back, the zebras let me walk right through their herd.

At the end of 2006, I took a party of friends to Rupurara for a mock-colonial New Year's Eve. After dinner we played a murder-mystery game. The staff giggled at us as we larked about in costume, then took a midnight walk, still dressed up like upper-class twits, hoping to spot a giant eagle owl hunting scrub hares. It was hard to believe that life could be so enjoyable in Zimbabwe. Everyone I met – villagers in round brick houses with thatched roofs, patient roadside fruit sellers, sculptors offering their interpretations of the striking and symbolic Shona style, hotel workers putting up with silly guests like me – seemed happy and at peace.

On New Year's Day, I bounced my Land Cruiser over steep, rough tracks, past occasional modest villages, to find the M'tarazi Falls – the seventeenth tallest in the world, twice the height of Victoria Falls. I was astonished to see in the visitors' log that only one or two people visited each month. Admittedly M'tarazi was hard to get to, but the lack of tourists coming to see such an astounding site had more to do with Zimbabwe's bad international reputation. When the road ran out, I had to hike eastwards alongside a small river for half an hour to reach the falls. Zimbabwe's weather is temperate, but during the rainy season, which coincides with European winter, sticky, pregnant afternoons are quite normal. So I was sweaty as I walked and strangely nervous, knowing that I was approaching the point where the plateau which forms the bulk of Zimbabwe abruptly ends.

At the end of the track, I stepped into the light to find that land had vanished. I could look down, almost between my feet, to see the Burma Valley and Mozambique borders a kilometre straight down below me. I could make out the circular green shapes of fields that used to be cultivated for coffee, but now lay fallow. The colours so far below seemed to swim, but I couldn't work out if this effect was due to vertigo or heat haze. To my right I could see the river I had been following disappearing over the edge, but it fell so far I couldn't hear it hit the bottom and the narrow fall was so steep I couldn't see much of its descent beneath me. I was right on top of a natural wonder of the world, but could get little sense of its scale.

I watched, queasy from the height, as a storm rumbled towards me from Mozambique. The cloud was isolated in the clear sky, initially below me, but moving right towards my position spookily fast. I couldn't feel the wind that was driving it into the escarpment and forcing it up, over, until it surrounded me and exploded, lightning suddenly striking something very close to me, the thunderclap the loudest noise I have ever heard, bouncing all around me. I ran back up the track, drenched now by monsoon rain as well as by sweat. I was terrified, convinced I was about to be hit, trying to make myself remember whether I should stop and shelter under a tree – I thought not – but too pumped up to do anything but run as hard as I possibly could.

Back to the car filthy and drenched, I dropped the keys and, after fumbling to retrieve them from the muddy layer of water on the ground, at last I was inside, feeling very safe and very alive – convinced that the rubber tyres would insulate me from a strike, and suddenly euphoric. Ten minutes later the storm had moved on and the day was clear again. I got out and could feel the trees spasm, almost see them grow, as thousands of litres of water flooded over their roots. Each year I loved the surging fecundity of the rains, which made the country impossibly green, squirming with frogs and insects, paradise for ten million migrant birds escaping winter in Europe.

I grew to know the Eastern Highlands well. During the hours I spent roaming over its tracks, it was impossible to imagine that the inert villages I passed would fall victim to a campaign of violence, arson and terror; or that my last visit to Manicaland eighteen months later would be to a refugee camp, into which I would have to creep after dark to avoid bloodthirsty gangs of indoctrinated teenagers.

But all that was to come later. My first year in Zimbabwe was gentle and peaceful. I fell in love with the country, the people and their benign, blessed-seeming place. Even my house was beautiful. It was unusual for Embassy accommodation, in that it was twenty kilometres out of town, in an area known as Borrowdale Brooke. The area felt entirely safe, and certainly I never suffered a break-in. The roof of my house was thatch supported on wooden poles, in the style of a boma, a traditional village structure, although the interior was much more Western. The large sloping garden was home to dozens of bird species – Abdim's storks grazed on frogs during the rainy season and the pair of spotted eagle owls, which nested in the thatch, ensured that rats never troubled me. I could not believe that the rent was only £600 per month. As I watched weaverbirds fly in and out of their nests – intricately woven, the size and shape of avocados, hanging from finger-thin branches – I liked to contrast my accommodation with what I would get for a rent of £600 in London. The greatest glory of the house was the grass tennis court at the bottom of the slope. Its bounce was sluggish and unpredictable and the net had more holes than mesh, but the players who contested our annual 'Zimbledon' tournament were not talented enough to mind.

However much I loved Harare, I loved the countryside more. One of many trips to rural areas, one which I honestly expect to relive in my head until the day I die, was in September 2007 during a lull in the violent anti-MDC campaign of that year. September is hot-hot, the perfect time to visit Zimbabwe's national parks, like Hwange which lies on the edge of the Kalahari Desert – places so large that I could wander all day with no sense of boundary. The sandy earth was parched and cracked. Trees put on the appearance of death, withdrawing juices to their cores while they waited for the rains. I had the park to myself – tourism had been depressed since the farm invasions began, but even the hardiest foreign visitors cancelled their holidays after the shocking images of March 2007. The predators and herbivores had called a ceasefire in their eternal blood war – neither the lions nor the buffaloes could think of anything more than the daily struggle to find water. I came across an adolescent elephant, three metres from foot to shoulder, lying dead of heat exhaustion, but still quite intact. I had a rare opportunity to touch the marbled smoothness of the tusks and the bristled sensitivity of the tip of the trunk. A row of white-backed vultures, unable to rip through such thick skin, stood in an orderly queue waiting for a passing hyena to allow them into the carcass. The sight of the pristine corpse was strangely upsetting. I had come to the park looking for a break from trouble, but it was the last place where I would escape from death.

Not all my trips out of Harare were personal. The most immediately rewarding part of my job was opening British-funded projects. Although working directly with people trying to advance their communities has gone out of fashion with development agencies – who prefer to hand huge quantities of financial support directly to national governments these days – we retained a small programme of such work in Harare. As well as helping some of the communities damaged by the country's economic decline, it was useful to have a visible assistance programme to generate good-news stories about the UK.

Late in 2007, a couple of months before the election campaign began, I set out on a typical trip to a remote village in

Manicaland to the south of the Harare–Mutare main road. The sound of the driver hammering on the door at 5.30 reminded me that I was supposed to have got up at 5.15. We drove overly fast for three hours, heading east, climbing into the mountains until the road ran out. We continued on a rough dirt track for another hour, fording rivers and bouncing over rocks. It was an exciting and beautiful drive. The villages we passed were basic – circular huts with brick or wooden walls and thatched roofs. Suddenly we turned a corner and saw an extraordinarily large number of people gathered next to the only substantial building I'd seen since the main road – the schoolhouse which I had come to open.

As our Land Rover approached, a stirring, ethereal noise rose up to meet us – the community choir, singing unwritten but well-known songs of welcome. A musician has explained to me why African singing, which thrills to the core and sets the pulse racing, is so unlike what a Western choir would produce. The difference is not just the product of greater passion and commitment; African singers also tend not to use vibrato and to sing in unison, both of which produce a powerful concerted delivery.

The next hour was a succession of handshakes with the smug headmaster and teachers from the new school and their envious colleagues from neighbouring areas, who asked for a new building of their own. I also met the headman – a short round expressionless fellow in a decorative ZANU-PF shirt – other traditional chiefs, local businessmen, the local ZANU-PF MP, who had arrived in a Mercedes, doctors, priests, an odd, spotty American missionary, dozens of local education officials and – finally – after all the important people had taken their turn – some children and parents. The children were sweet. The confident ones thanked me in their best school English. Some shy little ones held my hand and looked fixedly at the contrast of my pallid skin with theirs.

After a while the VIPs moved to plastic chairs in a shady area. Less important people, like the children, sat on the grass in the sun. The children danced. The young teenagers' performances were clearly sexual, which made for an uncomfortable spectacle. Five stern boys whacking monstrous, ancient hardwood tom-toms and a marimba player provided the music. Then the adult dancing group took their turn. Rural Zimbabwean women over thirty go one of two ways: they get HIV, thanks to their useless, unfaithful husbands, get thin and die; or they attain a substantial rotundity, particularly around the buttocks. The latter is a welcome development – a generous bottom is at the heart of the traditional Zimbabwean style of beauty.

The dance began with the women forming a tight ring, facing outwards, bending over and waggling their rear ends furiously. It was a vigorous and dramatic feat. I tried to reproduce it in front of the bathroom mirror later but fell over and hit my head on the toilet. One of the women was wearing a ZANU-PF sarong, tied on upside down, which presented me with the unforgettable image of Robert Mugabe's face, inverted and stretched tightly over a biggish and wildly oscillating derrière. The dance progressed, men and women taking it in turns to perform increasingly ambitious step sequences, while creating their own percussion by beating small sickles together. As the performers ended their segments they flung themselves brutally to the ground to roars of approval. It seemed like the dancing would never end, but it suddenly fizzled out and the villagers settled back into their non-VIP places.

Interpreting this interlude as his cue to speak, the ZANU-PF MP leaped up and began to explain how successful the country's education system was. He acknowledged that there was no money for textbooks, diesel for buses, school lunches or teachers' salaries. But that was due to illegal colonialist sanctions. It was Gordon Brown's fault. Then, through gritted teeth, he thanked the British for their generous support in paying for this school building. I gave the standard speech. The British people wanted the best for the people of Zimbabwe. That's why we were spending 400 quadrillion Zimbabwean dollars a year helping the country. (The figure was actually correct on that day – and it was fun to use it just to mock the economic mismanagement of Gideon Gono, head of the central bank, the Reserve Bank of Zimbabwe.) I wound up by saying how glad the British were to help the people of this remote and basic village by paying for this schoolhouse. The crowd whooped and the MP looked unhappy.

There was time for a little more fun: ribbon cutting; endless tours of the school buildings (wonderful, with colourful teaching aids everywhere – the first indoor teaching area the village had ever had) and the handover of extra goodies I'd brought: balls, sports gear, books. The lunch was a mound of sadza – Zimbabwe's staple food, similar to polenta – from the village's own communal maize plot. Everyone ate up, aware that in a few months food would be scarce. The headman stood and gave a lengthy vote of thanks in Shona. He gifted the MP and me a bag of maize meal each.

We walked to the cars. I asked the head teacher if he could use my mealie for school lunches, at least while it lasted. He gratefully accepted. We moved off behind the Mercedes, but after just a few yards the MP's car stopped. Locals ran up to the windows and listened to instructions being barked to them. They ran back to the school building and returned with what had briefly been my sack of maize, which they loaded into the car boot on top of that given to the MP. The Mercedes now roared off, leaving the village in its dust.

The Movement for Democratic Change – the opposition party led by Morgan Tsvangirai – launched its election campaign as early as February 2007. The March 2008 general election, which redefined Zimbabwe's politics, was more than a year away. But the MDC did not know when elections would be called and wanted its supporters to be warmed up.

A series of MDC meetings and rallies in Harare were well attended, demonstrating that the party retained great popularity in the capital. On 18 February, tens of thousands of MDC supporters gathered to hear Tsvangirai speak in Harare but were attacked by riot police with tear gas. The police then banned demonstrations in urban areas, though the Commissioner of Police, Augustine Chihuri, did not explain which power allowed him to do this. A rally in Bulawayo on 21 February was banned and peaceful demonstrations by civil society groups were greeted with the mass arrest of participants. Two hundred members of the Women of Zimbabwe Arise! organisation were arrested, made to lie on the floor of their cells, then beaten as a punishment for taking to the streets chanting their favourite slogan, 'Bread and Roses'. The regime rarely stooped lower than when it targeted these benign and dignified women.

Robert Mugabe was shocked and angered by the MDC's obvious popularity. He had hoped that the Murambatsvina campaign in 2005 would have neutralised the party's popularity. Urban people had seen their homes demolished and so understood the consequences of voting MDC. But despite the demolitions and despite the tear gas fired at them in February, tens of thousands were ready not just to vote MDC but also to turn out on the streets for Tsvangirai. Firmer action was clearly required to snuff out the MDC's spark of popularity. Mugabe had not remained in power for twenty-seven years by allowing rivals the freedom of the streets to express their views and build their morale.

Battle was joined on Sunday 11 March 2007. A civil society group, the Save Zimbabwe Campaign, called a meeting of prayer for the future of Zimbabwe. This meeting was in truth intended to be a mass rally, but the Campaign hoped that its ostensibly religious nature would exempt it from the ban on large assemblies. The streets of Harare's high-density suburbs – those blocks of houses I had admired on my first day in the country – were buzzing. One activist estimated that 100,000 people wanted to get to the stadium where the supposed prayer meeting was going to take place, in the expectation that Tsvangirai would speak.

But the police had no intention of letting that happen. They threw up roadblocks, turned away combis and warned people on foot to go home. As frustrated crowds gathered, they escalated their use of force, firing tear gas and then live ammunition. MDC supporters threw stones back. The police started making arrests and beating with riot sticks anyone they could get hold of. They fired into the crowd, killing a young activist called Gift Tandare and injuring dozens of others. Some people now fled in panic, but the arrests and beatings continued.

The police knew well whom they considered to be the principal troublemakers and singled them out for arrest. As well as hundreds of rank-and-file activists detained for a beating on the streets, or worse, sixty leading members of the MDC and of civil society protest groups were arrested. This group faced three nights of torture, injury and fear. The moment when ZANU-PF launched its own election campaign came a few hours later that night in a rank cell in Harare Central Police Station, when Morgan Tsvangirai's head was smashed repeatedly against a wall, fracturing his skull. That was not the end of Tsvangirai's suffering. He was whipped, kicked and beaten with sticks during three nights under arrest.

Almost all those arrested were brutally beaten, suffering fractures and other physical injuries, which generally healed, and mental traumas, which often did not. Grace Kwinjeh of the MDC, who fled to the UK after her detention, said that she suffered 'unspeakable torture. Each time that night when we heard the sound of boots returning, our bowels loosened.' Men in army uniforms beat Kwinjeh so viciously that her ear was almost severed. Sekai Holland, a sixty-year-old grandmother and MDC activist, suffered multiple fractures. The MDC took to referring to this bloody day as '3/11' to emphasise the terror which it brought.

Nobody knows quite who beat Tsvangirai and the other detainees apart from those involved in his torture. As Tsvangirai was under arrest and being held at a police station, the police were obviously complicit, if only by denying the most basic levels of care and protection to those in their custody. It could have been police or army officers who carried out the beating. But it is more likely that paramilitary thugs affiliated to Robert Mugabe's party were given access to the prisoners. Nobody involved in Tsvangirai's sustained torture has ever been arrested, even though Harare Central Police Station was full of officers supposedly committed to the rule of law and the defence of the constitutional exercise of power.

Three days later Tsvangirai emerged from the High Court, which had ordered his release for medical treatment. His appalling condition was apparent. His head was horribly swollen and misshapen, his eyes forced almost closed by large bruises. But he walked out and gave the open-handed MDC salute – a friendly gesture designed to highlight by contrast the aggressive nature of the clenched fist with which Mugabe greets supporters. Unlike much of the violence which takes place in Zimbabwe, these pictures of Tsvangirai emerging from detention and torture were carried by the global media and shocked the world. Doctors who examined him were surprised that he had endured so long with a fractured skull.

Remarkably, over the next few days Mugabe proved capable of repressive acts that were almost more shocking. On 13 March, agents stormed the house of the late Gift Tandare while his wake was under way. Two MDC activists were shot and wounded, but the real objective of the raid was to prevent a funeral that might become a pro-MDC rally. Mugabe's agents stole Tandare's body and buried it in secret in the country.

On the Thursday after Zimbabwe's bloody Sunday, a small cross-party group of Zimbabwean MPs was due to attend a routine meeting between EU and African parliamentarians in Brussels. En route to the airport for this meeting, the MDC's delegate Nelson Chamisa MP was stopped, dragged from his car, beaten and kicked by the side of the road. He lay in hospital with gaping head wounds while Zimbabwe was represented in Brussels exclusively by Mugabe's own party: the Zimbabwe African National Union – Patriotic Front, which is so often referred to as ZANU-PF that few people remember what the acronym stands for. The week ended as it began, with death. The body of another MDC activist, Itai Manyeruke, who had been missing since being arrested on 11 March, was found. He had been beaten to death and his body dumped outside Harare.

This week of violence and torture of oppositionists was widely condemned by Western governments. UN Secretary General Ban Ki-moon called for the immediate release of the detained. But what was less predictable was the attention of the Southern African Development Community, a group of fourteen governments to which Zimbabwe belonged. Tanzania held the rotating chair of SADC at the time of the 11 March events. President Jakaya Kikwete flew into Harare apparently to express the region's concern about Mugabe's violence. Mugabe was insolent and defiant. He told Western critics that they could 'go hang' and gave Kikwete similar instructions to keep his nose out of Zimbabwe's business.

The Tanzanian leader was not impressed by this snub and retaliated by adding 'unfolding events in Zimbabwe' to the agenda for a summit of regional leaders in Dar es Salaam on 27 March. Tanzanian Foreign Minister Bernard Membe, subtly distancing himself from this assertive action, told the press, 'Our President believes that SADC in collaboration with SADC leaders can solve Zimbabwe's problems.' Zambian President Mwanawasa also got involved, saying in a speech that Zimbabwe was sinking like the *Titanic*.

The Tanzanian initiative was a setback for Mugabe as it forced him to explain and defend his actions, albeit only to the audience of his peers and in private. But he was taken aback by the public criticism, particularly from his African colleagues. He showed his contempt for the SADC process on the day of the summit by ordering the police to raid the MDC offices in

Harare and to arrest yet again party leader Morgan Tsvangirai along with several of his staff.

While his security services were cracking down, Mugabe himself was in robust form at the summit. He told his fellow African leaders that Zimbabwe was under attack from Western-sponsored militias. The MDC was no more than a puppet of Western leaders like Tony Blair and George Bush who wished to destroy Zimbabwe. Their motives were clear – Zimbabwe had thrown colonial white farmers off their land and given natural resources to blacks. The West could not stand for such a defiant display of African nationalism in action. So the MDC had been instructed to launch terrorist attacks on the legitimate ZANU-PF Government. If it won, blacks would be subordinated to whites again. This kind of racially charged rhetoric would have worked in the 1980s and 1990s, but most Southern African states have moved on historically and psychologically from their liberation struggles: independence feels secure. Mugabe's claims of foreign interference no longer sounded credible.

However, even though Kikwete and Mwanawasa had broken ranks, most SADC leaders felt that it was not the done thing to criticise fellow governments, certainly not when led by a figure of legendary stature like Robert Mugabe. Some have since claimed that they spoke up and criticised to his face Mugabe's brutal treatment of the opposition. But no real sense of whatever criticism was expressed made its way into the summit communiqué, which read: 'The . . . Summit noted and appreciated the briefing by H.E. President Robert G. Mugabe on the current political developments in Zimbabwe . . . recalled that free, fair and democratic Presidential elections were held in 2002 in Zimbabwe . . . reaffirms its solidarity with the Government and the people of Zimbabwe.'

This innocuous text was supportive enough. The 2002 election, which Mugabe won, had been corrupt and bloody. Brutalised voters rejected Mugabe, who fell back on vote-rigging to secure his re-election. For SADC to call it free and fair demonstrated how far from the truth the organisation would deviate in order to avoid criticising one of its members.

Indeed the Dar es Salaam summit conclusions went even further to mollify and accommodate Mugabe. SADC called on Britain to 'honour its compensation obligations with regard to land reform' and appealed for 'the lifting of all forms of sanctions against Zimbabwe'. This was music to Mugabe's ears. His favoured version of Zimbabwe's troubles was that they were caused by the sustained hostility of Tony Blair's Government, which had reneged on promises made at the time of independence and had crippled the economy with economic sanctions.

But these friendly conclusions preceded one that was less acceptable to Mugabe. In implicit recognition that all was not as it should be and that external supervision was necessary, the summit 'mandated H.E. President Thabo Mbeki to continue to facilitate dialogue between the opposition and the Government'. Mugabe did not welcome this. He argued that Zimbabwe could solve its own problems without outside interference. But at least the mediator SADC appointed was somebody he could rely upon for loyalty. For decades before he became South Africa's president, Thabo Mbeki had been deeply influenced by Mugabe to the extent that he often seemed in awe of him.

South Africa, with its huge, fast-growing economy and aspirations to continental political leadership, dominates the Southern African region. And, as the most powerful politician in South Africa, Mbeki was the only candidate with sufficient clout to take on the thankless task of trying to influence Mugabe. He was also a man with whom Mugabe was prepared to engage, not so much on the basis of trust – by his eighty-fourth year Mugabe had learned to trust no one – but in the belief that *he* could influence and control Mbeki. It was awkward for the West to criticise the appointment. While giving a press conference alongside Thabo Mbeki in 2003, George Bush had described his South African opposite as his 'point man' on Zimbabwe. Mbeki was infuriated at the time by the implication that he was in any way a creature of the American President, reporting to him. But it was certainly true throughout the period of Mbeki's mediation that Western governments were careful not to criticise him, even as the situation in Zimbabwe went from bad to worse.

The MDC was dismayed by the outcome of the Dar es Salaam summit. The conclusions looked like a pat on the back for Mugabe. Nor could they see Mbeki as a balanced mediator. Since assuming his country's Presidency in 1999, he had religiously avoided any word of criticism of Mugabe, arguing, when pressed to defend the lack of results which his interventions generated, that only 'quiet diplomacy' would be fruitful. His refusal to condemn in public the beating of Morgan Tsvangirai alienated him from the MDC. For oppositionists facing brutality and persecution, his strategy of quiet diplomacy meant no more than inactivity. Some outside Zimbabwe were also unsure of Mbeki's ability to deal effectively with Zimbabwe's problems. Senegalese President Abdoulaye Wade said, 'It's a big mistake to always say that Zimbabwe should be left to Mbeki . . . this is a situation which just one person cannot resolve alone.' Desmond Tutu, Archbishop Emeritus of Cape Town and a consistent critic of Robert Mugabe's excesses, said that the mediation was not enough. Tutu's view is particularly important in Southern Africa because the post-apartheid Truth and Reconciliation process, which he led, is seen by many as a model conflict-resolution exercise.

Approaching from a different tack, the International Crisis Group, an influential British think-tank specialising in African politics, released a report arguing that the West might as well support the mediation as its own efforts had failed and there was nothing else to try. The ICG argued that Mbeki 'offers the only realistic chance to escape a crisis that increasingly threatens to destabilize the region', whereas, the report added, 'Western sanctions have proven largely symbolic . . . and general condemnations from the UK and US are counter-productive because they help Mugabe claim he is the victim of neo-colonial ambitions.'

Mbeki appointed a team within his Presidential office to handle the mediation. The work was effectively conducted in secret. Mbeki's office gave only the most superficial briefings to diplomats desperate to understand how the mediation was progressing. Even South African diplomats admitted that the Ministry of Foreign Affairs knew nothing about what was going on.

The mass arrests, torture and killing on 11 March marked the beginning of a concerted effort through the winter months of 2007 to detain leading MDC members. Forty were arrested in early April and charged with conducting a terrorist campaign. There was a string of Molotov-cocktail attacks after 11 March on three police stations, a passenger train and a supermarket. The MDC denied any involvement, stressed its non-violent credentials and suggested that the Government was carrying out the attacks itself as a pretext for a crackdown. The regime took the line that the MDC had perpetrated the attacks itself and put some effort into giving colour to these charges, even producing a dossier of photographs of alleged victims, which it posted on the internet. This dossier was a PR exercise for the consumption of regional governments rather than a legal docu-ment, as it contained nothing in the way of evidence against any of those arrested.

Exactly who did throw petrol bombs in March is another question that may never be answered. It is hard to think of any motive for the MDC to bomb a train or a supermarket, though it seems perfectly possible that activists were so enraged by police behaviour on and after 11 March that they looked for revenge. But if MDC members carried out one or more of the attacks on police stations, the action would have been free-lance and spontaneous, rather than planned and sanctioned by

leading party officials. The people in the dock were party officials, not enraged urban youths seeking payback. The charges
therefore looked improbable and politically motivated.

Part of the role of a British diplomat in a repressive country
is to attend political trials. This is ostensibly to monitor the
quality of justice being dispensed, but often – when the charges
are blatantly groundless – it's also a statement of protest. In
this ambiguous capacity I was a regular visitor through the
cold months of 2007 to the Harare Magistrates' Court, aptly
located in a street named Rotten Row. Initially I liked to walk
to the court. Harare is an uptight cartographer's fantasy, laid
out in standard blocks. After independence, the streets which
run north–south and the east–west avenues were renamed
after African liberation heros: Sam Nujoma, Josiah Tongogara,
Nelson Mandela and, of course, Robert Mugabe. (The renam-
ing did not extend to the suburbs, where streets are still named
after British royalty, Scottish towns and colonial trailblazers.)

Walking was a pleasure in Harare. The streets were wide and
lined with handsome trees, most famously jacarandas which
blossomed in lush pinks and purples. People were friendly and
loved to talk, but would not dream of hassling me, even if they
had something to sell. Traffic was light and speeds were slow,
partly to eke out scarce fuel, but also, unfortunately, because
some motorists are not entirely sure how to drive their vehicles.
The weather was predictable and lovely and street crime was
much less common than in London.

The court was hidden in a wooded park; the doughnut-
shaped building must have looked impressive when it was built
in the 1970s, but by 2007 its concrete walls were stained by years
of rainstorms and its windows were dirty or broken. Twenty
courts were arranged on two levels around a central courtyard.
This space was designed in different times for lawyers to sit
in the sun eating a sandwich while reading their briefs. But
nobody sat there in 2007. The public areas of the courts smelt
of urine and despair. The staff were friendly, although officers of

the Central Intelligence Organisation (CIO) used to check my ID and take notes, building their fatuous dossiers of evidence of Western support for the MDC's terrorism campaign.

I felt conspicuous observing the MDC cases. I was often the only white person in the courtroom. The rooms were small and seated only sixty, so there was nowhere for me to hide. As there were dozens of defendants, hundreds of relatives wanted to observe. I did not feel happy sitting down while worn-looking wives, sisters and mothers, who had been crammed on buses for hours to reach the court, stood. Nor did I want to sit on the floor, where some women spread their shawls, if the clerk was being lazy or permissive. So I would end up not only as the one white person in the room but standing in the central aisle, towering over the women sitting around my feet and staring straight at the magistrate.

The magistrate I spent so much time staring at was a young woman called Gloria Takundwa. I grew quite impressed with her as the weeks went by. She was under pressure to do exactly what the state wanted, but she regularly showed flashes of independence and courage. Her main drawback was that she was so softly spoken that the lawyers, let alone the observers, could barely hear her.

The proceedings were chaotic. It was routine for the prison service to tell Takundwa that there was no fuel for vehicles to bring prisoners to the court. She would have no alternative but to tut angrily and reschedule the hearing. Prosecutors often failed to turn up or did so but attempted to argue that they could not proceed, as they had no instructions. Takundwa would criticise them sharply for this and order them to return the next day fully prepared. As the weeks dragged by, it became ever clearer that the prosecution was struggling to produce any evidence. The case against one of the accused amounted to no more than a sandal found lying in a gutter. Takundwa was unimpressed. The prosecution stalled, saying that it needed time to collect more evidence.

On one occasion in court in May, I saw that a prisoner called Peniel Denga (who went on to become an MP for the Harare constituency of Mbare in 2008) was having difficulty walking and could not hear because of dressings covering his head wounds. When Takundwa, whose voice rarely rose much above a whisper, finally managed to make herself understood, Denga explained that he had been beaten about the head in his cell. Takundwa was visibly angry and ordered the police to investigate these allegations of torture. She and other magistrates made similar orders on a dozen occasions, but the police refused to investigate or to report back to the court. Zimbabwe's adherence to the rule of law and to judicial independence had been under threat for a decade, but the events of 2007 and 2008 showed that both principles were now discarded.

Leaving the court one day, I saw a strongly built but also overweight man arriving. His chinos, colourfully patterned Mandela-style shirt and white flat cap gave him an air of flamboyance which contrasted with the sober, understated style of normal Zimbabwean dress. It was Morgan Tsvangirai come to give support to his imprisoned party members. Tsvangirai impresses with his presence and courage. He exudes charisma and somehow the knowledge of his huge popularity shines out of him, making him credible and important. The resilience he has shown for a decade is little short of miraculous and serves to boost his standing and popularity further. But despite his dandy clothing that day, he does not pretend by his speech or opinions to be other than a manual worker who has come up through the trade union movement.

One well-to-do member of the MDC in detention was Theresa Makone. I saw her in June standing in the dock in a baggy prison-issue purple sweater, her hair messy and dirty from the stinking cells. The next time we met was after her release at the American Ambassador's 4 July reception. She was looking glamorous in an expensive dress and a sparkling collection of jewellery, and bemoaned her style-less prison costume almost as much as the horrible conditions and treatment she had endured.

After three months of procrastination on the terrorism cases, the prosecution changed tack and claimed that the police would need to travel to South Africa to explore the theory that the MDC had established terrorist training camps there. There was no evidence to support this notion. The magistrates saw through it as an attempt both to waste more time and to create a pretext for policemen to make expenses-paid shopping trips to South Africa. The magistrates ordered the release of the detainees. After a time lag, while the police and prison authorities calculated the extent to which they could defy such court orders, the prisoners did emerge. By August they were all out, though some had spent four cold, painful months in the cells of Chikurubi maximum-security prison. The prosecution had the option to continue its search for evidence. The accused could have been summonsed again at any time after their release. So the fact that the investigations were immediately dropped strongly suggests that the whole exercise of bringing charges was no more than an act of harassment.

After a run-in with Zimbabwe's police in mid-2007, my walks to the court were judged to be too dangerous. I had heard that the Combined Harare Residents Association – an organisation monitoring urban living conditions and opposing the corruption of the Harare city authorities – planned to raise placards and chant slogans on the steps of the Town House – Harare's seat of local government. Demonstrators in Zimbabwe were invariably treated roughly, so I arranged to share a vehicle with a colleague from the American Embassy and observe what happened. Perhaps our presence would deter a violent response to the demonstration; if not, we would at least be able to report accurately how the police behaved.

But we misunderstood the time of the protest and spent an hour circling the canary yellow Town House in a conspicuously huge Land Cruiser with US Embassy CD (Corps

Diplomatique) plates. Finally thirty brave people appeared and unveiled a large banner calling for local democracy for Harare. This was a reasonable cause, because the city's MDC mayor Elias Mudzuri had been dismissed by the Local Government Minister Ignatious Chombo and replaced with an unelected administration compliant to ZANU-PF. About fifteen minutes later, a squad of riot police wearing crash helmets and armed with sticks arrived on foot and charged the demonstrators, who fled nimbly in the opposite direction. We took some pictures and sped off, but our over-extended activities had attracted attention. As we approached the next junction, a police pick-up truck put on its siren and pulled in front of us. An officer came up to the car and demanded that we get out. There was an awkward standoff for about five minutes, negotiated through a one-inch crack in the window. We didn't wind it down any further in case the police tried to grab the keys. We insisted that the authorities had no right to interfere with us. They said that we were breaking the law. But the argument on this occasion was only verbal. The police made no threat or use of force and drove away when it became obvious that we had no intention of obliging them by leaving the safety of our vehicle.

This kind of confrontation with the authorities recurred in various ways throughout my time in Zimbabwe. In part it was a dispute about the rights and limitations of the role of the diplomat. The Zimbabweans considered that foreign envoys should confine themselves to attending national-day functions and passing back to their capitals whatever commentary on national affairs ZANU-PF chose to provide. The UK, among other concerned nations, had a more expansive idea of what it wanted to see and do in Zimbabwe. Both sides had their own favourite clauses of the Vienna Convention, which governs diplomatic relations. We liked to quote those articles which permitted us to 'ascertain by all lawful means conditions and developments in the receiving State' and guaranteed that 'The premises of the mission . . . and the means of transport of the mission shall be immune from search, requisition, attachment or execution.' The Zimbabweans preferred some of the treaty's other language: 'It is the duty of all persons enjoying such privileges and immunities to respect the laws and regulations of the receiving State. They also have a duty not to interfere in the internal affairs of that State.' When we photographed riot police attacking peaceful demonstrators and certainly when we made grants to the groups organising those demonstrations, the Zimbabweans argued that we were interfering.

As the show trials came to an end, Mbeki's mediation effort delivered its first results. He had managed to agree a number of electoral reforms with the two parties. He had negotiated rather cleverly. The MDC wanted wholesale reform – a free media, an independent electoral commission – but knew it wouldn't get these things. Mugabe wanted a convincing re-election, which meant winning a contest. He acknowledged that his mandate would be contaminated if the MDC declined to take part. Mbeki extracted some kind of commitment towards the elections from the MDC and persuaded Mugabe to agree to a package of reforms in return. Few independent commentators could understand why the MDC went along with Mbeki's proposals – the reforms seemed too modest to justify gratifying Mugabe. Some wondered if Tsvangirai was just too tired and broken to hang tough. But the commentators had got it wrong again. Time would prove that the concessions which the MDC wrung out of Mbeki and Mugabe were substantial and crucial.

The reforms were packaged as a constitutional amendment – the eighteenth since Zimbabwe's independence. Parliamentary debate on the amendment was extraordinary in that the two parties – particularly their lead negotiators Patrick Chinamasa and Tendai Biti – spoke to each other in a peaceable and constructive manner. Zimbabwe's Parliament had been a theatre of hate since 2005, so observers were stunned when Chinamasa referred to his MDC colleague as 'comrade'.

With support across the board the amendment sailed through in October 2007.

Mbeki's reforms altered the size and formation of Zimbabwe's two houses of Parliament. The Lower House of Assembly is the principal legislative body; the smaller Senate is intended to oversee and refine law-making.

The first substantial reform was the abolition of the President's entitlement to appoint 20 per cent of House of Assembly MPs. In 2005, the MDC had won 42 of 120 seats contested. This should have been just enough to prevent Mugabe from passing any constitutional amendment he wished by the required two-thirds majority. But Mugabe then exercised his power to appoint thirty more MPs, reducing the MDC's share of MPs to an entirely impotent 28 per cent. By means of amendment eighteen, the parties agreed that the next House of Assembly would be expanded to 210 MPs, all elected. The MDC was satisfied by this abolition of Presidential appointments, partly for reasons of fairness, but more because it assumed that Mugabe would continue to be the President. Both parties were happy with the expansion of representation, as it offered more jobs for their respective boys. Amendment eighteen also set out frameworks for defining constituencies, which looked impressively fair on paper. The MDC had complained that constituencies had been gerrymandered in 2005 to minimise its representation, so it was pleased with the principle set out in amendment eighteen that the Electoral Commission should become independent and apolitical. In addition the amendment created a Human Rights Commission 'to promote awareness of and respect for human rights and freedoms at all levels of society'.

Non-governmental organisations working on electoral and human rights issues were unimpressed. They argued that good-looking words on paper meant little if ZANU-PF politicised the Electoral and Human Rights Commissions by staffing them with party loyalists. Events broadly vindicated the NGOs' critique. The Electoral Commission showed a clear partiality towards ZANU-PF during the vexed electoral events of 2008, while the Human Rights Commission has not even been created more than two years after the amendment which mandated it. No state agent involved in the horrendous abuses which were to blight the electoral period has been officially named, shamed or disciplined, let alone prosecuted. Supporters of the amendment could perhaps argue that it was their role as legislators to create good-looking words on paper, but it was the task of the executive to make these aspirations reality.

Mugabe got some elements that he wanted too. The new amendment provided that in the event of his resignation a joint sitting of the two houses of Parliament should elect his successor. Analysts argued that this gave Mugabe extra room for manoeuvre in the event that he was forced from office. He might be able to influence the votes of an overwhelmingly ZANU-PF Parliament to choose a successor who would protect him from prosecution during his enforced retirement.

Curiously, the most important reform – and one that was wholly overlooked by everyone except the MDC negotiators who quietly secured it – was an obscure amendment to electoral regulations. The instructions for returning officers at polling stations were changed. Rather than sealing results and sending them up the chain of command, it was agreed that returning officers at the next election would announce their results and even post them on the polling station door for anyone to inspect. When the March 2008 election turned out to be far closer than anyone had believed possible in 2007, this reform proved vital. The MDC and independent election monitors were able to collect results and compare them with those officially announced. This greatly reduced ZANU-PF's ability simply to alter unfavourable results as it had done in 2002 and 2005.

The huge volume of arrests, torture and prosecutions in 2007 forced the MDC to set aside the task of planning for elections and to focus instead on protecting its existence. This need to work for physical survival as well as political gain was not new.

The MDC had repeatedly faced violence, including the murder of activists, in 2000, 2002 and 2005. Tsvangirai was arrested in 2000 and 2003 and charged with treason, among other things, which carried the death penalty. After a year of burying the dead, patching up the injured and getting the leadership out of jail, the party was broken and demoralised.

But Robert Mugabe's ZANU-PF party was also in disarray – a state from which it did not emerge until April 2008. Mugabe had made it clear throughout 2007 that he wished to be the party's candidate for the Presidency. Even at the age of eighty-four, retire-ment – a period when he would be exposed to the risks of exile or prosecution – was not an option he wanted to consider. This was an unpopular position. Mugabe's grasp on his party had weak-ened substantially since the previous Presidential elections in 2002, mainly because the country was sliding backwards so quickly.

The fast-track seizure of farms, which began in earnest in 2000, had initially been popular with the party faithful, who saw it both as a radical liberationist effort to overturn the continued white control of Zimbabwe's economy and as a chance to get rich. But by 2008 it was clear that the programme had had terrible consequences. Production of cash crops, like tobacco and coffee, had collapsed by 80 per cent. Production of the key staple, maize, had fallen by 50 per cent. Zimbabwe had moved rapidly from being a food exporter to a food importer. Foreign-exchange earnings had shrunk from more than a billion pounds a year to less than a hundred million.

Other sectors of the economy were also being damaged by low demand, by the predations of ZANU-PF members keen to appropriate valuable assets and by hyperinflation. In the context of what was to come, it is remarkable that annual infla-tion in January 2008 was 'only' 26,471 per cent, but even that was hard, almost impossible, for business to cope with. Money was halving in value every few days. The effort which shops and entrepreneurs had to put into handling such rapidly depre-ciating cash damaged their efficiency and profitability. These grim economic conditions shut many thousands of businesses and deterred mining, agricultural and manufacturing multinationals from investing in the country. Industrial facilities were running at 25 per cent of their capacity and visibly rusting. Multinational mining companies, which have the luxury of being able to play things long, were extracting the bare minimum, in some cases only 5 per cent of normal production.

All of this meant less wealth for the country and less patronage for Mugabe to hand out. The decline of his ability to distribute largesse weakened his grip on power, but it was not dislodged. He faced a crucial party congress in December 2007 at which his Presidential candidacy was the main, indeed the only, issue. Not for the first time, he outmanoeuvred his opponents, by showering one of ZANU-PF's principal power-brokers, Emmerson Mnangagwa, with praise and favours. Mnangagwa's chief rival, Solomon Mujuru, who was pushing for Mugabe's replacement, found himself isolated, unable to contest Mugabe's candidacy openly.

But divisions within ZANU-PF persisted and Mugabe was not able to have things all his own way. As well as promoting his claim to be ZANU-PF's Presidential candidate, he had also been pushing for the delay of Presidential elections until 2010 – a two-year extension of his term of office. He was not able to secure this. The compromise which emerged from ZANU's congress was that Mugabe could be the party's candidate, but that Presidential elections should take place at the same time as Parliamentary and local elections, which were due in 2008.

So ZANU-PF's internal politics drove the holding of an election at which every elected post in the country would be contested. Had the party been capable of imagining the possibility of defeat, it might have sought a hedge, some kind of staggering of elections so that the mood of the country could be judged. But the MDC seemed dead and buried and the mechanisms which had delivered victory three times since 2000 – a controlled state media, compliant ZANU-PF-affiliated quangos and an electorate easily cowed by the sound of gunfire – looked perfectly capable of doing so again.

It may seem remarkable that Mugabe was able to finesse his internal opponents, given the shambolic state of the country. But I had an early insight into his godlike status in 2006 when I attended the state funeral of one of his Ministers. ZANU-PF has created its own set of funeral grounds, Heroes' Acre, reserved for the band of brothers who had fought the revolutionary war, plus a few selected hangers-on. The most important of these Acres, earmarked for heroes of truly epic stature, is ten kilometres out of Harare on the Bulawayo road. These VIP funeral gardens consist of a long wooded driveway up to a hillside concreted over to accommodate numerous monuments, statues and graves. Some people claim that the arrangement of graves is intended to resemble a gun, if viewed from the air.

I arrived at the advertised time and found that my diplomatic ID got me a seat in the VIP area under a canvas shelter. I had a long chat with a senior engineer from Zimbabwe's Electricity Supply Agency. He reminisced about his undergraduate days at Loughborough University and bemoaned the wretched state of his infrastructure. The hours passed. The cheap seats filled up. Finally I heard the sirens of the elongated Presidential motorcade approaching from the city. An immense women's choir burst into stirring songs of resistance. A string of police cars, black limos, army trucks and an ambulance pulled up. Everyone leaped to their feet, ululating and chanting. My first glimpse of the great old man was when he reached the rostrum to give a eulogy that turned rapidly into a rousing political address.

I wasn't ready for how funny Mugabe was. He had the crowd in stitches as he went through his comic routine. Tony Blair was his favourite whipping boy. The crowd roared as Mugabe recalled 'all the gays' in his cabinet. 'Maybe that is why they meet in closed session.' The standard design of long-drop toilet used in Zimbabwe is known as a Blair toilet. Mugabe loves to play with this. 'The only Blairs we want in Zimbabwe are latrines.' He relished the word 'latrine', drawing out its two syllables and separating them with a comic pause of at least a second. It was not sycophancy that had the mourners in stitches. He may have been an ageing and corrupt dictator, but nobody could fault Mugabe's stand-up routine.

One of his best gags was at the expense of Cecil Rhodes: 'Some people say we should change our name back to Rhodesia to honour this white man. A man who loved this country so much he chose to live a thousand miles away in Cape Town. A man who only chose to live here once he was dead.' The crowd consisted mostly of party die-hards and public servants ordered or bribed to attend. But their affection for this old man was genuine. As he became more serious and spoke about the primacy of land in African politics, the need to take it from the colonial powers and give it 'back to we, the blacks', I wondered if I should re-evaluate my assumption that land seizure was a policy of greed, not principle. I was certainly convinced that there is at least a section of Zimbabwe's population whose loyalty to the old man is so great that they would support him to the death.

Mugabe's plan in 2007 was to create the type of electoral context he likes – a one-sided contest against a broken and demoralised opposition. But he didn't get things all his own way, because of the divisions within his party and because some other Southern African leaders held him partially to account. The MDC was a wretched wounded thing in late 2007, hammered by a state more or less identical in interest and guiding principle to the party that had ruled for nearly twenty-eight years. But it remained engaged by participating in Mbeki's mediation and played its weak hand as best it could, using the threat of abstention to secure some technical changes to the electoral framework agreed.

As the rains fell hard in December that year, the Combined Harare Residents Association reported what it believed was a case of cholera in Budiriro. Everybody thought this had to be nonsense; Zimbabwe had a supply of clean water and hadn't suffered an outbreak of cholera for forty years.

2

POSTURING AND POSITIONING

New Year's Day 2008 was the last painless and free day in the life of a man whose name we will never know. He lived in Mvuma in Zimbabwe's Midlands and, no doubt still nursing a hangover from a scud (a plastic container) of beer the night before, was arrested for theft. A succession of police officers tortured him over a space of three days. He was handcuffed and suspended between two tables in an agonising position known as 'the bridge'. Finally a broken bottleneck was shoved down his throat. Despite treatment at Gweru hospital, the man died. A post-mortem confirmed that his death was a result of his beatings in jail. Friends of his who reported the attack were too scared to give his name. Quite why this man, apparently just a petty thief, was so sadistically executed, we just do not know.

This death was not exceptional at any point of 2007 or 2008. Every month, human rights monitors recorded anything between several hundred and several thousand abuses. They ranged from physical assault, selective denial of food and demolition of houses through to terrible instances of mass rape, collective beatings and murder.

It seems incredible that three months before defeating Robert Mugabe and his ZANU-PF party, Zimbabwe's opposition MDC was contemplating boycotting the election. But as 2007 turned into 2008, the party was not ready either practically or emotionally. The MDC relied on donations from progressive and wealthy South Africans and did not believe lack of money would be a constraint. But its strategy was not defined, its internal communications were poor, many of its leading members were traumatised by violent abuse and its membership lacked confidence in victory.

Confronted with constant life-and-death dilemmas like the 11 March events, the MDC had started to opt out of a formal political process which was hopelessly slanted in favour of Robert Mugabe's ZANU-PF. The MDC believed that it had won the 2005 House of Assembly elections, but had ended up as a small minority party. The implications of Tsvangirai's decision to boycott subsequent Senate elections in November 2005 – deeming participation to be futile – had been unexpectedly serious. A group of MPs split off in protest against this decision, and against the autocratic manner in which Tsvangirai had taken it, and formed a new political party. Confusingly it insisted that it had the right to be called the MDC. To Robert Mugabe's delight, the opposition not only split, but also started a long and pointless argument about the ownership of its name.

The modest reforms set out in constitutional amendment eighteen had eliminated some of the grosser benefits of incumbency which Mugabe enjoyed. It had also created a better political atmosphere. Nobody in the MDC was likely to forget the events of 2007, but as the year closed there was no immediate threat of a renewal of violence. Yet nobody anticipated any electoral outcome other than the re-election of Robert Mugabe as President and of a Parliament compliant to his wishes. The MDC continued to argue that the lack of political freedoms and biases within the electoral system meant that a fair election was not possible.

At the turn of the year I wrote an analysis of the prospects for the 2008 Parliamentary election. My conclusion was that the MDC would do well to take 70 of the 210 seats in the House of Assembly. I felt this was both a realistic estimate of the prospects for the party – which, as we have seen, won about a third of the seats in 2005 – and a practical target, as securing more than a third of Parliament would prevent Mugabe amending the constitution at will. My expectations were perfectly in line with the standard wisdom of the diplomatic community and were, of course, completely wrong.

I wrote my first entry for the Foreign and Commonwealth Office's blog around this time on the topic of Mugabe's assumed electoral invincibility. Blogging was an innovation, championed by the new Foreign Secretary David Miliband. He was keen to get the Office's messages out in a less rigid way through the internet. The idea was that individual members of staff would write personal views for publication on the FCO's website. I jumped at this chance to say something about Zimbabwe's elections in a livelier style than was normal for Foreign Office reporting.

I argued that it was already obvious that the Zimbabwean election was not going to be fair, that Mugabe would employ ten techniques to secure his re-election:

1. Beating and terrorising his opponents
2. Electoral fraud
3. Giving food only to his supporters
4. Buying off the legal system
5. Monopolising the media
6. Patronising the traditional leaders (village chiefs and elders)
7. Looting and corruption
8. Fooling the rest of Africa
9. Fear
10. Keeping the urban people down and the rural people out

This list proved to be correct about the techniques Mugabe would use, but this was not evidence of any great prescience or insight on my part. I was simply summarising what Mugabe had done to win the last three elections. There was no reason to think he was going to change a winning approach.

The general assumption at the start of 2008 was that Mugabe could not fail to win re-election. It was true that city people hated him and would overwhelmingly vote MDC. Harare people of any profession were happy to say openly that the old man had to go, after all they had suffered at his hands. The Afrobarometer – a sample survey of views and experiences in various African nations – found in 2005 that 72 per cent of Harare's people reported that some part of their housing had been knocked down during Operation Murambatsvina, Mugabe's vindictive demolition of urban property that year. This fed straight through to a collapse in ZANU-PF's urban support, which was estimated to be no more than 19 per cent in 2005. It wasn't just Murambatsvina which drove ZANU-PF's unpopularity. Zimbabweans were getting poorer. As 2007 turned into 2008, independent economists believed that formal unemployment stood at 80 per cent.

But city constituencies amounted to only 20 per cent of seats in the House of Assembly. Rural people would elect 80 per cent of MPs. My assumption was that rural Zimbabweans were much more likely to vote for Mugabe. They had little access to information other than what the state media provided. These media did not report Zimbabwe's problems. They carried only praise for Mugabe and reports of his achievements. When the MDC was mentioned at all, it was described as a treacherous organisation working with Western governments to destroy Zimbabwe's independence and hand control of the country's resources back to colonial powers. International media which might report something different, such as the BBC, were banned.

Rural people (I assumed) were more traditionally minded than urbanites and more likely to support the party which had ruled the country for twenty-eight years. They were also strongly influenced by traditional leaders – every village has a headman and every area has a chief. These leaders used to be quite independent from official government structures. But Mugabe took control of their selection in the 1980s and began to impose leaders who supported him. He also used patronage to win the chiefs' favour, giving them cars and televisions. By 2008, the traditional leadership structure, with a few heroic exceptions, was little more than an organising network for ZANU-PF. I expected that tens of thousands of headmen would instruct their villagers to vote ZANU-PF and that this instruction would carry weight.

Rural voters were also generally poorer and less educated than residents of Harare, Bulawayo, Mutare and other large towns. As the economy shrank, and agriculture – which supported more than a million people in 1998 – collapsed, rural people became more and more passive and dependent on aid. Assistance came in various forms. As the state seized control of agriculture it also created a monopoly over the purchase and supply of maize through the Grain Marketing Board (GMB). This Board began to use food as a political tool, feeding only individuals loyal to Mugabe. Headmen again played an important role, identifying people in their villages who failed to show appropriate respect for ZANU-PF or even openly supported the MDC or belonged to a campaigning NGO. Such people were not allocated a share of maize supplied by the GMB.

GMB support was not the only type of donation rural people received. Many were supported by remittances from family members living in cities or abroad. And from 2005 onwards, after maize production fell below the level necessary to feed the population, the international community began to spend tens of millions of pounds each year to give out food directly to Zimbabweans. The Americans used a consortium of NGOs to distribute food imported from the US. Other donor nations, including the UK, channelled money through the UN's World Food Programme, which then bought food to hand out. This attempt by the international community to work around Mugabe to support Zimbabweans became a major point of conflict. ZANU-PF agents stole some international food deliveries and controlled the distribution of others, so that only Mugabe's supporters benefited. At various times the regime simply banned international agencies from working, so that their supplies could not frustrate ZANU-PF efforts to control people by means of their access to food.

The transformation of rural communities may prove to be the longest-lived and most ruinous effect of Mugabe's rule. In 1998 rural Zimbabwe was the most productive farming area in Africa and arguably the world. An enormous range of introduced crops grew vigorously, including lucrative products such as coffee, tobacco, sugar and citrus fruits. Zimbabwe's workforce was without doubt the most educated and skilled agricultural labour in Africa. By 2008, the average rural Zimbabwean had been reduced to a peasant. Travelling through small villages, I would see people sitting doing nothing, surrounded by dusty fields. Their children might be chasing a few goats about, but maize cultivation was in decline. The entire supply chain which equipped a nation for agriculture had collapsed. It was too much of a risk for a poor person to invest savings in seed, knowing that it would be impossible to get fertiliser to make the seed grow. Easier to wait for ZANU-PF or the UN to give out food. People's natural urge to feed themselves and advance their communities had been crushed out of them. Africa's premier workforce was now pacified, economically useless, aid-dependent and – I supposed – ready to support anybody, including Robert Mugabe, who promised to keep the food handouts, conveniently funded by the UK and other donors, coming.

In the face of such a body of reasons why Mugabe would surely win his re-election, Tsvangirai had to face down many who argued that the MDC should not contest elections held under Mugabe's crooked rules. It required substantial vision to see the possibility of victory despite ZANU-PF's control of the state media, politically partisan food distributions, the puppet court system and corrupted security forces. The alternative strategies of calling for street protests or appealing to Zimbabwe's indifferent neighbours within SADC had an emotional attraction.

This abstentionist tendency was to the fore at the start of January 2008. Many members and supporters of the opposition argued that the MDC could not win elections that year. John Makumbe, a political analyst at the University of Zimbabwe, who is deeply hostile to the Mugabe regime, set out this school of thought publicly: 'It is obvious that any opposition political party participating in this election will be legitimizing the Mugabe regime. It will obviously lose the elections. Under the current constitution, only Mugabe's party, ZANU-PF, will win the election.' Time would prove Makumbe and many others wrong. The MDC could win. But Makumbe's viewpoint was common in oppositionist circles at the start of the year.

Tsvangirai assessed that abstention would not secure the change that Zimbabwe needed. What few perceived was that ZANU-PF was in some ways in an even worse condition than the MDC. The lack of support for Mugabe's leadership was clear enough. But resources for campaigning were scarce too. ZANU-PF does not see a distinction between itself as the eternal ruling party and the state. Its normal practice is to appropriate public resources for party purposes such as contesting elections. But in 2008, after ten years of economic decline, the state coffers were empty.

Three events early in February transformed the election, galvanising the MDC and exposing the divisions within ZANU-PF which were evident enough at the time of the party congress, but which were covered over by gaudy expressions of support for Mugabe from die-hard supporters. The first was the belated announcement by the Electoral Commission that the 'harmonised' election – by which it meant simultaneous contests for the Presidency, Senate, House of Assembly and local authorities – would take place on 29 March. With less than two months to go, the Commission was criticised for not allowing itself enough time to prepare for the election and for denying the opportunity for a lengthy campaign. But the announcement did serve to set the clock ticking. Morgan Tsvangirai knew that the time for complaining about the conduct of the election and for posturing to the international community was over. He could abstain or he could choose to fight. He took the latter course and saw at once that there was no point in fighting unless he tried his utmost to win. Tsvangirai's idling and battered machine slipped into gear.

The Electoral Commission did not see fit to set a date for a second round of voting in the Presidential election, which would be required if no candidate scored 50 per cent on the first round. The retired military men who drew their stipend for acting as electoral commissioners considered any outcome other than a clear victory for Robert Mugabe impossible.

The second event (strictly speaking a non-event) was the collapse of an attempt by the two MDC factions to negotiate an electoral pact. Tsvangirai's group was clearly larger and more popular than the breakaway party led by Arthur Mutambara. (It was around this time that the factions first started to call themselves MDC-T and MDC-M, using the initials of their leaders to differentiate themselves for a confused electorate.)

Arthur Mutambara is a strange, isolated figure within Zimbabwean politics. He is tall, handsome and young enough to be Robert Mugabe's grandson. He returned from university in the US in 2006 to lead the MDC splinter party, which he has done with more eloquence and charisma than good judgement. Even Mutambara's friends concede that he is egotistical. He showed the extent of his self-regard, as well as a shaky grasp of grammar, in an interview with Shmuley Boteach in 2009: 'I think it's fair to say that I know better than Obama what is good for Zimbabwe ... If they, the political leaders of the West, were more reflective and decided to sit down and talk to me in this manner: "You are a young leader, a Rhodes scholar, you taught at MIT, you are smarter than me, tell me what's going on," because I am.'

Members of Tsvangirai's MDC tend to see Mutambara as a ZANU-PF stooge. It was fishy, they contended, that he was not tortured in March 2007. At key moments – such as when Simba Makoni announced his Presidential candidacy (see below), or when the 2008 Parliament elected its first speaker – Mutambara has broken with Tsvangirai and supported ZANU-PF candidates. The best one can say to date is that Mutambara may be trying to occupy a centre ground between the two main parties which does not exist. The risk he faces is that he will not make peace, but simply alienate everybody. Mutambara may be a man whose day is to come.

Mutambara's faction of the MDC is essentially a Matabeleland phenomenon. The 2008 elections showed that it had limited popularity in Zimbabwe's two Ndebele provinces and none beyond. Tribalism does not play as great a role in Zimbabwe's politics as it does in other African states where voting is along ethnic lines. But the effects of tension, often bordering on hatred, between the two largest tribal groups – the Shona and the Ndebele – are important. Robert Mugabe is Shona, as are around three-quarters of the population. The Matabele or Ndebele people are Zulus. They brutally dominated the Shona in Zimbabwe's pre-colonial history. During the liberation war of the 1970s, the Shona and Ndebele formed separate armies – ZANU and ZAPU respectively. On independence, these guerrilla forces became rival political parties, which gave the early years of the 1980s some sense of political diversity. But between 1983 and 1985 the Shona consolidated power and gained revenge for history. At least twenty thousand (nobody knows the number) Ndebele people were massacred during the Gukurahundi operation. ZAPU's leader Joshua Nkomo, his people crushed, was forced into a unity accord with ZANU. But this was no partnership of equals. Robert Mugabe's Government has been, among other things, an exercise in the Shona oppression of Matabeles. Nowhere is he hated more deeply than in Matabeleland's capital, Bulawayo (which aptly means 'the place of slaughter' in Zulu). The MDC has many roots in society: in the NGO sector, in the labour movement, but also in the strong support it enjoys from Ndebele people.

Zimbabwe's other smaller tribal groups, such as the Shangan and the Tongans, are profoundly alienated from the country's mainstream life. They have been thrust to the geographical and economic margins. Like many of Africa's weaker groups, they have been moved wholesale to make way for national parks, the flooding of the Zambezi valley or agriculture. The colonial and post-independence governments have treated them as an inconvenience to be managed roughly and denied basic rights.

Morgan Tsvangirai, like Mugabe, is Shona (though he was born not in the Mashonaland heartland but in Masvingo). As such, he was always mistrusted by some Ndebele MDC members. This ethnic tension widened and cemented the split over electoral tactics between the two MDC factions. Mutambara's grouping held its first party congress not in the capital but in Bulawayo, giving notice that, while it had no real expectation of nationwide appeal, it hoped to be a force to rival Tsvangirai in Matabeleland.

Nonetheless, many within both factions felt unified by a common purpose – the urgency of defeating Mugabe. Discussions between the two factions quickly concluded that reunifying the party could be ruled out. If anything, antipathy between the factions had intensified since 2005. Tsvangirai had not changed his style and there were even times when violence between the two MDCs broke out. Trudy Stevenson, a slight white woman who represented Harare North for MDC-M, was horribly beaten by youths who may have been part of the Tsvangirai faction.

Despite these hostilities, the factions could agree that they would be disadvantaged if they both contested the same Parliamentary seats, splitting the anti-Mugabe vote. Talks advanced to the point where a deal was on the table. MDC-M would be given a clear run in sixty-five seats, including thirty which were safe for the MDC. At working level this deal was agreed. Tsvangirai rejected the proposed electoral pact outright, a decision for which he was hammered. Mutambara's people saw it as more evidence of his dictatorial tendencies. Civil society groups were dismayed too. McDonald Lewanika of the

Crisis in Zimbabwe Coalition said, 'This parochial agenda will not benefit either formation of the MDC because the ruling party will use the division.' Bill Saidi, a political commentator, agreed: 'It's worthless going into the election divided because there is no chance they are going to win.' Saidi joined the long line of experts proved wrong by events in 2008.

MDC-M had been overplaying its hand in the negotiations. Tsvangirai reasoned that the 2008 election might not bring him to power, but it would certainly be a chance to put Mutambara's people in their place and show who the real opposition was. Strangely, the failure of the talks solidified Tsvangirai's instincts to fight and to win. Abstaining and letting Mugabe win an empty victory made some sense, but abstaining and watching Mutambara's upstarts assume the role of opposition party would have been intolerable.

The third catalytic event in February – easily the most unexpected and startling – was Simba Makoni's announcement that he was running for president against Mugabe and Tsvangirai. Simba Makoni is a telegenic and clever man who looks younger than his years (he was born in 1950). He did not fight in the liberation war, preferring to study at Leeds University and Leicester Polytechnic. He returned to independent Zimbabwe and took various cabinet and senior management posts within the regime. His reputation as a man of integrity rests on two occasions when he resigned after being overruled by Mugabe on a point of principle. After the last occasion, when he resigned as finance minister in 2001, Mugabe denounced him as an 'economic saboteur'. But Makoni never split from ZANU-PF and was a member of the party when he declared his candidacy for president. Indeed he said he wanted to run as a ZANU-PF member, but would stand as an independent if he had to.

As a senior ZANU-PF official, implicated in much of what the party had done, Makoni had to distance himself from Mugabe's repression and failure, in order to broaden his potential support. He used his declaration speech to do this, saying,

'The Zimbabwe of today is full of fear, in deep stress and polarised. The nation is also characterised by disease and extreme poverty.' Makoni attributed the nation's crisis to a 'failure of leadership' and promised 'national healing and reconciliation'. This was in fact the most shocking aspect of Makoni's declaration – that it made manifest the split in ZANU-PF which was normally concealed by shows of unity.

Makoni clearly hoped, perhaps expected, that leading members of ZANU-PF would publicly endorse him. He urged them to do so: 'I know there are a lot of people in the party and government who support what I am doing. The majority of ZANU-PF feels the same way. The time for decision has come. Jump off the fence.' Some suspected even that Solomon Mujuru, one of the biggest beasts and a man keen to unseat Mugabe, had put Makoni up to his challenge for the Presidency and had promised to back him. If any such promise was given, it wasn't kept.

Makoni was an exciting prospect as Presidential candidate because he was so widely acceptable. Those 'Rhodie' Zimbabweans who quietly lament the end of white rule, saw him as the ideal black man: clever, decent, steady, able to stabilise the country and sweet-talk the multinationals. Makoni was not acceptable to ZANU-PF's old guard, who considered only a veteran of the liberation war to be fit for leadership, but the younger generation of ruling-party supporters relished the chance of a generation shift. Plenty of MDC voters too were ready to admit that Makoni would be a great improvement on Mugabe. Makoni looked like a credible unity candidate, who could take large numbers of votes from each of the other candidates. Arthur Mutambara immediately jumped on to the Makoni bandwagon, pledging his party's support for the third candidate. In truth this was a relief for him as he did not relish the prospect either of endorsing Tsvangirai or of running himself and coming in a distant third.

ZANU-PF, divided and strapped for cash, was horrified by Makoni's disloyalty. The politburo of the party expelled him at the first opportunity on 11 February. The state media went to work on him, saying that his announcement was not a bombshell, but 'the loud fart all silently agree never happened'. Makoni was a Western stooge 'giving a black face to the voices from the White House and Whitehall'. Joseph Chinotimba, a spokesman for Mugabe's feral war veterans, implied that Makoni faced more than criticism from the party he had betrayed. 'Traitors should know that ZANU-PF has a history of dealing harshly with their kind.' Cruel words from the *Herald*, the government's daily mouthpiece, were actually helpful to Makoni. Harare's chattering class, ever paranoid and often right to be so, was debating whether Makoni was some kind of stalking horse for one of ZANU-PF's elderly hard men, rather than a reform-minded independent. The savaging he received from the ruling clique made that conspiracy theory less credible.

If Makoni had any thought that the entire party would defect to him, finishing Mugabe off, he soon found that the old man was still in control. Dumiso Dabengwa, the head of ZAPU's military intelligence during the war, was the only senior ZANU-PF man to break ranks and publicly back Makoni. Dabengwa gave Makoni some credibility with ruling-party voters in Matabeleland. But Makoni needed some of ZANU-PF's senior Shona to back him and deliver votes in the party's heartland.

A speculative hope that many entertained was that Makoni had links into the military – perhaps via his tacit supporter General Mujuru. If so, he might be able to curb any attempts by the regime to use violence during the elections. He might also be able to control any vote-rigging that the security services were planning. These kinds of ideas got Zimbabweans thoroughly excited in February. But my own sense was that Makoni never achieved the transfer of support from ZANU-PF that he expected. The electoral administration bureaucracy appeared to report only through structures loyal to Mugabe. There was relatively little violence or evidence of vote tampering while

Makoni stayed in the race, and plenty after he was knocked out. But there were other strong reasons for the upturn in violence and little cause to believe that Makoni was acting to muzzle the military during the March campaign.

After Makoni declared I (again in good company) was even less sanguine about the MDC's prospects. In mid-February I was telling people that Makoni had a 30 per cent chance of scoring enough votes to deny Mugabe an outright 50 per cent on the first round. I believed that most Tsvangirai voters would transfer their support to Makoni, as the candidate best placed to unseat Mugabe, meaning that the MDC leader would come a weak third. This prediction was even more inaccurate than my guess relating to the Parliamentary result.

Southern African commentators analysed the new three-way election in the same manner and urged Tsvangirai to with-draw so as to give Makoni a clear run at Mugabe. This was not wholly disinterested advice. A smooth technocrat and insider like Makoni looked a much better bet for stabilising Zimbabwe than a bloodied trade-union troublemaker. Makoni was the kind of man Mbeki would be happy to have tea with, free of Tsvangirai's working-class vulgarity.

Tsvangirai never even considered pulling out. His political instinct was that the race was now open and alive. ZANU-PF was wounded. Anything could happen. In any case, Makoni was not the saviour many took him to be. He had sat in cabinet in 2000 and so was complicit in the violent agricultural inva-sions taking place at that time. 'I would like to be among the first to welcome Mr Makoni to the opposition in Zimbabwe,' Tsvangirai said. 'Opposition leaders in Zimbabwe face arrest, beating, tear gas, treason trials and the shock of seeing their supporters murdered. Mr Makoni knows this because he has seen it from the safety of the ZANU-PF politburo.'

With less than a month to go before polling day, an opinion poll was published. Polls are rare in Zimbabwe and invariably suspect. It is hard enough to sample Zimbabwe's large rural areas in a representative way and all but impossible to persuade people that they can safely say what they really think. Within those constraints the results of the poll were dynamite. Tsvangirai had 28 per cent; Mugabe 20 per cent and Makoni 9 per cent; 24 per cent of respondents refused to say whom they would vote for; the remainder did not know. It was hard to know which figure was more surprising. Makoni's surge through the centre was not yet happening. Mugabe's level of support was shockingly low. Tsvangirai, against all odds, seemed to have opened up a clear lead.

Nobody could quite believe the poll results. Could Tsvangirai really be doing so well? Maybe the sample was heavily skewed towards his urban voters. Some felt Makoni had to be doing better than estimated. Even the head of the polling agency, MPOI, felt that Makoni was still a credible candidate: 'Makoni has a lot of latent support. Those in the shadows, particularly the senior figures who are being talked about, need to gather their courage before election day and declare themselves.' But the MDC began to throw off its doubts. The poll vindicated the sense it was getting from the country. 29 March, the day when Tsvangirai might just defeat Mugabe, could not come soon enough.

3

MARCH 2008: THE DEFEAT OF ROBERT MUGABE

It was time to hit the road. The Harare-based political clique had manoeuvred as best it could, but now it was time for the parties to win and lose the election, time to campaign in the real Zimbabwe: the rural areas where most people live, largely isolated from political news from the capital.

I wanted to hit the road too and observe what was going on. But before I could do so I had to spend a sticky morning at Harare's polytechnic waiting to pay the Zimbabwean Government US$300 of British taxpayers' money so that I could call myself an officially accredited election observer. I tried some banter with the team issuing the accreditations. First I offered to pay the fee in worthless Zimbabwean dollars, which raised a laugh. Next I tried pointing out that observers of British elections are accredited free of charge. This prompted a grin from the young lad taking my picture. He pointed out that my US$300 got me not only an official pass but also a Chinese-made t-shirt and baseball cap saying 'Election observer'. What a bargain.

Along with other Embassy staff, I set off on a series of two- or three-day field trips. Visiting every part of the country, even once, was an impossible task. After all there were going to be almost 10,000 polling stations. Main roads are pretty good, but the villages I needed to get to, if I really wanted to understand the election, often took hours to reach along slow dirt roads. The British Embassy used every vehicle it had to send out monitoring teams and we shared information with other embassies doing the same, but even so we knew that our coverage could not possibly be comprehensive. Rather than making short token visits to many places, I decided to pick a particularly interesting and significant area and visit it repeatedly, so as to gain an understanding that was both in-depth and dynamic.

I used to love driving through Zimbabwe. The country is green and open. There's always something interesting to see – and if time did drag, I could always pass it by deciding whether to pick up hitchhikers. Throughout March I saw people waiting by the roadside to travel with no definite idea how they were going to achieve this. There were often several hundred people waiting at major road junctions. They were hoping for an infrequent bus or a passing pick-up truck ready to give a lift. But bus companies had been badly hit by hyperinflation. During the Government's periodic (and disastrous) attempts to implement a Communist-style price-control policy, the companies were required to stick to artificially low fares equivalent to only a few pence. It was impossible to maintain and fuel buses with so little revenue, so buses often stopped running until the price control was loosened and bus companies could charge a viable market fare again.

The situation during the elections was even worse. More people than usual wanted to travel – to go home, either to vote or in case there was trouble. But ZANU-PF, the Electoral Commission and the security services often requisitioned buses for their own purposes, which further disrupted the limited service. So the crowds waiting for a ride were even larger than normal. Some people, of course, did not have the money to pay for a bus journey at any price, but still needed to travel. They were waiting by the roadside for a miracle and I liked to help when I could. The main problem was that hitchhikers could easily turn into carjackers. For this reason the Embassy Security Manager had forbidden Embassy staff to pick anyone up. So I had to be cautious to avoid both being carjacked and being found out – which would lead to a vigorous reprimand back in Harare.

At first I adopted a policy of picking up only women or children. Once on the road to Mutare in 2006, I had picked up two children who couldn't have been more than eight years old – one was too terrified of me and my large car to utter a single word; the other admitted her name was Blessing, but could say no more until she let out a shriek as I roared past where she wanted to get out. Blessing offered me $20,000 as a fare, which was at that time worth 10p, and blessed me with a smile when I turned the money down. It was a touching moment. I was concerned also by the vulnerability of those two tiny, shy children, travelling several kilometres by themselves. I then read in the paper about 'honey-trap carjackers' who placed siren women at roadsides to lure drivers into the clutches of waiting gangs. So I amended my policy to one of picking up only *plain* women or children.

The area that I chose to visit repeatedly during the campaign was Masvingo. Jestina Mukoko, a leading human rights campaigner, had identified a number of communities in Masvingo as likely hot spots for electoral violence, based on her analysis of what had happened there during previous elections. Electorally, Masvingo would be fascinating too. It was a marginal, battleground area. The MDC would not be able to win a national election without doing well in Masvingo.

Ethnically too, there were interesting dimensions to the contest in the province. While Zimbabwe might look tribally homogeneous – some three-quarters of its people are Shona – its politics of ethnicity are more complicated. Both Robert Mugabe and Morgan Tsvangirai are Shona, but Mugabe belongs to the Zezuru clan, while Tsvangirai is Karanga. As well as profoundly alienating other tribes, such as Ndebele people, by brutal social engineering, Mugabe had antagonised many Shona people by preferentially advancing people of his own clan. Tsvangirai, who was born in Masvingo and belonged to a different clan, was in a good position to take advantage of any ethnically based anti-Mugabe sentiment.

In addition to visiting the city of Masvingo itself, I spent time in quiet towns hiding in rusty-coloured hills packed with uranium and copper, minerals which thousands of miners, like the young Morgan Tsvangirai, dig for. Masvingo's soil is a rich red colour, and in the course of several visits in March I began to love that country and those towns – places like Gutu, Zaka, Bikita and Chivi.

I wanted to make the most of my accreditation – the Zimbabwean Government's permission to observe the election. Meeting Electoral Commission (ZEC) people was a core part of this function, as it was my business to assess whether the election would be well organised. Many ZEC people I spoke to recognised this. For example, in Gutu, ZEC officials were friendly and welcoming and gave me all the time I needed to ask questions. They looked organised – their offices were obviously temporary, typically borrowed spaces in local council offices, but were productively cluttered with manuals, large plastic ballot boxes and maps. They told a convincing story of how well their preparations for election day were going. They had the materials and transport they needed. They had found polling stations, almost always schools, and recruited polling station staff, almost always the teachers who worked in those schools. They were – rightly – confident about putting on a good show on the day.

But not everyone was so helpful. I found that other ZEC officials were skilled at hiding in toilets or behind bogus excuses when I came to visit. I would turn up to discover that the ZEC officer had just gone out, without his mobile, to an unspecified place for an unspecified length of time. Some ZEC people would at least dare to show their faces but would then refuse to talk or to answer questions. Occasionally an official – I particularly remember a district electoral officer in Zaka – would invent reasons why he couldn't talk to me. He would say that he had orders not to talk to observers. I would ask if these orders were written down. No. So who gave the orders? Any disclosure of that information would breach national security. I never let this nonsense drop – I was determined not to let them get away with it and anyway it was too much fun to fire a long series of pedantic questions. Did the orders come over the telephone or at a meeting? Was the person who gave the orders a man or a woman? Why did nobody else have similar orders? I said I would have to report this obstruction of accredited observers to the Provincial Office. At this point the poor man at Zaka simply shut down, sitting motionless and saying nothing until I left, unable to work out whether it would be more terrible to be seen helping the British Embassy man or to be reported to his superior.

The lack of co-operation, which I and other observers received from about a third of ZEC officials, was particularly silly because the story that ZEC had to tell was generally such a good one. The chief elections officer of the province, who was friendly, open and generous with his time, gave me a picture of a remarkably smooth operation. With two weeks to go, he said, ZEC had already recruited all the polling station staff it needed. It was to hold three days of training courses for these staff. There was plenty of transport to ferry around ballot boxes and papers, which had already arrived. A multi-party liaison committee was meeting each week to ensure a free and fair election. The committee was happy with progress and did not anticipate any problems. Of course I tried to push at the boundaries of this account by probing into areas that weren't really ZEC's responsibility, but the elections officer rebuffed my provocative efforts charmingly. He did not know if there was any political violence (ask the police), but thought not. He did not know how many people had registered to vote (ask the registrar general). He did not know who was going to win (ask the political parties).

Most of ZEC's mid-level officials – who were usually civil servants within the education system drafted in to manage the election – were a credit to the superb education Zimbabwe used to provide and to the traditions of a civil service that used to be the best in Africa. Despite the political bias of the senior levels of ZEC and the economic chaos in the country, they went on to deliver a credible election.

However good election day was going to be, one aspect of the pre-election preparations that was not well administered was the registration of voters. Zimbabwe's system is modelled on Britain's, but customised to favour ZANU-PF. Voters need to register with their local authority to be on the electoral roll. They are then entitled to vote in their home area. In practice, large numbers of Zimbabweans – probably more than 50 per cent of adult Zimbabwean citizens – were either not on the electoral roll or unable to get to the area where they were registered to vote.

The most obviously excluded group was the diaspora. By 2008 an estimated three million Zimbabweans were living outside the country, seeking to escape the effects of the economic decline or of a sudden collapse in their living conditions, such as the mass evictions that followed the farm invasions or the demolitions of urban property during Operation Murambatsvina. The large majority of these refugees and economic migrants had moved to South Africa, though tens of thousands also tried their luck in the UK, Botswana, Mozambique, Zambia or Australia. Although some Zimbabweans abroad landed on their feet and secured skilled work as nurses or teachers, most refugees from Mugabe's regime were homeless or in temporary accommodation in South Africa, and survived by working illegally for low wages. The presence of so many illegal workers antagonised South Africa's townships and sparked a series of vicious lynchings in Johannesburg and Durban during 2008. Zimbabweans saw two ironies, both cruel. It was appalling that refugees who had fled violence in Zimbabwe should have met horrible deaths in South Africa and perhaps just as appalling that even the import of civil unrest from Zimbabwe did not galvanise Mbeki to resolve the crisis there.

Zimbabwe's electoral laws do not allow citizens living abroad to vote by mail or at polling stations in Zimbabwean embassies, thus excluding three million Zimbabweans at a stroke. It is safe to assume that expatriate Zimbabweans – people who have already voted with their feet by leaving the country – would strongly prefer Tsvangirai as president. If as few as one in ten diaspora voters had voted, assuming that eight out of ten would have preferred Tsvangirai, the MDC would have won the Presidential vote by a decisive 20 per cent margin.

It is likely that deregistering and otherwise disfranchising opposition voters by pushing them to the edges of society – even out of the country – was part of the reasoning behind farm invasions and the Murambatsvina urban house-destruction campaign. It is no coincidence that these brutal initiatives were rolled out in the years after the electorate first showed its displeasure with Mugabe, by rejecting his proposals for a new constitution at a referendum in 2000. Urban voters – hundreds of thousands of whom were driven from their homes by Murambatsvina – had begun to reject Mugabe consistently since the creation of the MDC. In the late 1990s several white farmers were brave and foolhardy enough to support the MDC publicly. Mugabe reasoned that black farm workers were coming under the unwholesome influence of their bosses. By authorising his supporters to invade farms, he dispersed agricultural workers, thereby dramatically reducing their ability to vote against him.

Even voters still in Zimbabwe found registration awkward. A large number of people born in rural areas, but working in the cities, had to travel home (a time-consuming and expensive business) twice – once to register and once to vote. Many did not bother and lost their votes. Zimbabwe's restrictive nationality laws also exclude from the electoral roll anybody whose grandparents were not born in Zimbabwe. Many people who were born in Zimbabwe and know no other country came to vote on 29 March only to be told that they could not, as they were foreigners. The restriction particularly affected Zimbabweans of Malawian origin, whose parents or grandparents moved to Zimbabwe in the good old days, for work.

The registration system worked smoothly only for Zimbabweans who lived permanently in the areas where they were born. In practice this meant poorer, rural people – the group among whom Mugabe enjoyed strongest support. It is surely no coincidence that members of other demographic groups, who tend to vote MDC, faced awkward hurdles if they wanted to vote in 2008 – hurdles that often proved too high. As I contemplated the desperately close results of the March 2008 Presidential and House of Assembly elections, I thought how much more comfortable the MDC's winning margin would have been if millions of the Zimbabweans who have lost most from Mugabe's rule had been permitted to vote.

I made a note to monitor the proportion of voters turned away from polling stations on election day. I was sure the percentage would be high. To see for myself how electoral registration was working, I visited the registrar's office in Gutu. The place was in chaos. A queue of 200 people was slowly advancing through the hot midday sun. Once inside the office, people were trying to achieve a range of bureaucratic objectives: asking about scarce public works jobs and Government training courses, registering births, deaths and marriages and so on. About half of the people, who had gamely spent their day queuing to register to vote, found they had wasted their time. The registrar told them they were too late to register to vote in March. As well as those who were turned away from polling stations on election day, it was clear that many thousands of Zimbabweans had no idea about the deadlines for registration (which kept changing and were poorly advertised) and so missed their opportunity to register and vote. I had plenty of reason to conclude that, while voting might well go smoothly on 29 March, the mass exclusion of the bulk of Zimbabweans from the election dramatically weakened its value as a democratic exercise.

Part of my job was also to meet members of the political parties. I always tried to visit ZANU-PF's local offices but, in the days before the election, I often found they were closed up as if the local party was inactive. If I did come across anyone there, it would be an old man who looked at me blankly as I asked how the canvassing was going, and just shrugged his shoulders in response. So it was usually something of a waste of time attempting to meet ZANU-PF local officers, though I could tell myself that I was showing courtesy and balance by seeking their views.

I was able to persuade a retiring ZANU-PF senator to meet me for dinner at the lodge where I was staying. I pushed plenty of wine his way, which was part of the deal as well as the standard diplomatic technique for extracting the maximum from – to use a classic Foreign Office phrase – unhelpful interlocutors. Like most ZANU people privately meeting 'unfriendly' diplomats, he was keen to prove that he was only a semi-detached member of the regime. He was full of apology for the state of the country and Mugabe's continuing Presidency. Things were very bad. Food production had really collapsed. The one sure way to make people angry was to make them hungry. ZANU-PF was in for some bad results. My guest rattled on in this vein for some time. Mugabe ought to retire, but who could make him do so? Most people in ZANU were – like himself – benign academic types with no involvement in violence or corruption. They were just frustrated technocrats who wanted the country to work properly, but were having to wait for the old man's exit before taking over. The MDC were an ignorant, disorganised rabble by comparison. We should not imagine that Morgan Tsvangirai would make anything better. There were some good people in his party but most lacked experience or education.

Another cork popped. Of course the British Government played into Mugabe's hands by continuing to interfere in Zimbabwe like a colonial power. Clare Short started things off when she wrote that letter in 1997, saying that she was Irish and would not take responsibility for Zimbabwe's problems any more. Mugabe had been enraged, not least that a pathetically minor British minister should dare to write in such arrogant terms. The British just did not understand African politics. Every time Tony Blair criticised Mugabe the old man got a new lease of life. Who could attack a liberation hero who clearly continued to rile the old colonial power?

Somewhere towards the bottom of the second bottle, I was made privy to the full master plan. Living in Zimbabwe was no longer really tolerable; retirement with the family, judiciously located already in Wolverhampton, was a much better idea. Luckily the travel ban applied only to the Zimbabwean Government, not to Parliamentarians and certainly not to established friends of the British Embassy. ZANU-PF's finest: slyly negotiating with 'the enemy' for an exit from the country they had trashed.

MDC-T people were by contrast generous with their time and opinions. On my first visit to Gutu, the party put together a raft of candidates to brief me, led by Crispen Mudzuri, a friendly man – clearly the elder of the local party – in a dashing trilby. Mudzuri (a member of what turned out to be quite a clan of MDC Mudzuris in Masvingo) did all the talking; the young men – they were all men – running for various council seats supported him by nodding vigorously, but were clearly not yet empowered to open their own mouths.

Mudzuri was confident and expansive – he was enjoying the campaign. The MDC was doing well. Its rallies in rural areas – which would have been impossible in previous years – were each attracting more than 200 people, including old folk who had never previously dared to listen to the opposition's message. ZANU-PF was occasionally sending hecklers or hooligans to disrupt rallies, but there was no real violence. The worst that had happened in Gutu was a ZANU-PF councillor making threats and singing aggressive songs. Fickle young men, who used to ally themselves with ZANU-PF for no other reason than that it had the loudest voice and the best t-shirts, now supported the MDC. ZANU-PF was inactive. Mudzuri's forecast was that the MDC was on course to win four out of five Parliamentary seats in Gutu. This confidence appeared again in a later meeting with Alois Chaimiti, executive mayor of Masvingo town, who forecast gains also in Zaka, Chivi and Bikita. Chaimiti himself expected to become a senator (which he duly did).

Mudzuri and Chaimiti were not too concerned about ballot stuffing or abuse of postal votes. They anticipated two problems with the poll. They feared that the police would exploit their duty to assist illiterate voters, by attempting to monitor and influence them. This was a perfectly valid suspicion. In 2005, village headmen had instructed all their villagers to ask for police assistance, so that their compliance with the order to vote ZANU-PF could be monitored. The MDC men were also concerned about soldiers under orders to vote several times, either by exploiting weaknesses in the registration process or by using fake IDs. Voters were supposed to dip their fingers in purple indelible ink, so that returning officers could readily see people trying to vote twice. Chaimiti's theory was that returning officers would be instructed to use ink that washed off easily instead. He also alleged that some polling stations had been placed very close together to facilitate multiple voting.

Trying to familiarise myself with the buildings that would be used as polling stations and people who would staff them, I visited schools and talked to teachers. I remember particularly a long talk with a chubby, greying, bearded head teacher in a village near Gutu. We sat in the centre of the schoolyard, in the shadow of a lone tree, happy that nobody could eavesdrop. The head candidly set out the situation. Teachers were angered and disillusioned. They were qualified educated people but their pay was a disgrace. Official salaries were not enough to feed a goat, let alone a family. All his staff had been on strike for more pay; he had sympathy with them, but the Government did not care that the schools were closed. Feeling against Mugabe was very strong in Gutu. There would be a very high turn-out against him on election day.

But when it came to 29 March, the head assured me that teachers would set aside their problems for a day. The polling process itself would be smoothly efficient. No equipment had been delivered yet and teachers recruited as polling station staff had not yet been trained or paid. But they already knew what to do. The building had been used as a polling station before, during the 2006 local council elections. Staff had gained experience at that time. The headmaster's confidence reinforced the sense I got from ZEC people that there would be no glaring mistakes in the mechanics of the voting.

Despite the public anger against Mugabe voiced during my field trips to Masvingo, despite the buoyancy of the MDC and the invisibility of ZANU-PF, my reports before the election continued to assume that Mugabe would win. I just could not shift my mindset swiftly enough. I was mesmerised by the myth of Mugabe's invulnerability: a kudu in the headlights of his reckless motorcade. I thought that the country was forever to be a one-party state. I thought the Government would be able to muffle the opposition's voice. I thought the people themselves incapable of the courage and imagination to act to change their miserable futures. My intuition was telling me that a change was coming, but I reported in line with the diplomat's standard cynical assessment of human capability.

The MDC was keen for me to see real electioneering in rural areas. The party's local activists tipped me off about a rally at a growth point in Zaka. 'Growth point' is the grandiose term for the small collections of commercial buildings that form the nucleus of low-density rural areas. People living out in tiny communities and smallholdings will walk to their growth point to shop or catch a bus. The tiny place thirty minutes south of Zaka where the rally was to be held consisted of an unmarked bus stop, two tiny grocery shops selling the same basic goods, a hardware shop with a surprisingly impressive range of mobile phones, and a bench, bearing the substantial weight of six middle-aged women, all of whom were displaying – with superhuman patience – tomatoes that they had grown in their own gardens and were selling for a few pence to generate a tiny income.

By the bench, but uninterested in the tomatoes, was Harrison Mudzuri, a short robust man in his early forties, wearing smart trousers and a leather jacket – the MDC's candidate for the Zaka Central Parliamentary constituency. Harrison turned out to be a relation of Crispen Mudzuri – my jovial informant in Gutu – and the brother of another leading MDC man, Elias Mudzuri, the former mayor of Harare. Unlike Crispen, Harrison was a serious, intense man. He briefed me on his constituency with an impressive authority.

Mudzuri felt 80 per cent confident of victory. He felt he ought to be 100 per cent sure, because people were utterly fed up with ZANU-PF. The reasons were simple: no food and no jobs. Hospitals and schools had deteriorated. Inflation made everyone poor. Everyone knew the country had failed and that Mugabe had to go. If the vote were really free and fair, Mudzuri would win with a large majority. But ZANU-PF was using traditional leaders to undermine rural voters. Headmen were telling people that they should vote ZANU-PF. Any not doing so would have their houses demolished and would be thrown out of their villages. Headmen said they could monitor how their people voted. It didn't matter if this was true or not. Some people were influenced and altered their votes out of fear.

After talking to Mudzuri, I walked across the road to attend his rally. Two hundred people were seated in a neat circle. There was no sign of any police presence, though two dozen MDC activists in t-shirts provided some security, by standing in a ring around the circle of participants. The programme was varied. The MDC's numerous local authority candidates took it in turns to lead humorous chants about the state of the nation or political songs. One of the songs went, 'The fist which liberated us is now a hammer destroying the nation.' The words sounded grim in English translation, but there must have been some extra spice in the Shona, because everyone was laughing. Members of the audience spontaneously sprang up into the space inside the ring to offer a few words, an amusing variant on a chant or some nifty dance steps. Their contributions were greeted with a deep ululation that set my heart racing. I wrote at the time that the space inside the circle was the embodiment of a piece of jargon diplomats like to use. It was a democratic space. And people were enjoying using it for the first time in ages.

When Harrison Mudzuri, the Parliamentary candidate, began to speak, his delivery reminded me of Martin Luther King's 'I have a dream' speech: slow sentences, long pauses populated with moans of appreciation from the crowd, building to a climax: the country was hungry and dependent on food from Malawi (the crowd laughed, because for decades Zimbabwean farmers had fed Malawians with their surpluses). People were dying and others were leaving. But the Government was saying it was stronger than ever. At this point everyone got to their feet and started to sing and dance – Harrison looked like he had a bit more to say, but it was clear that the singing was going to be sustained, so he shrugged his shoulders and called it a day.

At key moments during my time in Zimbabwe I realised that I did not know the country nearly as well as I thought. In a couple of months I was going to be confronted by some Zimbabweans' desire to carve each other up at times of national stress. But in March I was being shocked again by the country's ability to hold something like a national debate about its future and something close to a fair election.

The final stop on my last monitoring trip before the election was quite a coup. I had persuaded Linda, the charming and excellent elections officer for the Chivi District, to let me sit in on the training course for polling officers that she held, five days before the election. It was a valuable experience. First and foremost, Linda's behaviour convinced me that there was no centralised Electoral Commission conspiracy either to obstruct

observers or to play a role in an electoral fraud. If Linda had
instructions to keep observers at arm's length she would not
have allowed me to sit in on such an important and sensitive
event. Similarly she would not have allowed me to listen to her
final briefing to polling officers, if she had any politically biased
instructions to issue. Secondly, I was able to look through (and
even pinch a copy of) the Electoral Commission's manual for
conducting the election. It was a long, dull document, overwrit-
ten with numerous errata slips, but impeccably thorough and
fair. Nobody could possibly get to grips with it during a one-
day training course, so I decided that any errors or variations
in electoral practice that I saw on election day would probably
be the result of different returning officers understanding the
regulations differently – or not understanding them at all – and
taking their best guess.

There was a moment of familiar gender-based humour to
the event too. The teams being trained consisted of a returning officer and up to a dozen subordinate polling officers. The
boss was invariably a man, of course; most of his team were
women. Linda presented each team with a voting booth in kit
form: cardboard sections with instructions for assembly. The
male leaders immediately leaped on to the task, pushed the
cardboard pieces at each other for a few moments, then threw
them down and started complaining. The women quietly took
over, read the instructions and calmly assembled the booths.

In the event's imperfection, in the head-scratching befud-
dlement of returning officers when confronted with reams
of bureaucratic guidance, in the openness of Linda and her
colleagues, I saw that there was plainly no conspiracy between
these people. I saw the goodwill and cleverness of Zimbabweans
at grass-roots level and their determination to deliver the best
election they could. I was immensely encouraged.

What I had seen was not perfect. The Electoral Commission
was politicised and corrupt at the top, though it improved
further down its hierarchy. I had seen enough of the experience,

quality and readiness for hard work of tens of thousands of people – generally teachers – to expect the election to be administered well and with integrity at the grass roots. Underpaid polling officers had little reason to keep Mugabe in office by participating in widespread fraud.

Violence was undoubtedly less common than in 2000, 2002 and 2005. Nonetheless, human rights monitors reported seventy-six credible, documented acts of political violence in March. Some of these were punch-ups between rival supporters, where both sides were to blame for what happened. But most of the incidents reported followed a more one-sided pattern: ZANU-PF members in packs attacking MDC activists as they went about the business of campaigning – administering some kind of beating, usually causing only minor injuries, but sometimes worse. There was a patriarchal and territorial dimension to some of the attacks. As the two parties' young supporters battled physically for ownership of the streets of Epworth, a group of women returning from a Tsvangirai rally were kicked, punched and stripped of their MDC t-shirts. In three months' time, I was to meet three Epworth women who suffered worse punishment for their political views.

The MDC was undoubtedly guilty of some of the violence. Three Tsvangirai supporters set upon a member of the Mutambara faction in a shopping centre in Glen Norah, a suburb of Harare. In a few cases ZANU-PF members reported attacks on them by the MDC. I cannot be sure that ZANU-PF's apparent greater aggression was a true reflection of the situation. There might have been a response bias in the human rights data. Perhaps ZANU-PF members did not tell human rights groups (routinely described by the state media as being part of a Western-funded, pro-MDC conspiracy against Zimbabwe's national interests) when they were attacked by the MDC.

However, my judgement overall – based on what I could see as well as what people told me – was that the most typical act of violence was a spur-of-the-moment attack by ZANU-PF gangs on unlucky and isolated MDC party workers. But the violence was not sustained, widespread or savage enough to cause popular terror. This was a little strange, given the much greater brutality of Mugabe's 2005 election campaign. The threat and fear of violence, hunger and eviction seemed to be a potent weapon for ZANU-PF that the party was choosing not to use. Ordinary Zimbabweans were not living with fear and were feeling largely free to engage with the election in the way they chose.

There was certainly a new tone and style to the conduct of the election. The state media generally excluded the opposition from its news pages – the activities only of Mugabe and his Ministers were deemed newsworthy. Certainly editorials mentioned the MDC, but only to recycle as fact the propaganda message that the party was Western-funded and committed to rolling back independence.

That obviously biased approach changed somewhat in February and March 2008. State-funded media accepted adverts from the MDC; journalists toned down the vehemence of their denunciations of the opposition. It was even possible occasionally to see MDC figures on television, of which the state had a complete monopoly. But despite improvements in balance, coverage remained biased. An NGO which monitored Zimbabwe Television's coverage found that during March 2008 the state channel carried 189 reports of ZANU-PF activities, 31 reports of the MDC's campaign and 14 of Simba Makoni's. The NGO also felt that ZTV gave more of a platform to ZANU-PF and 'allowed ruling party officials lengthy sound bites to discredit the opposition, often employing excessively offensive and inflammatory language to do so'.[1]

Most government officers got the message – whether by osmosis or instruction – that they should at least pretend to be independent. The police in Bulawayo had a hard time catching on to this. They detained a trade-union activist, Tabitha Kumalo, accusing her of putting up MDC posters. Kumalo admitted the charge and asserted her right to put up posters. The police tried to insist that the MDC give three days' notice of all its political activities, but finally let Kumalo go after six hours of verbal sparring. Zimbabwe's civil society groups – professional cynics, owing to the length of their experience of disappointment – continued to tell me that they smelt a rat: ZANU-PF was not going down easily. Most contacts believed that ZANU had a major pre-ballot fraud in preparation, such as sending soldiers to vote several times using faked IDs. There was no particular evidence for these lively theories, other than Mugabe's track record.

Taking advantage of the limited but noticeable new pluralism, the MDC, now full of self-belief, was campaigning strongly, even in areas of Masvingo, Midlands and Mashonaland where it would have been violently repelled in previous years. Most MDC people thought they were going to win. However, Simba Makoni, whose dramatic announcement had first galvanised the campaign, was going nowhere. ZANU-PF was strangely absent. Mugabe looked a wooden and angry figure in his dull monotone posters, whereas Tsvangirai's were up-beat, colourful and adorned with the big man's hearty smile: 'Morgan is More! Vote for the Change You Can Believe in!' I saw few ZANU t-shirts or party workers. Team Mugabe was either confident or apathetic and disillusioned – I wasn't sure which. Had Mugabe been completely thrown by Makoni's declaration? Or did the old man have an ace up his sleeve that he would play only on election day?

It was still dark when I woke at 5 a.m. on 29 March, Zimbabwe's election day. I had travelled down to Masvingo the night before so that I could reach a rural polling station by the time it opened at 7 a.m., but, even pre-positioned, I had to start early. The road east from Masvingo was dark, but wide and empty. As usual the Zimbabwean night was warm and comforting to me. I was excited to be part of such an important day in such a strange but wonderful country.

Every few kilometres I saw activity at polling stations. Most made use of school buildings, but some were being set up in tents along the roadside, to service rural areas too thinly populated even to merit a school. As usual work was divided along gender lines – women were stirring up fires to cook a breakfast of tea and maize porridge – a more liquid form of sadza; men were moving papers around trying to look important. Just as they had said they would, tens of thousands of polling officers had slept uncomfortably at their posts to guard their supplies of papers and boxes and to be sure they were ready to open at 7 a.m. After an hour I reached a deserted crossroads that I knew well. I could continue east to Bikita or turn south to Zaka, but I had already decided to go north then west on to a dirt road that ran thirty kilometres into the countryside – the real Zimbabwe. A couple of policemen stood at the crossroads, but they were so languid about their work that they hardly constituted a roadblock. They waved me on without interference.

It was still night. The car lights showed the way ahead clearly but the sides of the road were in darkness. I started to glimpse people, thousands of people, walking to vote. They were hard to see, as they generally wore dark clothing, but I could sense their movement somehow. They weren't walking fast or racing to get ahead of each other, but rolling along steadily, using a minimum of scarce energy, in great numbers. The people of Zimbabwe – rejecting passivity, rejecting a fatalistic assumption of a grim destiny – had woken in the middle of the night, eaten breakfast, if food was available, and begun to walk, perhaps fifteen kilometres, to join a queue that might take four hours to clear, so great was their desire to shape the nation's decision on its future. I marvelled at the resilience and stamina of so many people with poor shoes, insufficient food and little intellectual cause for optimism. Where did their basic desire to vote come from? Did they all know something – a collective secret, a shared hope – that I did not? I sensed that something was happening that my brain had not thought possible.

The dirt road was slow going in the half-light of the fast-approaching dawn. It was cambered so steeply that it would be easy to slide off into the ditches on either side. Every few kilometres, it angled down sharply to ford a gully – dry now, but gushing in November. I realised that I was going to be late reaching the very end of the road – thirty kilometres of dirt would take more than an hour. So I decided to stop at a smaller polling station after fifteen kilometres.

The sun was up by the time I reached Nerupiri primary school at 6.45. I counted 300 people in the queue. Inside, a full team of election workers, smartly dressed despite a dirty and uncomfortable night's sleep on the floor of the polling station, was already hard at it. The polling station staff had at least eighteen hours' work ahead of them.

Over the next three hours I saw the same pattern at half a dozen polling stations around Gutu. Hundreds of voters waited calmly, without harassment by party or security personnel. Once inside the station, they found their names on the register, collected four ballot papers – for the Presidential, Senate, House of Assembly and local authority elections – dipped their fingers in ink to prevent any attempt to vote twice, went into private booths to mark their choices and placed one paper into each of four translucent but opaque plastic boxes. Voting was brisk and efficient. I immediately realised that my fears of a glacial pace of voting were completely unfounded. Nearly all polling stations cleared their 7 a.m. rush by mid-morning and were then quiet. No election observer reported any case where a voter was prevented from voting because he was still waiting at 7 p.m.

During the morning, I was able to get a sense of the seriousness of two other problems I had worried about. The first issue was the proportion of people turned away, which was invariably significant. At one polling station in Masvingo, 84 out of 153 people – 55 per cent of those who had hiked through the night and queued through the morning to try to vote – were turned away. Returning officers cited all kinds of reasons for their behaviour. Voters were in the wrong place, not on the list, lacked appropriate ID or were not true Zimbabweans. Once I had been able to compare notes with other observers, I estimated that the proportion of people refused was on average around 20 per cent. Rather more than two million people were allowed to vote, which implies that election day must have been soul-destroying for around half a million people whose big effort to influence their country's course had been rejected.

There was also the question of unwanted assistance. Only a few illiterate voters – which meant older, poorer people, as primary education had been universal for over thirty years – should have needed help. But most pro-democracy activists believed that the police had imposed assistance upon voters during elections in 2005 so that they could pressurise them to vote ZANU-PF. There were areas where the percentage receiving assistance was surprisingly high, for example in Chivi, where the proportion at a number of polling stations ranged between 15 and 25 per cent. But there was nothing about the way the police did their work that aroused my suspicion. On the one occasion when I was able to eavesdrop and watch as a policeman assisted a tiny, ancient woman, she said that she wanted Morgan Tsvangirai and the policeman pointed to the correct box for her to cross. I, like other observers watching the process, felt that there might have been local conspiracies to intimidate in some places, but that police behaviour was not part of a systematic fraud.

Midway through the morning I turned east off the north–south road between Gutu and Zaka to try to find a polling station in a remote village called Chipangami. The road was exceptionally poor, non-existent in places. I had to drive over rocks and through a shallow stream before arriving at what turned out to be a double polling station: two set-ups in different areas of a large primary school.

The atmosphere in this place was immediately suspect.

Several hundred people were waiting to vote in very slow-moving queues. Most polling stations dealt with the 7 a.m. rush in two to three hours, so it was unsatisfactory and peculiar that so many people were still standing around in the growing heat of the day. I tried to chat with people in the queue to ask how long they had been waiting, but nobody would catch my eye or say more than a stifled 'Good morning'. Youths were hanging around the queues. They weren't wearing ZANU-PF t-shirts, but they carried an aura of trouble about them. The police presence was heavy. There were six officers sitting inside each of the polling stations, staring blankly at the voters as they crawled through. The presiding officers were nervous and evasive. They noted details of my accreditation carefully, but refused any conversation. I stood and watched for half an hour, walking around to allow everyone to see I was there. I felt that party-political influence had infected the whole process. I hoped (vainly, I am sure) to give a little confidence to anyone being influenced by the oppressive atmosphere.

If I had been a voter at Chipangami, I would have felt scared to vote. I reflected that a monitor randomly touring polling stations could not detect many potential electoral frauds. The headman in this village might have told his people to vote ZANU-PF and said that a team of police and party youths would be watching to make sure people did as instructed. Human rights groups told me that such instructions were common. What proportion of voters would be affected?

There were other polling stations which observers thought strange. For example, at the Masvingo Showgrounds, there were long queues right into the afternoon at a polling station set up especially for a nearby police and army barracks. My colleague observed that few people were turned away and that a high proportion of voters had certificates, indicating that they had registered to vote only very recently. The result at the Showgrounds was nine to one in ZANU-PF's favour on a heavy turnout. Again, I could not be sure that there was anything suspicious about the results. Perhaps soldiers just really liked Mugabe. But I had heard credible reports that military units had been ordered to vote ZANU-PF. If that were going on at the Showgrounds, it would be consistent with the last-minute registrations and the overwhelming vote for Mugabe.

This kind of qualitative assessment that management of some polling stations was suspect is not, of course, a rigorous proof of electoral fraud, particularly when voting looked reasonably fair at nine out of ten stations. But if ZANU-PF had made special arrangements to deliver a strong positive vote at 10 per cent of stations, that would have been enough to alter the result in a close contest.

After a lengthy stay in the virulent atmosphere of Chipangami, I headed for Bikita – a scattered community to the east arranged around mines which pull lucrative minerals out of Masvingo's red soil. I had spent more time around Gutu than I had planned, but I really wanted to show a face in Bikita. In the end I visited only one polling station, because a local human rights activist texted me a report of an MDC member who had allegedly been detained and beaten. I thought I would spend some time investigating, but ended up on a wild-guin-eafowl chase that lasted two hours. After several interviews at different police stations – including with the District Chief, a female officer trained at Hendon in the 1980s – I was no nearer the truth, but hoped that my inquisitiveness would prevent any further brutality.

I had suggested to the whole team of British Embassy moni-tors around the country that they should start the day early, observe the opening of the polls at 7 a.m. and tour several other polling stations through the morning, when I expected voting to be busy. After that I reckoned that we would all need to take a break, ideally a siesta, as we would be working right through the night, observing the count. But when it came to it, I was so pumped up by the reality of election day that I couldn't sleep in the afternoon. The lodge I was staying at was right next to

Great Zimbabwe, an archaeological site near Masvingo, which had provided the new name for independent Rhodesia. So I went there instead.

Calling the site an ancient city is generous, as it is a collection of no more than a dozen structures. But it is a thought-provoking and impressive place – its stone tower, hilltop citadel and extraordinary curved walls clearly built for the elite of a sophisticated medieval civilisation. Nobody knows quite who was responsible. Before independence white children were taught that no Bantu African could have built such structures, so Egyptian or Arabic visitors must have constructed them. Since independence, children have learned that a powerful society of indigenous Africans created the city, demonstrating that Africa was civilised more than a thousand years ago while Europe was fumbling through the dark ages. Nobody is interested in scientifically resolving the question of who built the site and when. It is much more galvanising to use it as a backdrop for projections of prejudice.

I drove out to Zaka in the late afternoon. I looked round a couple of polling stations, which were now deserted. At the first, the officials were bored and pleased to talk. They reported that several hundred people had voted early and peacefully. They had no idea if the turnout was heavy or light as they had no reliable total of the number of people registered to vote. At Zaka Number One secondary school an awkward and evasive presiding officer refused to tell me how many people had voted or to give me any other useful information, even his impressions of how things had gone. Maybe I was getting tired already, but for the first time in a long day I was irritated by his unnecessary rudeness. I wanted to tell the returning officer what I thought of him, but I wasn't supposed to be making any scenes, so I moved on instead.

It was now 6 p.m. Dusk was falling and everything in Zaka was quiet. The smoke of cooking fires rose only slowly through the still air. Everybody who was going to vote had done so. But the count could not begin until 7 p.m., so polling staff were taking the opportunity to cook some evening sadza, sit quietly with a cigarette or stretch out for a nap. I phoned round some other observers to collect impressions of how the day had gone. Everyone's experiences had been similar to mine – peaceful voting by large numbers of people, an exemplary effort, a few places where something funny was going on, but no obvious large-scale fraud.

While I was on the phone night fell – as it does in Africa – with a bump. It was suddenly pitch-black. With so many demands on Zimbabwe's scarce electricity that night, there was none for Zaka. The Embassy tells its staff not to walk around at night, but I felt happy doing so. Zaka had felt benign to me all day. I couldn't see any danger coming from the people I had met.

In the darkness, I heard rather than saw people gathering at the registration office where I had decided to observe the count. I had talked a few times to Harrison Mudzuri after attending his rally, so I chose a polling station in his constituency. I knew that once I was inside the returning officer would not want me to leave or use my phone until the counting was finished. There were some observers in 2005 who were locked in their counts until dawn. So I hid my mobile and some food and water in my day sack and went inside.

The polling station was a small official building constructed of breezeblock with asbestos roofing sheets – the ugly but functional norm for rural Zimbabwe. At the centre of the room was a large trestle table, surrounded by a dozen participants in the count – the returning officer and his assistants, agents of the parties, an independent observer and me. As I had expected, the returning officer (whose name was, I think, Tobias) warned me politely enough that if I wanted to observe the count I would have to stay until the end.

Tobias worked slowly and carefully through the instructions in his manual. The guidance was long and complicated, and hard to read by candlelight. Tobias stood gripping the edge of the table, looking intently down, moving the process along one small step at a time. First he removed seals from the ballot boxes, then locks. Then he asked his assistants to count the number of votes in each of the four ballot boxes. There were about 200 in each. Tobias began a painful process of matching the number of votes in the boxes with the number of names ticked on the electoral roll. One vote for the Senate election was missing. After a long search, the stray paper turned up in the local council box. I was frustrated by the drawn-out process, but Tobias knew what he was about. In the weeks after the election returning officers accused of any kind of irregularity were roughly treated.

More than two hours had gone by. Tobias showed no sign of losing bladder control, but I was not feeling so comfortable. I tried following people who disappeared occasionally through a door in the back and found there were toilets there, which hadn't been cleaned in a long time. I started making regular visits, so that I could text reports back to colleagues in Harare, who emailed them on to London. I had to be concise though as the stench was appalling.

Some time after 10 p.m., Tobias suddenly told the slumbering polling officers that they could now count the votes for each candidate. The women sprang to life and grabbed ballots chaotically, shouting out and flinging papers at each other:

'Mugabe!'

'Makoni!'

'Tsvangirai!'

Tobias tried to referee the frenzy and finally persuaded his colleagues to collaborate in producing three piles. I was so captivated that I found I was trying to hold my breath for an impossibly long time. The piles took shape. One was just a few papers; the second was a decent pile, an inch tall. The third was a tottering tower.

Even after everything I had seen, I was still sure that the large pile had to be Mugabe's. But I was so, so wrong. The smallest pile was Simba Makoni's – eleven votes. The middling pile was Mugabe's – forty-four votes. Amazingly, incredibly, the tallest pile belonged to Morgan Tsvangirai. The polling officer, drooping with fatigue after sixteen hours of work, kept losing count. At one point she became tongue-tied at 'one hundred and twenty-seven' and had to start again. She sighed desperately, but finally managed to finish her count: 167. Tsvangirai had won about three-quarters of the vote.

It was midnight when Tobias finally said we could all go. I stepped out of the stuffy building into the rich darkness outside. There were a few lights 300 metres away in a building where results from all the polling stations in the district were being added together, but otherwise I was surrounded by the kind of dense blackness in which I could hardly see my own hand. The Milky Way stretched over me. I just stood staring upwards not really sure what I wanted to do next. I jumped when a policeman who had walked very quietly up behind me whispered in my ear, 'Mr Philip, we are so pleased you are here, but do you really think there is hope?'

For the first time in more than two years in Zimbabwe, I thought the answer might be yes. I didn't know if the authorities would ever dare to release these results. I didn't know how a country that had only ever transitioned by means of violence could accept peaceful change. But I had finally caught up with the simple truth that had been staring me in the face for six months, but which I had been too slow and stupid to accept – Zimbabweans did not want Mugabe any more and were going to vote for Tsvangirai. The enormity of that simple, suddenly obvious fact was unnerving but thrilling.

I was back at my hotel around 2 a.m. I was unbelievably tired, but not sleepy. I felt a bursting, teary pride. Diplomacy is so often futile, but I had spent the day among real people who were trying to improve their own lives. Perhaps I had given them some confidence. Monitoring the election had been a marathon of driving, talking, watching, cajoling and waiting.

But I had been right on the spot, hearing the first results of the election the moment they were announced. And I knew I could communicate those amazing results not just by reporting back to the Foreign Office, but widely through my blog. I sat for a few minutes looking at the results I recorded as Tobias finally read them out:*

Presidential Election

Candidate	Votes	Percentage
Makoni	11	5
Mugabe	44	20
Tsvangirai	167	74

House of Assembly Election

Party	Votes	Percentage
Independent	4	2
MDC-M	14	6
MDC-T (Harrison Mudzuri)	155	70
ZANU-PF	47	21

Local Council Election

Party	Votes	Percentage
MDC-T	168	76
ZANU-PF	54	24

I knew that extrapolating conclusions from the results at just one of 10,000 polling stations was unreliable. But I couldn't help drawing a few conclusions. The MDC was doing incredibly well. In 2005, ZANU-PF had won a constituency similar to what is now called Zaka Central with about 60 per cent of the vote. Yet at my polling station Mugabe had scored only 20 per

*I have omitted the Senate election result.

cent. Of course my polling station could have been atypical for some reason. But I didn't think so. Looking at the voting figures alongside the MDC's vibrant campaign in Masvingo province, I sensed that the party was going to make dramatic gains. Just as remarkably, Mugabe scored worse in the Presidential poll than his candidates for other offices. Even those voters who had remained loyal to the ruling party seemed to be sending a message that he should go.

There also seemed to be a pattern in the way that people who supported different parties in different elections split their votes. Mugabe had scored ten votes fewer than his local authority candidate. It looked like those missing ten voters had defected to Simba Makoni, who scored eleven votes. Similarly the 167 votes cast for Tsvangirai fell to 155 for Harrison Mudzuri. Those twelve missing votes surely went to MDC-M, which scored fourteen.

I suspected a nationwide pattern – Makoni would take some votes from disaffected ZANU voters, while Mutambara would take votes from Tsvangirai. Mutambara's recommendation to his voters that they should support Makoni had apparently been ignored – not the last time that Mutambara's people would refuse to support his efforts to make common cause with elements of ZANU-PF. Clearly neither Makoni nor Mutambara was going to do well, but I wondered whose rebellion would do more damage to the parent party.

I made phone calls – there were people sitting up all night at the Foreign Office desperate for news about the elections – and drank a couple of beers as I typed up my report to induce some sleepiness. I finally managed a quick nap before waking for an early breakfast and heading for home.

Zimbabwe is gorgeous in March. It's the end of the monsoon season, so rain is possible, but usually it comes only in the afternoon. Mornings are warm and fine, and the countryside is green and bursting with life after months of rain. Storks stalk frogs. Prey animals hide their newborn young in the long grass.

On the morning of 30 March everything seemed symbolic – the bright morning, the renewal of fertile life, the hope of an African sunrise.

I drove back through the centre of Masvingo town. All the results for the Masvingo Urban constituency had been posted outside the civic centre. The MDC had won comfortably. In the large car park at the front of the civic centre, MDC activists and candidates were gathering to compare stories and marvel at the great results, which were coming in by text message. I spoke to a party co-ordinator who reckoned that the MDC had taken more than a dozen seats and become the largest party in the province (he was right – Tsvangirai secured fifteen MPs to ZANU-PF's eleven). People were relaxed and happy. There was not a riot policeman, a soldier or a ZANU-PF t-shirt to be seen. Hope and excitement were so real I could taste and smell them. I finally believed what my heart was telling me. I was standing in a new Zimbabwe.

4

WAITING FOR GONO

At the beginning of April I felt euphoric – giddily excited at what I had just witnessed and hopeful that the feverish uncertainty about what would happen next would resolve itself into a positive future. I was experiencing the flighty and breathless effects of something Zimbabwe had not known for a decade: optimism.

My feelings were synchronised with the country's pathway through that month. Zimbabweans were captivated by the prospect of change, but unclear how and when it would become a reality. Anyone who had witnessed the count, as I had in Zaka, knew that the MDC had scored unexpectedly well and that ZANU-PF had done amazingly badly. News and rumours of the results rippled out even to rural areas, which the regime tried to isolate. Ordinary people could gauge the extent of Mugabe's defeat in their areas, as results had been posted in polling stations on election night. These snapshots of local voting patterns were augmented by text messages from relatives in the cities, where the MDC's dominance was almost complete.

Election officials had done much more than simply count votes at individual polling stations. They had totalled up the figures at collation centres and announced the results of local council and House of Assembly elections to the candidates and their agents. So the results in the lower chamber of Parliament were semi-public before the regime had any chance to assess or alter them. By the simple expedient of speaking to all its prospective MPs, the MDC was able to work out immediately that it had broken through. It was not quite clear if the party had become the largest in Parliament, but it had certainly denied ZANU-PF its majority and, more importantly, had demonstrated that Mugabe's party was not all powerful, for ever and ever, amen.

The Electoral Commission, which was to be tortoise-like throughout April, shrank into its shell. Its provincial officials had announced hundreds of results locally on election night, but the national authority hesitated to confirm even what the candidates already knew. It took three days for the formal announcement of Parliamentary results to begin. When the announcements started, they were ponderous, theatrical and stretched out over two days. ZEC selected successes for each party in turn, so that the running total of seats won remained level. Announcing results so slowly bought the regime some initial thinking time, but was an act of succour in another way too. The MDC was convinced that it had taken control of Parliament and that this presaged an outright Tsvangirai victory over Mugabe in the Presidential race. By making clear that Parliament might be hung, with no one party in a clear majority position, ZEC raised expectations that the Presidential voting would be indecisive too.

The MDC was deeply suspicious of the re-announcement of results nationally, suspecting that they were being altered to ZANU-PF's benefit. When Harrison Mudzuri's result was announced I texted congratulations to him. He sent me back a terse reply: 'I have already been the MP for four days.' But fears of crude alteration of results proved unfounded – the MDC and independent election monitors could see little evidence of tampering, though the MDC did claim that ZANU-PF had exaggerated its vote in seats which the ruling party won comfortably in Mashonaland. If true, this tactic would have reduced only the MDC's margin of superiority in terms of total votes, not its number of elected MPs. The only sensible reason why ZEC might have engaged in such apparently inconsequential fiddling would have been to suppress the fact that the MDC's overall vote was greater than ZANU-PF's, which had obvious implications for the Presidential race.

When all the results were finally confirmed, the MDC found it had won a narrow victory. Elections were postponed in three seats after the deaths (not through foul play) of candidates during the campaign, meaning that 207 rather than all 210 MPs were elected. The MDC won more of these seats than any other party.

Party	Seats
MDC-T	99
ZANU-PF	97
MDC-M	10
Independent (Jonathan Moyo)	1

Regionally, the MDC dominated Harare, Bulawayo and other urban areas, as expected. Much more surprisingly, it had made dramatic advances in Masvingo (taking most of the seats around Zaka and Gutu and even achieving gains in Chivi and Bikita) and Manicaland. These areas used to be solidly ZANU-PF, but were now overall MDC provinces. ZANU-PF scored heavily in rural areas of the three Mashonaland provinces and its vote also held up in Midlands. Mutambara's successes were in Matabeleland.

Like other observers who had seen tottering towers of MDC ballot papers, I was initially surprised that the party's margin of victory was not greater. But I reflected that I had been observing in the battleground areas of Masvingo where the MDC came through strongly. Few observers went to Mashonaland as ZANU-PF's victory there seemed beyond doubt. Had I observed in Mount Darwin or the villages around Marondera, I would probably have seen piles of ballot papers for Mugabe and his candidates.

MDC-T performed well in the senate elections too, precisely sharing the sixty elected seats within the upper chamber with ZANU-PF. All parties then had some opportunities to appoint additional senators, but that process favoured ZANU-PF – ultimately fifty-seven out of ninety-nine senators were more or less loyal to Mugabe.

The effect of Tsvangirai's decision to pull out of an electoral pact with Mutambara became apparent. Had he agreed to the deal, he would have secured around eighty-three seats while Mutambara might have taken thirty-four. The opposition as a whole would have been stronger in the House of Assembly, but ZANU-PF would have remained the largest party. The popularity and clout of Mutambara's group would have been much exaggerated. So Tsvangirai's decision to reject the deal was surely vindicated in hindsight, proving wrong the doubters who had accused him of putting his ego ahead of the opposition's chances. The deal would have cost his party dear and have benefited his two main rivals. By rejecting the deal, he was able to push ZANU-PF into second place and to substantiate his belief that his party was the true, popular and mass opposition and that Mutambara's group was the splinter.

Conversely, the impact of the Mutambara faction's decision to fight on despite its feeble levels of support was dramatically negative for the opposition as a whole. Voters were confronted with two candidates both calling themselves MDC. Some were undoubtedly confused. Had Mutambara's candidates not been splitting the vote, Tsvangirai would have secured eighteen more MPs (Mutambara's ten, plus eight which ZANU-PF won on a split opposition vote), giving him a clear Parliamentary majority and an advantage of almost thirty seats over Mugabe. Such a decisive Parliamentary victory might have mitigated the national disasters that were to come, particularly if it had convinced ZANU-PF that the game was up. Part of the assessment of Mutambara's role in the 2008 elections must acknowledge that he obscured the will for change in the country expressed by voters. This enabled Mugabe to argue in the coming months that the country was evenly divided and that a unity government was therefore a fair and pragmatic way forward.

But, even without the hypotheticals, the results marked a dramatic change of direction for Zimbabwe. Mugabe had always enjoyed a compliant legislature loaded with representatives of his own party. Even after the launch of the MDC in 1999, he had been able to secure an impregnable majority in Parliament one way or another. The combined effect of electoral reform and the MDC's vigorous campaign was that Mugabe could no longer treat Parliament as a rubber-stamping body, staffed with his placemen. Despite its fears that the delay in announcing the Parliamentary results was designed to allow the Electoral Commission time to fiddle the results (as it had done in 2005), the MDC had no substantial disagreements with the results announced.

My excitement was becoming even greater than it had been a week earlier, on election night, which had already taken on a mythical and glittering quality in my memory. If the MDC was now the largest party in Parliament, was it possible that Tsvangirai might have won the Presidency? Mugabe was invisible, whereas his usual style would be to claim victory and be sworn back into office immediately. What was going on?

Harare's coffee-drinking classes discounted the possibility of Mugabe accepting defeat, secure in their belief that ZANU-PF would not surrender power to such an impotent process as democracy. But the MDC's ownership of Parliament was already a fact on the ground, so discussion turned to the prospect of cohabitation between such a legislature and a ZANU-PF executive. In fact there was no reason why Zimbabwe could not function in this way. Under Zimbabwe's present constitution, the President enjoys substantial executive power. He is able to do most of what he wishes without much reference to Parliament. In any case, the differences between the overt manifestos of the two parties were not great. If he could learn the new tricks of a little consultation and compromise, there would be no reason why Mugabe could not operate as president despite lacking the full control of Parliament.

The country's attention now shifted on to the Presidential race. There was no technical reason for delaying an announcement of the outcome. The constituent figures of the result were available to ZEC as early as 31 March. All the national body had to do was to add up the provincial results and announce the totals. But it failed to do this, fuelling speculation that Mugabe had not won a clear victory. Indeed most observers suspected that not only must he have failed to secure 50 per cent of the vote, but he must have come second to Tsvangirai. Otherwise why delay a favourable announcement? Beyond all expectation, coffee-drinkers started to wonder out loud if Tsvangirai had himself scored 50 per cent or more, defeating Mugabe outright.

The MDC was certainly quick to claim victory in the Presidential as well as the Parliamentary vote. Just three days after election day, I went to a packed press conference at the Meikles Hotel to hear Tendai Biti, the party's secretary general, claim that the MDC had collated results nationwide and was ready to announce that Tsvangirai had scored 57 per cent. The official reaction to this was furious. Biti was charged with treason, charges which were baseless but which hung over his head for months before finally being dismissed. Mugabe's spokesman and principal attack dog George Charamba (who wrote a hateful column in the state press throughout the elections, using the pseudonym Manheru) said that Tsvangirai would be guilty of an attempted coup if he declared himself president. Charamba's subsequent threat was not even veiled: 'We all know how coups are handled.'

Although Biti's claims seemed possible in the heady aftermath of the MDC's astounding performance, they became less defensible as more data was collected. Indeed a few weeks afterwards, the MDC revised its estimate of Tsvangirai's vote down to 50.3 per cent, barely enough to make him the outright winner. But the sharp revision in the MDC's estimate of its own vote made it clear that the MDC had not really collated all results in the way Biti had claimed. Its credibility suffered as a result.

Filling the void in more authoritative and less partisan style, an election-monitoring NGO, the Zimbabwe Electoral Support Network (ZESN), attempted to predict the Presidential result four nights after polling day. The Network had asked its monitors to report results from a large sample of polling stations and used these as the basis of an estimate of the actual result. The figures were announced late in the evening in a packed function room in Harare's Holiday Inn – a hotel that has been free of holidaymakers for about a decade. As usual the start of the event was delayed – on this occasion while ZESN's officials huddled together and tried to guess how the regime would react to their announcement. This was no idle worry; it was quite possible in the light of Charamba's menacing remarks about Biti that the organisation would be criminalised and its members arrested.

I was at the Holiday Inn waiting for hours while this was going on. I passed the time buying beers – which cost $120,000,000 each – for contacts. The attraction of a free beer from the Brits drew over quite a number of personalities of various sorts all ready to give an opinion. Everyone believed that Tsvangirai had scored around 60 per cent of the vote, but that the Electoral Commission was suppressing this unacceptable figure. So great is the speed of Harare's gossip and speculation machine that a Tsvangirai win was already being treated as a certainty and a crude ballot-rigging exercise in response taken to be inevitable.

Once the doors of ZESN's press conference opened, I elbowed my way to a seat near the front, amazed at the number of international film crews and journalists, politicians and diplomats jammed inside. The scene – journalists interviewing each other, diplomats swapping flippant observations – was normal enough for a press conference during an international crisis, but Zimbabwe had not tolerated the media for years. Clearly the usual rules were not being applied. There was not a policeman to be seen. Was the regime losing its grip? Was a shift in power, a change of governing culture, already under way?

ZESN's spokeswoman, looking tense but aware of the historical importance of what she was doing, finally announced the estimates at around 9 p.m.: Tsvangirai had scored 49 per cent, Mugabe 43 per cent. There was a margin of error of +/- 2 per cent on those figures. There were gasps and applause. Some were horrified that the 49 per cent forecast of Tsvangirai's vote was so much lower than Biti's 57 per cent. Others were tearfully euphoric at this first credible confirmation that Mugabe had lost. The international journalists were most interested in what would happen next. When would the official figures be out? What would happen if neither candidate had 50 per cent of the vote? Of course, nobody knew. The panel of brave folk – the board of ZESN – looked anxious as they fielded these questions and were right to do so. Over the next months, the organisation paid a heavy price for its commitment to openness.

With information about the Presidential vote ever more widely available – including a growing collection of local result notices scanned on to the internet – ZEC needed a good reason to continue to withhold the actual figures. The solution was a series of appeals conveniently filed by twenty-two losing ZANU-PF candidates. ZEC decided that the results in each of these constituencies would have to be recounted and that the Presidential results would have to be withheld until after those recounts. ZEC however showed no urgency about arranging the recounts, thereby achieving the desired delay of a few weeks.

As with every part of the prolonged and opaque process in April, there was contention about these appeals. The law was that objections to results needed to be filed within forty-eight hours of the election; the ZEC Chairman George Chiweshe confirmed that they had been filed within this deadline. Both MDC parties disputed this and claimed that the ZANU-PF appeals had been made several days later when the scale of the defeat became clear. If this was true, ZEC should have set them aside and moved ahead with announcing the results.

Chiweshe, a retired member of Mugabe's ZANLA guerrilla force, stuck to his guns, knowing that Mugabe needed a few weeks to work out his next step. He supported appeals, saying it was possible that 'the votes were miscounted and that the miscount would affect the results of this election'. In fact none of the ZANU-PF appellants gave any grounds for believing that their counts were badly done, other than their plain horror that they had lost seats that were supposed to be safe.

The MDC took legal action to compel ZEC to release the Presidential results. High Court judges have done well out of Mugabe. In 2008 alone they were given German cars, Japanese SUVs and plasma-screen TVs, purchased at the expense of Zimbabwe's poor and sick, using the monopoly money emerging from the printing presses of central banker Gideon Gono. It was unlikely that such a compromised judiciary would back the MDC's case, even if they thought it had merit.

In order to go to court to hear how a senior judge would react to the MDC's application, I had to walk 500 metres from the Embassy along Samora Machel Avenue, Harare's main east–west road. The road took me past the Reserve Bank – a modern, expensive-looking building decorated with an artful sculpture of Zimbabwe's national bird – and the blocky Parliament and up to a ring of riot police – brown uniforms, crash helmets and sticks – surrounding the High Court.

I usually tried to carry off interactions with the police with a self-confident swagger, as if a line of big cops looking mean was an everyday hurdle. As I reached the thick police line I managed a cheerful 'Good morning! How are you, sirs?' in the Zimbabwean style. This usually elicited some tentatively cheery responses and a gap in the cordon big enough to walk through. Inside the police cordon was a scrum of journalists, observers and lawyers all struggling to get into a tiny room to hear the judge rule whether Zimbabwe's election results should be released, more than two weeks after the people had voted.

After a long hot wait, the judge appeared, flung a copy of a written judgment at the lawyers and made his escape. The judgment was fifteen pages long – enough reading time for him to escape the building. It said that the election authorities must act legally, but that the courts could not question the authorities' decisions. So the court could not make any comment on ZEC's actions. The human rights lawyer next to me was disgusted, as he believed this opinion was intellectually and morally bankrupt.

Outside the court, I hared across Samora Machel to avoid the cameras. I did not want to appear in the next day's state newspaper described as a British agent on hand to give orders to Gordon Brown's alleged puppets – the MDC. But in my haste I tripped over a man sitting on the roadside selling apples (twenty million dollars each). I had a short chat with the man – everyone is ready to talk in Zimbabwe. He asked me, 'What is going to happen to us, sir? I am waiting and waiting and I cannot sleep. I am sure I will die if we carry on like this.'

Internationally Mugabe's delaying tactics fooled nobody. Regional leaders started to call for the release of the results and for a solution to Zimbabwe's 'problems'. Even this conservative language was a step-change for most leaders in Southern Africa who had grown used to seeing no evil. Mbeki kept quiet, refusing to make any public comment on Zimbabwe's elections. Attitudes hardened in other fora too. The G8 and Ban Ki-moon, Secretary General of the UN, called for the early release of the election results. The UN Security Council discussed Zimbabwe in April for the first time in a year. As usual, the discussion led to no action. Russia, China and South Africa (a temporary member of the Council in 2008) made clear that they would block any critical resolution or action against Zimbabwe, such as sanctions.

Tsvangirai was incensed by the public stance of Mbeki and South Africa, which continued to be helpful to Mugabe despite his election defeat. For the first time he said publicly that Mbeki was not able to mediate and that Zambian President Mwanawasa – whose public statements were becoming hostile to Mugabe – should take over in that role. Zimbabwe started to become a domestic political issue in South Africa too. Jacob Zuma, who was in the process of replacing Mbeki as head of the African National Congress (ANC) and president of the country, criticised the electoral process. Zuma is a Zulu, as are Zimbabwe's much put-upon Ndebele people.

Zuma's public criticism of Mugabe was certainly more in tune with the popular South African mood than Mbeki's quiet diplomacy. If this needed to be proved, the Confederation of South African Trade Unions (COSATU) confirmed it by taking industrial action to block a Chinese shipment of weapons to Zimbabwe, which was due to be offloaded in Durban. Following COSATU's action – and similar popular support for Zimbabweans by trade unionists in Angola and Mozambique – the weapons were turned back to China. The shipment became an international story. Most journalists assumed that the weapons were intended to supply a post-electoral purge. But ZANU-PF is organised in such matters and would not have left it so late to secure essential supplies. The delivery was simply poorly timed. Zimbabwe's order had been long-standing and was not stimulated by the prospect of elections or the immediate requirements of repression. ZANU-PF was soon to demonstrate that its party militias and the armed forces had more than enough bullets and AK-47s to bring the disobedient country into line.

The arms shipment was an embarrassment to China because it became so public. The real embarrassment, of course, should be that China is prepared to supply bullets for Mugabe's guns. As multinationals have fled Zimbabwe, China has entered, offering the regime things it wants – cheap pick-up trucks and weapons – in return for broad and open-ended concessions to exploit mineral reserves. One conservationist watched the progress of a Chinese labour gang in 2008 as it built a fence around a pristine area of wilderness, slaughtered all wildlife inside, cut down the trees and dug a monstrous open-cast mine.

The recounts took three weeks of snail-like work to organise and did not begin until 19 April. I went to observe. After the usual 6 a.m. start and long drive south, I ended up in Zaka again, covering the Zaka West constituency recount at the district administrator's office – a large, single-storey building up a dirt road. I had not seen the place in daylight before. It must have looked grand when it was built in 1985, but had become grim – broken panes, piles of rat droppings and a strange photo of Robert Mugabe from two decades ago – a young-looking sixty-five, headmaster glasses, trying to smile. The security presence was more obvious and menacing than on election day. Soldiers stood around chatting, waving large assault rifles as if they were breadsticks to make points in their conversation. The compound was packed with bored policemen, tense party activists and anxious presiding officers.

The election officers had reason to worry. The work they had carried out by candlelight, three weeks before, was going to be checked. The methodology for checking was not clear, but the consequences of any mistakes were. Several presiding officers had already been arrested on implausible charges of electoral fraud and accepting bribes from the MDC. Those waiting in the heat in Zaka knew they too could soon be going to prison, accused of corruptly inflating the opposition vote, if their tally of votes for Tsvangirai should be deemed to be too high. It was going to be a long hot wait for them in the sun. Some stayed in the arid compound for five nights, sleeping and eating as best they could, waiting for their turn. I stayed about five hours, which seemed like an eternity.

Nothing happened quickly. After an hour, a team of police extracted a first set of ballot boxes from a storeroom and brought them to a dusty meeting room furnished with wobbly tables and broken chairs where the recount was going to take place. The boxes were in a sorry state. After finishing the count on 29 March, presiding officers had inventoried and sealed them with padlocks and wax. But there were problems even with the first few boxes. One had a hole bashed in the side; others were not securely fastened. The first set of presiding officers summoned to watch their boxes being unsealed looked horrified, either because of the damage the boxes had sustained while in storage or because the last tired act of an extraordinarily long working day three weeks before was to be exposed. The MDC's candidates and agents, packing the room, looked aghast too. If the boxes were not sealed, anybody could have stuffed extra ballot papers inside.

Sometimes in Zimbabwe it's impossible to know who's in charge. But there was no problem on 19 April. A smart and authoritative woman, 'Just call me Priscilla', was clearly the boss. She carried her authority well. She said she was from Harare and worked for 'a Government agency, not the Electoral Commission, but I'm acting for the Electoral Commission'. She was courteous and welcomed foreign observers. I sat next to a spherical Angolan from the SADC team, who spoke only Portuguese and understood little of the proceedings. He soon fell asleep, which was not too surprising as the sun, the throng and the activity pushed the temperature well above thirty degrees.

Priscilla was starting to give instructions when Dongo Festus, the new MDC Zaka West MP, elected by 4,734 votes to ZANU's 4,030, spoke up. He objected to the recount. It was illegal and he demanded that it be stopped. He and Priscilla, who was determined to press on, argued for an hour. They were both tenacious in defence of their positions, but logical and respectful. They reached a typically Zimbabwean compromise. Priscilla would proceed, but Festus would explain to the room what was wrong.

I was developing some respect for Priscilla, who was emerging as a negotiator and manager of considerable skill and sensitivity. Festus cleared his throat theatrically: 'Respectfully, madam, I want the Electoral Commission to say who called for this recount – was it themselves or the ZANU-PF? And I want to see the written application for a recount to check that it was submitted less than forty-eight hours after the original vote. If it was not, this recount is illegal. I also want to know if the original results recorded will be produced. And where have these ballot boxes been kept? And who has had access to them? And if there are any differences between the original results and what we see here today, I want you, madam, to hold an inquiry to find out why. Until these questions are answered we take part in this recount under protest.'

Priscilla happily ignored these questions and bustled around to get things moving. She had handled things well. At Gutu – where the chaos and tedium were tripled, as three recounts were taking place – the senior ZEC official threatened to bring in the riot police unless the MDC stopped making what were nationally co-ordinated protests against the recounts.

I spoke to MDC party workers to find out more. Their story was that the party had won the seat despite intimidation of voters and attempts by ZANU-PF to monitor how loyally villagers supported the ruling party. Now ZANU-PF was trying to overturn the result – part of an effort to snatch back a dozen marginal constituencies and regain a Parliamentary majority. The MDC claimed that on 9 April, eleven days after the election, a group of ZANU-PF officials, helped by the Electoral Commission and the police, broke into the ballot boxes, took out MDC votes and replaced them with forged papers marked for ZANU-PF. Witnesses were ready to testify to this in court, but their safety needed to be guaranteed. I spoke to Festus too. He was a careworn man, his eyes twitching about nervously, who could have been anything between forty and sixty years old. Having won a surprise victory, he was worried that his future in Parliament would be taken from him.

I had got used to taking what MDC people say with a pinch of salt. There is an unfortunate tendency within the party to exaggerate for effect – unnecessary when the truth in Zimbabwe is shocking enough already. The outcome of the recount process made clear that the story party workers had told me of a multi-agency break-in to the ballot boxes on 9 April was untrue. So the witnesses the party was offering to produce were people ready to lie for the MDC cause.

Meanwhile Priscilla had got the first ballot box open. There were problems – first a security tag had the wrong serial number, then the number of votes did not exactly match the number of names ticked off the electoral roll. Priscilla looked balefully at the presiding officer, but he managed to talk his way out of trouble. Indeed the discrepancies soon proved to be minor. Progress was paint-dryingly slow. The presiding officer, sweating out his terror, held each vote up for scrutiny by party agents. There were protracted arguments about individual papers – did a cross made with red ink mean that a ballot was spoiled? The ZANU-PF agent was hyperactive and questioned everything that might possibly take an MDC vote out of play. But Priscilla was robustly sensible. She showed no bias and did not disallow any ballots on which the voter's intention had been clear. Her decisions generally matched those the presiding officer had made on election night.

After three hours the Presidential votes had been verified in just one of thirty polling stations under review. The process was repeated for the Senate, House of Assembly and local council elections. By this time the presiding officer looked as if he wanted to vomit his fear up, as he painstakingly went through the electoral roll, checking that the number of names ticked off equalled the number of votes cast. It was 1 p.m. – five hours after we had started – before the first complete set of boxes was finished and the poor presiding officer was allowed to leave.

Priscilla announced her recounted results, which matched what Festus had noted down on election night: Tsvangirai 164, Mugabe 106, Makoni 5. There was a stir of animated conversation. Even in this poorly connected rural area, everyone had heard rumours that Tsvangirai had won. But surely the purpose of these recounts was to cast doubt on that victory by altering or disqualifying some of the votes cast? So why was Priscilla allowing the original results to stand? What was going on?

Festus looked pleased. We chatted. Tsvangirai was out of the country and he was frustrated by that, but what else could

Morgan do? He might be killed or arrested if he returned. Ordinary activists were being beaten and burned out of their homes by ZANU-PF youths. Festus feared that Mugabe planned to grind into submission those who supported the opposition, and then call for a run-off Presidential vote. That would give the MDC a desperate dilemma – whether to try to win a dirty fight or to boycott it and hand Mugabe a default victory. Even with such a feeble mandate, Mugabe might try to soldier on for a few more years, at least while he had Mbeki's strong backing.

I spoke to the ZANU-PF candidate, Makonese Muzenda, too. Muzenda was a skinny and eloquent young woman sporting trendy little dreadlocks who explained to me that ZANU-PF was modernising and reaching out to women – the disempowered 52 per cent of the population.

It was obvious that the recounting would be going on for days and that it would be unlikely to change the electoral arithmetic. There had been no fiddling with the ballot boxes or other administrative heists. ZANU-PF was not making any serious attempt to challenge enough MDC votes to overturn any of the Parliamentary results. The whole exercise was simply intended to buy a dying regime time to plan.

Two people were notably absent from April's events. Morgan Tsvangirai, as he tends to do in times of crisis, embarked on a global tour lobbying countries – who were generally supportive already – for help. Even Tsvangirai's supporters were regularly frustrated by his readiness to spend weeks out of the country, particularly when he spent them visiting European capitals. For all Europe's condemnations of Mugabe, it was clear that any plan to remove him from office would need to begin in Zimbabwe and to be facilitated by other Southern African governments playing a supportive role. European governments were impotent onlookers throughout the 2008 events. Of course I had some sympathy for Tsvangirai. His time in Zimbabwe was hard, characterised by pain, harassment and disappointment. A few days being fêted in Brussels and Berlin must have boosted his spirits. But sadly, while the time he chose to spend in Europe may have been restorative, it was not productive.

The other more surprising absentee was Mugabe himself, who shut himself up in his Harare home after his defeat at the polls and didn't emerge for a month. He had been given the results denied to his people soon after the polls closed. He was shocked and saddened. Until that moment, he had believed he was a hero to the loyal majority of his people and that he had been on course for a solid victory.

Mugabe wobbled. He told his advisers he was ready to go, as the people did not want him any more. For two days at the beginning of April he was on the brink of resigning the Presidency. The consequences of resignation and retirement for Mugabe were reasonably certain and benign. He could not stay in Zimbabwe in case he was caught up in a Tutu-style truth and reconciliation process that might lead to his prosecution. But he could retire quietly to one of several Asian countries. He had spent plenty of time in Malaysia, Thailand and China and would be tolerated by any of those regimes if he chose to live there in low-key luxury. Money would not be a problem. Members of the Zimbabwean regime are estimated to have stashed one billion US dollars outside the country, of which Mugabe has taken a large part.

But the consequences for those around him were more uncertain. They had no claim on the immunity behind which heads of state try to hide. Indeed, Mugabe's security chiefs were more vulnerable to prosecution than the President himself, as they had carried out atrocities and could not deploy the defence Mugabe often uses during intimate conversation – that he did not know what was being done in his name. So Mugabe's security chiefs took their wobbling President in hand. The Joint Operations Command (JOC) assumed charge of the country while Mugabe was wringing his hands. The members of the JOC are the hardest of ZANU-PF's hardliners. They include Major-General Paradzai Zimondi, who has turned a term in Zimbabwe's prisons into a

death sentence, allowing 20 per cent of prisoners to starve and
rot each year. Air Marshal Perence Shiri led the 5th Brigade's
Gukurahundi purges in Tsholotsho in the 1980s, during which
his forces murdered at least 20,000 Matabeles. Commander
Constantine Chiwenga announced in March 2008 that he
would never salute any 'sell-out' who defeated Mugabe. During
the period of Police Commissioner General Augustine Chihuri's
leadership, Zimbabwe's once exemplary police force has mutated
into a corrupt and hated rabble that will act politically to thwart
the regime's critics, use torture, carry out extra-judicial murder
and rob poor people of what little they have.

These men spent the 1970s fighting Zimbabwe's brutal guerrilla war of liberation and have spent the decades since running
Zimbabwe's security services. They are true believers in the power
of the gun and the primacy of the African nationalist one-party
state. But their hands are also dirty. They have corruptly taken
a share of what the regime has looted from the country and are
implicated – in a direct and leading fashion – in its atrocities.
For them, there is no plan B, no Asian retirement, no alternative to moving directly from their grandly titled positions to
their pre-designated spots in Heroes' Acre. The JOC did not
immediately know how to respond to the electoral defeat, but
its members did know that they would not allow Mugabe to
resign. So long as he stayed in place in State House, there was
no need for panic. There were plenty of tactics to buy time and
plenty of strategies which would keep ZANU-PF in power.

While making its plans, the JOC tried to revivify Mugabe by
showing him films of white farmers resisting eviction in 2002.
As I had seen when he spoke at Heroes' Acre, Mugabe believed
his own propaganda when it came to the importance of black
control of Zimbabwe's soil. Nothing enraged him more than a
defiant white farmer – the epitome of racism, colonialism and
the attempts of the UK and its puppet MDC to reassert power
over the black man. The JOC also fed Mugabe information about
evicted white farmers who returned to their former farms in the

days after 29 March to assess the prospects of reclaiming their property. These individuals were not many, but their inflammatory and stupid actions were reported, exaggerated and held up as the reality of life under the MDC – a government that would evict black settlers and give Africa's land back to the whites. The thought of the reversal of Zimbabwe's liberation began to pump revolutionary blood back into Mugabe's dry political veins.

This version of what happened in State House in the days after the election is necessarily based on second-hand accounts. But it has been widely confirmed and never denied. For example, Enos Nkala, a former ZANU-PF defence minister, said, 'I have information from very reliable sources that, on 1 April, everyone had the results including those of the Presidential elections. The President wanted to go, but there are people surrounding him who have committed heinous crimes against the people of Zimbabwe and they are afraid of a change of guard.'

After three decades of one-party rule and ten years of all too predictable decline, Zimbabwe's future was for once unclear. Rumours of Mugabe's wobble spread. Could he really steel himself to continue? Or would the country's security forces embark on a period of military rule? The members of the JOC had engaged in violent repression, including mass killing, in the past. Their reputations were ominous. But in 2008, after the horrors of Rwanda and Kenya, would they still be able to get away with such brutal techniques? The country was starting to bleed, but the violence was not yet so awful or so widespread as to negate wholly the optimism of 29 March. People were hanging on for the Presidential results. The recounts had not affected them. The violence did not alter the reality of how people had voted. ZEC eventually announced that it had finished the recount and would be able to announce the results soon. Was it still possible that Morgan had won and that his victory would be announced? And if yes to both, what would that mean for a country that was declaring war on itself?

5

THE UNCONQUERABLE WILL

Three weeks after his electoral defeat, as yet unannounced, Mugabe remained dazed, searching for his political mojo, showing his age. The JOC became a de-facto military leadership – some called it a junta. Still unsure how to address the problem of electoral defeat, the JOC used the window created by the delay in announcing the Presidential results to launch two campaigns to improve the prospects of Mugabe's survival: one subtle, one brutal.

The subtle side of the JOC's activity was to open the door for a power-sharing government. The *Herald* began to carry op-ed pieces arguing that a unity agreement between the parties was a viable model for Zimbabwe. African leaders had watched developments in Kenya in 2007 with great interest. There opposition leader Odinga had defeated President Kibaki at the polls – though this fact was obscured by some ballot rigging. However, Kibaki simply refused to relinquish power and, after a good deal of bloodshed, Odinga could secure nothing more than an agreement by which both men divided executive power in a ramshackle way. The Kenyan model had attractions for ZANU-PF. Given that it had lost the election, clinging on at least to a share of power might have been a pretty good outcome. Tsvangirai (speaking from abroad) appeared to be opening the door for some kind of unity deal – or other non-standard transfer of power – when he suggested that Mugabe should be found a graceful and honourable way to go. In South Africa, Zuma also said that a national-unity government was worth trying.

But allowing tame journalists to float the idea of all-party government was no more than a hedging activity for the JOC. Power-sharing was not its first choice of outcome – absolute control was obviously more desirable – though an accommodation with the MDC might be a short-term expedient. The JOC calculated its electoral options. Tsvangirai had come dangerously close to an outright victory. If his vote was over 50 per cent, or even very close to that magic number, it would be hard to deny him the Presidency. In that case the results would have to be challenged and altered or suppressed – a messy business. If, however, Tsvangirai's victory could be portrayed as less than decisive, then a second round of voting became a viable option. This was preferable, as it opened the possibility of Mugabe winning a clear victory second time round and being indisputably re-elected.

The JOC recognised from an early stage that a second round of voting could take place in a radically more favourable electoral climate – one in which people were afraid to vote against Mugabe. Indeed, whatever strategy it settled upon, the JOC knew that the spirit of the people and the opposition they had shown to Mugabe on 29 March would have to be broken. Otherwise a confident MDC could lead nationwide protests against the theft of its victory which the regime might not be able to resist. Whatever else was to be done, launching a nationwide offensive against the MDC and its voters was essential. As early as a week after the election, the JOC was set on this path.

As a sensible first step towards this offensive, the JOC decided almost immediately to activate ZANU-PF's youth militias by channelling money, vehicles and weapons to them. Gideon Gono, who had allocated few resources to ZANU-PF's 29 March campaign, was told in words of one syllable that his Reserve Bank had to produce large amounts of foreign currency to get the militias mobile and motivated.

Most of ZANU-PF's wet work in 2008 was carried out by its youth militias. In Zimbabwe, as elsewhere in Africa, mind-controlled children have shown the greatest capacity for subhuman cruelty. Grown-ups are required to manage logistics, deliver materials and insert incendiary propaganda into damaged minds. But when it comes to the intimate job of torturing to death – heaping beatings on to knife work on to partial incineration for days on end – crazed, indoctrinated teenagers have an unparalleled talent. The youth militias in 2008, many of whose personnel were actually children, often called themselves war veterans or war vets – bizarrely so, as most were not even born when the liberation war ended in 1979. The term war vet was first applied to any ZANU-PF militiaman, regardless of age, during the farm invasions which began around 2000. One evicted farmer's wife recalled the bemusement she felt when a twenty-year-old with a machete told her that he was now the rightful owner of the property as a reward for his military service.

The true war vets were getting rather old for fighting. The twenty-year-old guerrillas drafted into action in 1978 were now fifty. Certainly some retained a revolutionary spark. ZANU-PF's veterans' association specialised in menacing and bellicose statements about the MDC throughout 2008. But Mugabe could not expect his ageing warriors to go into battle again. Indeed, it is a mistake to believe that all true veterans of the liberation war were supporters of Mugabe. I know some genuine and senior war vets well. They occupy the role which retired military officers take in many countries – speakers of a traditional common sense, bemoaning the excesses of the younger generation and harking back to the good old days. Many liberation fighters were well educated in Moscow and Beijing. The best among them are erudite, dignified and appalled by what Zimbabwe has become.

The militias which the JOC powered up were entirely different from such greying gentlemen. A typical squad consisted of a group of young ZANU-PF members from a Mashonaland village, dazzled by the gift of a vehicle and a daily allowance for party work. A designated leader – a senior party man or an agent of the Central Intelligence Organisation – would provide leadership and briefing. The message was simple. The revolution was being betrayed. The MDC was killing ZANU-PF people across the country. It was time to make things right. Sometimes a militia would be given clear instructions – a list of names of MDC activists to be disciplined. Other teams would get only vague instructions – that a group of villages had supported the MDC or that all presiding officers had been paid by the British to steal the election from Mugabe. Whether given exact orders or a broad remit to punish, ZANU-PF militias proved to be a terrifying weapon. Their lack of discrimination contributed to the breadth of the fear they created.

There were plenty of fist-fights and run-ins between rival supporters in the week after the election, but attacks on the MDC began in earnest around 7 April. That night, 180 war vets crashed through Chitungwiza, just south of Harare, issuing threats to MDC agents. Armed ZANU-PF youths rounded up a large group of people in Mudzi and threatened them: 'There will be a re-run, and if you vote for MDC again we will go to war.' The next day the MDC reported to the police eleven different incidents in which its supporters had been attacked either singly or in groups. No arrests were made. The attacks at this stage were no more than beatings and aggressive or threatening behaviour, causing some fractures and other relatively minor injuries, but no deaths.

The police not only refrained from arresting ZANU-PF youths but also acted alongside them that April as agents of politically motivated violence, albeit in a different role. The police tended to take the lead in suppressing MDC victory celebrations and political organisation. On 12 April, two MDC supporters carrying party leaflets on a bus in Harare were arrested for doing so, taken to Glenview police station, beaten with riot sticks and kicked. The two were quite certain that their assailants were policemen, not ZANU-PF youths.

In contrast, the youth militias delivered more proactive intimidation. A good – and unusually well-documented

– example is the onslaught on the town of Mudzi, on 11 and 12 April. Of all the disappointments of its electoral performance, ZANU-PF was most shocked by the frailty of its support in Mashonaland – the tribal and political homeland which Mugabe expected to deliver absolute loyalty. However, of sixty-three Mashonaland seats, the MDC had taken twelve. Some of these gains should not have been complete surprises, as they occurred in semi-urban areas like Marondera, Chegutu and Chinoyi. But ZANU-PF strategists were not in a mood to tolerate any losses in the heartland. They were quick to see that if the party had secured a clean sweep of Mashonaland, to which it surely had a divine entitlement, it would have retained its overall Parliamentary majority.

ZANU did not actually lose any seats in Mudzi, but the MDC took 6,593 votes in the North constituency, just 1,500 fewer than the ZANU victor. Neither this, nor the fact that over 10,000 Mudzi inhabitants across the area's three constituencies had voted for Tsvangirai, could be tolerated. The militias were sent in to re-establish complete party loyalty. The militias rampaged through Mudzi's public areas on 11 April. In Chivaka village, they beat a sixteen-year-old girl, five women and six men on the buttocks with sticks. In Kanjanda village they beat a known MDC supporter, whereas they chose a random member of the public for a beating at Makanjera shops. They found one of the MDC supporters whom they were targeting at his home. They taunted him, 'We will put you in your grave,' then burned down his house and beat him viciously, fracturing his bones in four places. Another MDC supporter reported that he was taken that night with party colleagues to a ZANU-PF meeting. A terrifying mob of 150 ZANU youths told the MDC activists that they were going to be taught a lesson. They were ordered to lie on their stomachs and were beaten by a succession of members of the ZANU gang for over three hours.

Despite their evening of hard work, the youth militias went into action again the next day. But they were now hungry and on the lookout for a free meal. A group of sixty raided and looted two small shops belonging to Paradzai Chimutsa, justifying their actions by claiming that Chimutsa was an MDC member. Another group of twenty invaded the smallholding of an MDC supporter, beat him and his wife and stole his harvest of maize. Restored by their purloined foodstuffs, the youths began another protracted punishment beating on the evening of 12 April. To encourage others, the youths detained three MDC members at an ad-hoc camp in the centre of the town – now deserted, as nobody wanted to be on the streets where the militias were roaming. The three men were detained there for over two weeks and subjected to a series of beatings on their backs, legs and feet, which left them severely injured and traumatised.

It may have been in Mudzi that the first murder of the run-off campaign took place. Certainly, two days later, on 14 April, ZANU-PF youths killed Temba Muronde as he was being carried to a clinic for treatment after being beaten the day before. Soon I saw my first political funeral. The victim was carried through his village in an open casket, his young, bearded face puffed and ripped, his body covered with MDC regalia to hide the punctures in it. His comrades sang wildly but in tune – songs of struggle and victory but sung with rage and despair.

Seeing the corpse made the violence real to me as it had not been before. The forensic language of human rights reporting is deliberately restrained so that nobody can accuse the monitors of exaggeration. But the measured terminology hides the most important effects of the militias' rampages – the sleepless gnawing fear of being seized, of facing – while helpless and immobile – pain, even mutilation, that is just too much, but which goes on until time is a fuzzy notion; life becomes measured in episodes of agony, with comrades, wives and daughters being punished and abused. I wept that day for the brave, bloodied young man, too young to be lying in his casket.

From mid-April onwards, quantitative assessment of the spread and severity of the violence became difficult. It was clear that the JOC's onslaught, which began in those areas of ZANU-PF's Shona heartland which had voted MDC, was becoming more widespread. It was also clear that people were being killed. But the flimsy networks reporting human rights abuses could not cope with the volume of reports or with threats and violence against the few, brave monitors in each area. Yet despite failing communications, every day I heard dozens of reports of incidents ranging from the brutish to the atrocious.

Often I got the impression that large numbers of abuses affecting whole communities were being carried out without any outside knowledge. A refugee fleeing Murewa on 19 April said that there were multiple beatings and house burnings in his village. Chillingly, he said that young people were being taken out of the village for 're-education'. Other communities must have suffered similarly, but had nobody to tell their tale.

The nature of ZANU-PF's murders necessarily meant that many were undetected. During Zimbabwe's 2008 troubles hundreds of people simply vanished. Some perhaps drowned while trying to swim the Limpopo to the doubtful sanctuary of South Africa, but many others were surely killed and dumped in lakes or game parks so that their bodies were not discovered. Dozens of bodies were found in lakes when their levels fell during the dry months of August and September, though by that stage nobody could be sure of the cause of death.

In late April, my hope that the uncertainty might end well died. I started feeling frightened for Zimbabwe. Violence was spreading and becoming more vicious. But nobody knew quite why it was happening or what the aggressors were demanding. Was the JOC acting so that a cowed populace would accept a crude adjustment of the Presidential results? Was a military coup under way? Was there to be more voting? Or was this just revenge?

In the middle of growing terror, the Harare International Festival of the Arts (HIFA) at the end of April seemed incongruous, almost impossible. In previous years, the festival had been tolerated, even when musical performers and plays criticised or ridiculed the regime. Mugabe knew that Harare's cultured young people were never going to vote for him and allowed them their annual weekend of pretended freedom. But despite a general assumption that the 2008 HIFA would be cancelled, Mugabe did nothing and the show went on. It was beyond strange to sit in Harare watching the opera, while 100 kilometres away people were being beaten as punishment for their political views.

But HIFA soon ended; I woke up from the dreamland of freedom. The tolerance shown to the international media during the elections had already come to an abrupt end. A British journalist was arrested in Bulawayo on 9 April and detained for a terrifying week of threats and physical abuse. Journalists left either to avoid harassment or to cover other stories; Zimbabwe's election was becoming old news. Accounts of violence therefore went unreported.

As early as 20 April, the MDC claimed that 500 of its supporters had been attacked and ten killed. But the party's internal communications, which have never been effective, deteriorated rapidly once the violence started. The estimates of victims it released were not reliable. In this case, the estimate of ten murders looks like a figure plucked from the air (though the death toll certainly climbed to, and beyond, ten victims quickly enough), whereas all the reports I was hearing of collective beatings suggested that many more than 500 people had been assaulted.

Certainly, thousands of people were fleeing rural areas and coming to the towns to shelter with friends, relatives or anybody who could possibly help. Many turned to the MDC for assistance and formed a squatters' camp within the party's central Harare offices. The police turned the screw on the refugees and the MDC by raiding these offices on 25 April and arresting 250 squatters. Absurdly, it charged these folded-up and dispirited people with an arson campaign in Manicaland. Harassing refugees was only a secondary motive for the raid, giving it some apolitical cover. The police's primary goals were the MDC's computers and files, containing documentary evidence of voting patterns on 29 March. The police took the party's data and IT equipment away, severely hampering its efforts to stay organised.

On the same day, the police raided the offices of ZESN – the NGO which had boldly forecast the Presidential result. Again the stated target of the raid was the individuals who had supposedly broken the law by announcing results before ZEC. The actual target – just as at the MDC's offices – was ZESN's IT and its records of voting figures. By targeting the data of the two organisations which had attempted to record the election results, the regime was clearly trying to remove the means by which whatever results it chose to release could be challenged.

Having given the JOC over a month to restrategise and having done everything possible to ensure its figures could not be checked, the Electoral Commission ended its five-week silence on 2 May and announced the Presidential results:*

Candidate	Percentage of Vote
Tsvangirai	47.9
Mugabe	43.2
Makoni	8.3

If the Parliamentary results had left an impression of a country uncertain of its mind, the Presidential figures gave a clearer picture. After almost three decades of Mugabe's rule, Zimbabwe's people had said plainly that they did not want their great leader any more.

Mugabe had known about this shift in Zimbabwe's political tectonics for a month already and it had shaken him off his feet. Others in ZANU-PF were just as horrified but less incapacitated. But even the old men's suppression of the result

*I have omitted the negligible share of the vote secured by a fourth candidate.

throughout April, and the campaign of violence which then began, could not negate what the people had said at the ballot boxes in March. Tsvangirai's enormous popularity ultimately had to be admitted and his bid for power could no longer be denied. Though the cruel old men fought, and fight still, the historic courage Zimbabweans had shown on 29 March marked the beginning of their end.

Even more humiliatingly, the complete results now available demonstrated that Mugabe was ZANU-PF's weakest link. Way back on 29 March, which seemed like a year earlier, I had seen in Masvingo that ZANU-PF's candidates for Parliament had attracted a few more votes than Mugabe and that the party's local authority candidates had performed best of all. This pattern had been replicated nationally. Some voters were happy with ZANU-PF's performance locally, yet rejected Mugabe as president. ZANU-PF, which had served for so long as a vehicle for Mugabe, had to face the fact that the eighty-four-year-old leader was now impairing its electoral performance.

The results were also a crushing disappointment for Makoni. Yes, the third candidate did break the political mould. He had rattled his own party and galvanised the MDC; the small number of votes he took – most, presumably, from moderates or progressives within ZANU-PF – was enough to allow Tsvangirai to beat Mugabe. But Makoni had to be content with shaking things up for others' benefit. He himself did not score well enough to be able to claim a slice of the future division of power.

The MDC was disappointed too, as it had hoped for an outright win. But the official figures were compatible with the independent estimate, that Tsvangirai had scored 47–51 per cent, made a month earlier. The general view was that they had not been heavily adulterated. The Electoral Commission had perhaps shaved a couple of percentage points off the MDC's vote to support ZANU-PF's assertion that the voting had been inconclusive, but no more. Morgan Tsvangirai probably scored between 49 and 50 per cent of the vote, a whisker away from an absolute majority. ZEC could chip away at this total around the edges, but could not do anything too drastic, as a large proportion of the actual results – showing how well Tsvangirai had done – were on the internet and in the hands of the opposition, civil society and the foreign media.

The MDC cried foul, claiming that Tsvangirai had actually scored 50.3 per cent, but had been robbed of somewhere between 50,000 and 170,000 votes during the electoral process. This might have been true, but the party was not able to substantiate its claim and did not sound convincing. After all, the MDC had initially claimed that Tsvangirai had scored 57 per cent, a dramatic exaggeration. The MDC tried to argue that Tsvangirai had won outright and that – even if he had not quite secured 50 per cent – he should become an interim president. But if Tsvangirai had scored less than that magic number there was little basis for the claim. And Tendai Biti, MDC secretary general, soon moved the national debate on (implicitly accepting that he could not prove that Morgan had scored more than 50 per cent), arguing that the country was not prepared for more elections and that Tsvangirai should be allowed to form an interim government for a couple of years.

ZANU-PF cried foul too and accused the UK and USA of tampering with the electoral process. Nobody took this seriously. ZEC had controlled the voting and had every incentive to exaggerate Mugabe's vote to the maximum figure that could possibly be justified.

ZEC changed its position on the question of when a re-run would take place several times during May. Before the results were made public George Chiweshe said that the re-run would be within twenty-one days of the announcement. That changed after the announcement came on 2 May, because the JOC needed more time to soften the country up. Chiweshe first claimed that he did not have enough resources to administer a second round. This was obviously legally indefensible, so a Presidential order was rushed out to relax the deadline for holding a second round from twenty-one to ninety days. ZEC exploited this relaxation fully, ultimately announcing that the re-run would take place on 27 June.

The country collectively groaned. The prospect of three more weeks of violence before an early run-off had been grim, but three months of burning, beating and butchering would be intolerable. It was perhaps at this point that the people's will to hang tough snapped. Nelson Chamisa MP drew the obvious conclusion that the long delay before a re-run was intended to 'give Mugabe and ZANU-PF time to torment the MDC'.

The prospect of a re-run of the election provoked international comment. The US position shifted as the weeks passed. In April, the State Department had claimed that a re-run was not justified as Tsvangirai had won. But when the MDC's claims of an outright win began to look less defensible, the US position changed accordingly: a re-run ought to be conducted without violence under the inspection of a large multinational monitoring team.

SADC's position was not too far away from this in the end. The organisation wanted to avoid a re-run which would clearly trigger conflict, but if Mugabe forged ahead, SADC planned to deploy a team of several hundred observers. Given the way it intended to fight the election, ZANU-PF was keen to minimise the number of observers in-country. Patrick Chinamasa announced that observers only from friendly countries – defined as those not imposing sanctions on the regime – would be permitted. But ZANU-PF could not possibly exclude SADC observers unless it was prepared for the winner of the re-run to be shunned by his Southern African counterparts.

I felt desperate. Mugabe had won. Despite losing the election, he had retained power. He could instruct supposedly independent bodies like the Electoral Commission to delay his removal from power and provide them with bogus legal cover by means of ex-post executive orders. He could postpone a run-off until he was confident that the people were so weary of suffering that they would re-elect him just to end their misery. Alternatively, if he lacked that confidence, he could delay the run-off indefinitely, perhaps for years. If all else failed he could simply resurrect the allegation that the MDC was a terrorist organisation and declare martial law. In other countries, a display of people power – a mass demonstration – might have forced the dictator out. But the Zimbabwean security forces were numerous and remained loyal. They would put such a demonstration down with whatever excess of force they saw fit. Mugabe had all the cards and there seemed no way he could lose.

During this crucial period Tsvangirai remained absent. Between 8 April and 24 May, he spent more than a month out of Zimbabwe. This was a strange choice for a man who was ostensibly the front-runner in a desperately close Presidential election. The MDC claimed that it was not safe for Tsvangirai to be in Zimbabwe. Tendai Biti, for example, claimed that there was an official plot to kill him: 'We know there are eighteen snipers, and the military intelligence directorate is in charge of this.'

It is true that Tsvangirai was under threat at any time he was in Zimbabwe. The regime had shown its readiness to arrest him, beat him and prosecute him on flimsy evidence. Whether he was under greater threat following his victory in the March election is not so clear. Obviously he represented a greater danger to Mugabe's continuation in office than he had at any point before. But he was also visible as never before, which made him safer. It is hard to imagine that the JOC would have risked the unquantifiable international reaction that assassinating Tsvangirai would have brought, particularly as its plan B – a concerted and violent effort to overturn Tsvangirai's victory at the polls – was credible and well tested.

Such calculations were obviously nerve-racking for Tsvangirai, but he should have reasoned that he could protect himself from assassination only by staying out of the country indefinitely. If he meant to take the risk at some point and return before the run-off, he should have done so as early as possible to maximise his opportunities to campaign and sustain his embattled supporters. Whether or not Tsvangirai was justified in absenting himself from his country for so long at such a time, the effect on his supporters was serious. A leading article in a pro-opposition newspaper criticised Tsvangirai's decision: 'If you are not in front of your people, then you weaken the struggle.'

Certainly Tsvangirai's supporters were in a struggle. In early May I again met Jestina Mukoko, the director of Zimbabwe's principal human rights monitoring network, the Zimbabwe Peace Project. Jestina is a smooth and professional woman, a former state journalist who, after the regime went seriously astray, turned poacher by joining the NGO sector. I always like talking to Jestina as she has a sense of humour and a ready, gappy smile as well as access to hard information about human rights abuses. She – like so many other civil society activists – was to suffer as a consequence of her fearless and high-profile work. Jestina confirmed my impression that violence was going though the roof, but that corroboration was becoming harder to obtain: 'There were over four thousand abuses in April 2008, compared with eight thousand in the whole of 2007. Ten political murders took place in April. The MDC has said that even more of its members were killed, but we are careful only to report cases that are verified.' Despite the difficulties of her work, Mukoko was able to give a clear sequence of events: 'The violence started in Masvingo, following allegations that white commercial farmers were returning to Zimbabwe to reclaim their land. Farm invasions were followed by attacks on villages in areas which ZANU-PF used to control, but which were taken by the MDC on 29 March. The worst of the violence is now in Mashonaland.'

More qualitatively, Mukoko also described how rural Zimbabwean communities were experiencing the violence. 'Typically, ZANU-PF militias arrive at night. They go door to door, seize householders and force-march them to militia camps for "meetings" that can last several days. Many houses are burned. The militias burn ID cards and accreditation materials to ensure that villagers will not be able to vote, to monitor the election or to act as party agents. At these camps,' Mukoko said, 'militia members claim that the whites are trying to take over again and are being helped by enemies within the community. A list of these enemies is read out. These people have to identify themselves and are beaten with sticks and whips. Initially these beatings were just on the buttocks and legs, but lately militias have started beating heads and private parts. We are seeing corpses that have been mutilated and tortured before death. This goes back to the liberation war of the 1970s when sell-outs were brutally punished.' Jestina Mukoko's ability to combine statistics with vivid accounts of what was happening made her one of the regime's most effective critics, and soon a target of violence herself.

The violence, and fear of it, drove whole communities to flee. The UN estimated that, by early May, 30,000 people were homeless. The rumours of violence were bad enough, but the regime's blatant threats were even more chilling. Jubulani Sibanda, head of the war vets, was explicit about what the regime now required from its subjects: 'We are looking forward for every Zimbabwean not only to pledge their votes but to cast them for Robert Mugabe. People should know that each vote is no longer secret, but a responsibility put in the hands of each Zimbabwean by pain and death.'[2] These became ZANU-PF themes. The re-run would not be conducted as a secret ballot; rather, votes would be closely monitored. Only patriotic votes would be tolerated and patriotism meant support for Robert Mugabe.

Jestina Mukoko had said that Zimbabwe's white farmers were one of the regime's first targets in April. I already knew this was true from direct contact with many of the forty farmers in Masvingo who suffered invasions by ZANU-PF militias that month. For about a week militia units blockaded their gates,

destroyed their crops, killed their cattle, threatened and beat
farm workers and told the farmers themselves to leave before
they were murdered.

The onslaught on Masvingo farmers ended after about a week.
In Mashonaland, where ZANU-PF had felt most confident,
and then most betrayed by the March results, the youth militias
had been immediately directed to attack disloyal communities,
like Mudzi. But in Masvingo, where ZANU was now a minority party, the youth militias were warmed up with the familiar
task of destroying agricultural facilities and terrorising farm
labourers. Once inflated with revolutionary zeal, the youths
were redirected to higher-priority but less accessible targets –
MDC activists and the teaching profession. In Masvingo, these
people were embedded into communities that were now explicitly hostile to Mugabe. Cutting the traitors down to size was to
be a protracted and bloody business.

As so often happens on Zimbabwe's farms, a politically
motivated Government offensive in one area triggered copy-
cat violence by looters right across the country. The Masvingo
attacks were carried out with the elections, rather than Mugabe's
bogus land-reform agenda, in mind; but they signalled that seizing farms was acceptable and indeed Government-approved.
Acquisitive characters in all Zimbabwe's provinces took the
opportunity to try to grab some of Zimbabwe's few remaining
valuable assets.

I saw the reality of the violence that resulted when I spoke to
Bruce and Netty Rogers, a British-Zimbabwean couple who live
near Chegutu, an hour west of Harare. I saw them on 9 May,
three days after they had suffered a terrible beating. Bruce is a
strongly built man of about fifty. His skin has been coarsened
by decades of African sun, the bristles of his moustache look
as tough as wire, but despite his rugged appearance he is softly
spoken. From his scalp down to his neck, his face was covered
with overlapping bruises, some plum purple, others quite black.
He sat and moved gingerly, feeling the pain of his broken ribs

much more than he admitted. Netty is usually the livelier half of the couple, but she was subdued and clearly still suffering from their experience. Her face was terribly discoloured and her head looked misshapen and out of alignment with her neck. Her ear was bandaged. Bruce appeared to be coping better, but had male armour to hide behind. They sat together as they told their story, helping each other to remember all the details and the sequence of events. I was struck at the time by the way that neither criticised nor questioned any of the life-or-death judgements their partner had made during their ordeal. They had an impressively absolute faith in each other, which must have helped their recovery.

Two local men warned Bruce and Netty at lunchtime on 6 May that they should leave their property 'within two minutes' or face trouble. They thought about moving out, but Netty decided, 'This is where we live, we're not getting out of our house. We have no other home and if we leave they will loot and trash it.' She described how their attackers soon arrived: 'Just after 5 p.m., ten or twelve men drove up to the gate in a white pick-up truck. There were three guys in their thirties in charge, accompanied by youths in their teens and twenties. They said they were war vets and demanded to be let in. We went inside the house, locked the doors and closed the curtains so they couldn't see our movements. The guys broke the lock on the gate, drove on to our lawn and began to smash our windows and hammer on the door. I shouted to them that Bruce was armed. I said if they came inside we would not hesitate to kill to protect ourselves.'

From the top of the stairs, Bruce and Netty saw the war vets smash down their front door. Just in time, Bruce told Netty to move backwards in case they fired. 'I felt the rush of the pellets over my head,' Bruce said. 'They went just past Netty's left ear, where she'd been standing just before. Then we knew we were in very serious trouble – we knew they intended to kill us. I wondered if I should return fire, but I knew if I started firing

I'd have to shoot all of them. Also I was worried that they might have AK-47s, which they could use to shoot us through the floorboards from downstairs. And all the time in the back of your mind you know that the justice system here is corrupt and that we might be charged for defending ourselves.'

A complex struggle took place over the next hour. The war vets did not dare to enter the house knowing that Bruce was covering the front door with his shotgun. They tried to use farm workers as human shields, forcing them to advance up the stairs at gunpoint. Bruce couldn't shoot without risking innocent lives, but Netty used a pepper spray when the group of war vets hiding behind farm workers neared the top of the stairs, which drove the attackers back out of the house, but also roused them to fury. She described what happened next: 'They shouted that we should stop being stubborn and come out. But we knew they would beat us. Things went quiet for a minute, but then they broke down the back door and started throwing burning logs into the house. A fire started in the lounge. Bruce decided that we had to get out or we would be burned alive.'

As she came out of the house a war vet grabbed Netty and began to beat her. 'They throttled me and I started to lose consciousness. I thought I was going to die. I bit the arm of one of the guys holding me, then they really started laying into me. They started beating us and kicking us. I could see an outline of four guys on Bruce jumping on his head, kicking his back. The blows on my head were so hard that I thought it wasn't a fist and then saw it was an iron bar. I drifted in and out of consciousness as they attacked us like that three or four times.'

Incredibly, the Rogerses were rescued and, though terribly beaten, the worst injury was Netty's perforated eardrum, which may never heal properly. More incredibly, they resolved to stay in Zimbabwe and in their home. 'Initially I thought I'd never go back,' Netty said, 'but it is my home and we have nowhere else to go. My dad bust a gut to buy that place. It was just bush and tall grass. I'm not going to let some thug take all that hard work.'

The suffering in May extended well beyond white farmers. Later in the year I found out that huge numbers of black farm labourers had suffered even more than the Rogerses. Nobody knew quite what the death toll was, but it was climbing. The authoritative Zimbabwe Association of Doctors for Human Rights reported on 9 May that twenty-two people had been killed and 900 had been tortured. This was a defensible and conservative estimate. Amnesty International, which has no monitoring network of its own in Zimbabwe, but which speaks with international resonance, drew on the Association's estimated death toll and issued its own report of twenty-two deaths a week later, by which time the figure was a clear under-estimate. Amnesty also accused ZANU-PF of recruiting young people for violent operations and accused the police of doing nothing to stop the killing. At the same time the MDC claimed that thirty of its supporters had died and the union represent-ing farm workers – one of the few organisation with a genuine feel for rural Zimbabwe – estimated that 40,000 people had been driven from their homes and were sleeping rough or flee-ing to the cities.

The statistics hide the pain of individual cases, such as Tonderai Ndira. Ndira was a high-profile MDC party worker in Harare. He was thirty-two years old, tall, eloquent and char-ismatic, with a rakish smile often accessorised with a woolly hat and a cigarette. He had been sleeping away from home for several nights – many activists did this to reduce the chances of abduction. But on the day before he was taken Ndira had come back to his own home to sleep; his wife said he was exhausted by weeks of round-the-clock party work. A standard ZANU unit – ten men in a pick-up truck, some armed with assault rifles – arrived at his house. They dragged him out of bed, beat him in the street and took him away wearing only his underwear.

There were dozens of witnesses to all this. Human rights groups were immediately alerted. The police were informed at once. The Combined Harare Residents Association, for which

Ndira used to work, produced a bulletin demanding his release. Diplomats took up the case. Amnesty International issued an early press release saying that it feared for Ndira's safety. Even the UN bodies in Harare, which were usually fearful of irritating Mugabe and so were silent about his abuses, issued an appeal for Ndira's release. Harare held its breath. We knew that hope had to be slim. But we so wanted something good to happen, something to make us believe that anything other than the worst was possible. He was already dead, of course. He had been killed hours after his abduction, while the UN was still circulating drafts of its appeal for his release for internal clearance. Before the mercy of death, the ZANU militia beat him, breaking his neck, his jaw and his hands. They sliced out his tongue and hacked out his eyes. They stabbed other parts of his body several times.

The police found Ndira's body on a farm in Goromonzi a week later. Typically they did not bother to identify it, merely taking it to the mortuary of Parirenyatwa hospital. A human rights lawyer, touring the mortuaries to find the missing, came across the corpse, which was now badly decomposed, the head crushed. Ndira was identified mainly by the funky jewellery he liked to wear.

We all knew what was coming. But the impact of the death of such a bright spirit after such an effort to prevent it was devastating. A friend of Ndira's, Daniel Molokele, blogged on the news of his comrade's death:

> I never thought we could turn to each other with such brutality, after the bitter and protracted struggle that our people went through to be free. It pains me.
>
> Oh rest in peace, Tonderai. Your blood will water the revolutionary tree and keep the revolutionary garrison going.
>
> Tendai Biti asked if the international community was only going to react after dead bodies littered the streets of Harare. Little did he know that even with a Harare littered with dead

bodies no one was going to respond either. Probably only Hollywood responded by investigating if the genocide was bad enough to warrant scripting yet another *Hotel Rwanda*.

I became used to the bitter demands of Zimbabweans that the world do something to end their suffering. I also became used to the impotent sense that there was nothing I could do.

As the country burned, Tsvangirai spent time everywhere except Zimbabwe – Ireland was his most unlikely destination. But when he did finally return to the country on 24 May, he at least showed readiness for the contest with his own take on the state of the union address, delivered to his newly elected MPs on 30 May. He began by setting out the problem: 'Our nation is in a state of despair . . . We are an unmitigated embarrassment to the African continent. We have the world's highest inflation rate, 80 per cent unemployment, an education sector which has plummeted from one of the best to one of the worst.' He envisaged for the country government 'based on the return of fundamental freedoms to the people of Zimbabwe'. But he offered no prospect of reconciliation or immunity for those attacking his supporters: 'The violence that is taking place must stop. There will be no tolerance or amnesty for those who torture or injure or kill other citizens. We as the leaders have a historic responsibility to reverse the tide on intolerance, violence, corruption, inequality, discrimination, hatred division and patronage.'

Tsvangirai's words were spoken in anger. But, even allowing for that, they sound hollow now, as we shall see. But he was at least back in the country and back in action. Tsvangirai finished May as he should have spent the entire month – energising his supporters and setting out a strong vision of a post-Mugabe Zimbabwe. But with less than a month to go before the re-run, had he left it too late?

6

RED SOIL

By the start of June 2008, the MDC claimed that forty of its members had been killed. Monitoring networks were reporting collective beatings in remote villages, mass evictions and an unseen refugee crisis as thousands fled their homes. It was hard to be sure all this was true. But whatever was happening was beyond the reach of television cameras and so invisible to the world.

On 3 June I drove again into Masvingo province with an Embassy team to see for myself if the reports of horrific violence were true. I wasn't ready for the viciousness and callousness to which I would be exposed over the next two days. It was immediately obvious that large numbers of security personnel of all types had been called up from their barracks to exercise tight control over the country. I had to pass through six police checkpoints during my 200-kilometre journey to Gutu. For the first time in my three years in Zimbabwe the police did not wave me through when they saw my white diplomatic number plates. As a diplomat, I was officially allowed to travel where I wished in the country without interference. But I was pulled over at every roadblock and asked a series of questions. Who was I? Where was I going? What was I doing? The checkpoints were more militarised than before. As well as police in their brown uniforms, I saw soldiers with assault rifles. And the purpose of the checkpoints had clearly changed. Rather than simply shaking local people down – stealing their goods and extorting bribes – the police were now acting politically, restricting the movements of the MDC and of people like me.

At each roadblock I handed my papers to a policeman who carried them directly to a stony-faced man in plain clothes. Typically he would be wearing jeans and a t-shirt. But despite his casual dress he was obviously a member of the internal security service – the CIO – and very much in charge. Sometimes the CIO man would simply make notes before flicking my papers wordlessly back to the police, who would then let me go. But other roadblocks were more diligent. One CIO agent quizzed me for ten minutes about my movements. He wanted to know the names of everyone I was going to meet. Clearly I couldn't tell him without putting my contacts in danger, so I said that I was going to meet government officials – local administrations, police, the Electoral Commission and so on. He could hardly object to such meetings and could not reject my accreditations and notifications of travel, which were all Government-issued, so he had to let me go on.

I passed through the market town of Chivu, which usually hums with people breaking journeys and selling vegetables, but was now ominously quiet. The bus station, which doubles as a market square, had been transformed from its usual concrete grey to yellow, as if it had been repainted. But we had ZANU-PF to thank for the new splash of colour. The youth militia had plastered bright yellow posters, carrying a new picture of an airbrushed and uncomfortably grinning Robert Mugabe. People were keeping their heads down to minimise the risk of being pulled into an all-night ZANU-PF rally by these fly-posting zealots.

An hour later as I approached Gutu I passed a group of a dozen young people – women as well as men – jogging along the road. They were singing, in the way a squad of soldiers under training might, and waving sticks and knobkerries. They were wearing the bright yellow ZANU-PF t-shirts which appeared all over the country seemingly overnight. They were clearly a paramilitary formation – armed, uniformed, controlling a space.

The politics of t-shirts in Zimbabwe are serious, sometimes a matter of life or death. International donors are often infuriated to find that NGOs wanting, for example, to combat the spread of HIV include a large amount within their budgets for t-shirts. But NGO leaders are adamant that the investment pays off. And politicians also know the effect that distributing thousands of shirts can have. In Zimbabwe, a t-shirt does four things:

It communicates. Political t-shirts carry party slogans: 'Vote ZANU-PF for 100% empowerment'; 'Vote Tsvangirai for the change you can believe in'. Civil society t-shirts can carry longer and more complicated messages. I have one which reads, 'The Domestic Violence Law-Bill – Support the Law that promotes domestic harmony.' Another produced by a group campaigning for the abolition of the death penalty says, 'Who is supposed to kill who???' then switches to Shona to condemn execution as a colonial and unAfrican form of punishment. In a society where most have no television and do not read newspapers, where even a radio is a rarity, direct communication by t-shirt can penetrate communities that cannot otherwise be reached.

It shows affiliation – membership of an NGO or a political party.

It claims territory. In March, I had seen ten MDC t-shirts for every ZANU-PF one. That public display of ownership foreshadowed the MDC's strong gains in the town. In June the MDC was invisible and the bright yellow of ZANU-PF was everywhere. The message was clear: the ruling party had retaken the town.

It intimidates. Pluralism is barely acknowledged as a concept in Zimbabwe, let alone a reality. The line between political opponent and mortal enemy is routinely confused by the hate speech of the state media and the use of violence as a central tool of political campaigning. The sight of twenty ZANU-PF supporters, in their yellow uniforms, armed, was a clear message, and a threat, to any opposition members who wanted to campaign on Gutu's streets.

In all I saw three groups of ZANU-PF youth, thirty people altogether, marching or jogging around Gutu's streets. One group carried axes, a chilling warning that I was going to witness the use of lethal force for the first time. I could immediately tell that the overt allegiance of the town had changed. It was no longer acceptable to belong to the MDC. I saw only one brave soul wearing one of the t-shirts the party had issued in March. It looked faded and worn, as if reflecting the MDC's threadbare prospects.

I revisited the MDC party office where I had met a dozen buoyant and optimistic candidates in March. There were just two this time. The MDC, which had been so vibrant, was now passive and disorganised. The two candidates complained about poor communication between the central party organisation and the provinces. They had not been told what approach to take to the June elections in the face of violence. Should they carry on campaigning despite the risk of attack? Should they try to hold rallies? In practice they weren't doing much.

I spoke to Harry, who stood for the Chatsworth council on the MDC slate. Eight armed soldiers had picked him up on 27 May with four party colleagues while at a butcher's in Chatsworth. He had been beaten with sticks, accused of supporting the MDC and taken by truck to the 4th Brigade army base at Matisha. En route the truck stopped several times to allow troops to dismount and beat people on the streets. Harry was beaten again at the army base, had icy water poured on him, then taken back to Chatsworth and handed over to police. The police detained him for two nights, accusing him of possessing drugs and destroying property, before releasing him.

I heard numerous other complaints of violence, some first-hand and credible, some no more than rumours. Seven men had just visited the house of another MDC official and beaten him with logs, taken his ID and birth certificate. ZANU-PF youths were abducting, beating and burning houses. MDC spokesman Nelson Chamisa's family home in Masvingo was attacked. Soldiers shot the husband of an MDC councillor in the arm, and in Zimuto live grenades were used. There had been another shooting in Mwenezi. There was little room to doubt that ZANU-PF had taken a decision to militarise the campaign of intimidation against the MDC. It was never clear if the people carrying out the violence were regular army officers or ZANU's own militias. But the military were at the least playing a supporting role, containing and isolating communities that ZANU militias could move into and terrorise.

The MDC officials I met in Gutu and elsewhere were unsure of the impact of violence on voter turnout and the popular readiness to defy Mugabe again. Initially they tried to take the line that the people would still vote heavily for the MDC on 27 June. They even claimed that popular anger and determination to vote out Mugabe would be strengthened by the campaign of violence. I heard some evidence for this point of view from victims of violence, who said they were not afraid to vote MDC again, even as they sat outside clinics waiting for treatment. But, as discussion went on, the strong doubts of the MDC's people on the ground started to come through. They acknowledged that their voters were scattered, that no system was in place to transport people who had fled their homes back to the areas where they were registered to vote on election day. Many voters' ID cards had been confiscated or destroyed and it was going to be hard for poor rural voters to get fuel and money to travel to a registration centre and replace them.

Civil society groups that I met in early June, most of whom were more or less sympathetic to the MDC, were fully convinced that ZANU-PF was doing more than enough to steal the election. They claimed that ZANU personnel were touring villages saying, 'There will be war if MDC wins.' ZANU was also claiming it would be able to monitor individual votes and punish anyone who supported Tsvangirai.

On 4 June I made an early start to meet contacts in Bikita. I arrived at a tiny parade of simple shops where I had arranged to meet a teacher. But the place was not safe for a rendez-vous. A truck loaded with maize meal was parked by the road, surrounded by men wearing ZANU-PF t-shirts. They didn't look too scary, so I ambled over for a word, hoping that a big smile and a friendly 'How are you?' would be disarming. We had a chat and the ZANU guys explained that the food was there to feed people who attended a party rally later in the day. A free plate of sadza would be a major attraction for people in rural Masvingo who were struggling to muster one meal per day. I asked if I could come to the rally, but this was a step too far. The senior man in the group shifted uneasily and said it might not be safe for me.

I spoke to my teaching contact on the phone and arranged to meet him at a remote point on the road. He emerged from a hiding place behind a tree and got into the car. He was abso-lutely terrified, his hands shaking, his eyes darting around looking for anyone who might see us. He quickly told me his story, quivering with rage and terror at the danger his family was facing. The consequences for him if he was seen with me would obviously be serious, so I ended our talk quickly and let him get away safely.

At that moment, the provincial chair of the MDC called to tell me that the party office in Jerera, near Zaka, had been fire-bombed. I drove as fast as possible to Zaka and went into the police headquarters. The officer in charge said he had heard nothing about an attack, but would investigate immediately. The officer was a superb liar and I believed him. But he was actually just trying to put me off the scent. The moment I left he must have told two policemen to get to the site of the attack as quickly as possible and ensure that I couldn't inspect it.

I drove on to Jerera, another ten kilometres down a wide empty road. I was going fast, but the police Land Rover that overtook me was going much faster. I found the place easily, partly because the building was a blackened shell and partly because the speeding police jeep had pulled up in front of it and two policemen were stationed fifty metres away waving their arms telling me to turn back.

For the only time in the whole sordid campaign I lost my temper and let it show. The policemen were doddering rural plods and I wasn't scared of them. I said I was going to see the building as an accredited observer and they couldn't stop me. I asked them who they had arrested for this attack. They shrugged and I called them war criminals complicit in concealing serious human rights abuses. I took out my camera and photographed the MDC office, which was completely gutted. They told me to stop, but I could keep them away simply by swinging the camera at them and asking if I should take their pictures too. They were scared of this, knowing – I believe – that they were acting in a grotesquely immoral and illegal way. They weren't the type of ZANU-PF thugs who would carry out such an attack, but they were covering it up and they knew it.

I drove on to the local mission hospital, where I found a Swiss doctor. He had courageously come to Zimbabwe for a year as a volunteer, but was shaken by what he had got caught up in and was desperate to flee the country. He brought in his patient, one of three men who had survived the attack and the least badly injured. The survivor I spoke to was Peter, the Secretary General of the MDC in Zaka District. His hands were thickly bandaged, his arms and legs raw and burned, his hair and scalp charred and blackened. He spoke very quietly, with remote, disengaged eyes. I had no doubt that he was telling me the truth.

Armed men, not in uniform, had come to the MDC offices at 4 a.m. the night before. The MDC had decided that party members should sleep at the office to protect it from break-in. The armed men smashed the door open and told the six party members who had been sleeping there to lie down. When they started to pour petrol over the MDC men, three resisted and were shot. Peter hoped they had been killed instantly, because the militia then set all six men alight and left, blocking the doorway. Peter was able to beat the flames out with his hand and tear off his burning clothes, before fleeing through the back of the building. He escaped with burns to his head, feet and hands. His two colleagues who had not been shot also survived but had suffered terrible burns, 30 and 40 per cent respectively. They were in an ambulance travelling to Masvingo's larger hospital, but it was not at all certain that they would live. The three men who had been shot were all dead, one way or another.

There was a strange symmetry between ZANU-PF's election slogans '100% empowerment' and its terror campaign in Masvingo that was 100 per cent ruthless and 100 per cent effective. The attack in Jerera was a clear statement to everybody who had escaped with nothing worse than a beating, an eviction or a threat: cross the party and it would react, even burning opponents alive. Afterwards nobody in the province could doubt what a vote for Tsvangirai might cost.

With less than four weeks to go before the re-run, Morgan Tsvangirai tried to get his stuttering campaign moving by touring rural areas. But he was effectively prevented from doing so by repeated harassment. He and his entourage were detained for eight hours in Lupane on 4 June – the same day I was witnessing the firebombing in Jerera. Two days later, the police held him at a checkpoint and prevented him from addressing a rally near Bulawayo. Tsvangirai's scared and faltering voters needed to hear words of reassurance and conviction from his own lips. The police, again working hand in glove with the ruling party, harried him and wasted his time to ensure that he could not deliver that message.

A week later a teacher in Zaka sent me a text message: 'At a meeting called by soldiers teachers threatened with death if polling stations they man come out in favour of Tsvangirai many people now homeless after their homes burnt down.' It was becoming clear that, along with MDC activists, teachers were a key target for ZANU-PF action. They were being subjected to a two-pronged attack.

Firstly, they were being arrested in large numbers – I heard of seventy-two teachers or headmasters arrested in Masvingo province alone. Most faced the same charge of electoral malpractice – the implication being that, while acting as returning officers and other polling officials, they had displayed bias towards the MDC. These charges had little merit and, though some were detained for over a month, no teachers were in fact successfully prosecuted. However, I had seen examples of returning officers irritating the authorities by attempting to apply the rules of the March election rigorously. In Zaka, a senior provincial official marched into a polling station in March and instructed the returning officer to allow his friend, who was not on the electoral roll, to vote. The returning officer said he could allow an unregistered person to vote if he had a certificate of registration from the provincial registrar general. This may have been the right thing to do, but crossing a senior ZANU man is not the done thing. Once the state abandoned even the limited impartiality with which it had acted in March and reverted to its normal partisan role, conscientious and impartial returning officers became a problem that needed to be solved.

The second element of ZANU's attack on teachers was, of course, violence. I remembered the story of the frightened teacher in Bikita. His wife, also a teacher, had been attacked. On 19 May, she and other teachers had been woken up by men in army uniform, some with guns, ordered to gather in one place, then to lie on their bellies. The uniformed men beat them across the back and buttocks, accusing them of voting for the MDC and of teaching politics to their students – inducing them to vote MDC too. ZANU's readiness when under pressure to resort to violence and to target educated people shows its Maoist origins. The type of ideas that inspired Pol Pot – that the rural peasant is the heart of the revolution and that intellectuals and urbanites are petit-bourgeois betrayers of socialist ideals – come up time and again in Zimbabwe. The regime's suspicion of teachers' influence over the pupils – and its readiness to destroy an entire school system to neutralise that influence – is typical.

The action against teachers dealt Zimbabwe's education system a blow from which it has never recovered. Of course education had been on a downward trend since 2000. Until then it had been normal for children to receive a free, good-quality education up to O-level. Even in 2006 and 2007, school attendance was the norm for most children.

All that changed in 2008: an international donor estimated that 70 per cent of children attended primary school at the start of the year, but only 30 per cent by December. There were several reasons for the collapse of education: hyperinflation which destroyed the value of salaries, poaching of staff by South African schools and the implementation of fees which excluded the poorest households. But the Government's decision to attack teachers physically was a key stimulus for tens of thousands to abandon their jobs, their profession and even their country. Certainly, on my travels in early June I found many schools closed, particularly in Chivi, Mwenezi, Chiredzi and Bikita, places where teachers were being harassed or beaten.

Each day in June brought a new horror. A settlement near Marondera was raided by fifty ZANU youths carrying sticks and axes. Twenty people were injured. Attackers apparently looking for Emmanuel Chiroto, a leading member of the MDC in Harare, instead raped, tortured and murdered his wife Abigail, in front of their young son.

It seemed there were no limits to what Mugabe would do. Having decided to win at all costs he had fuelled up and unleashed indoctrinated and violent young men who now saw large numbers of the population as valid targets. MDC officials were terrified and thousands hid, but this left their families exposed. ZANU-PF youths coming to get an MDC man were capable of beating, torturing and killing wives and children if their target was not at home. In mid-June I went to a clinic in central Harare to meet three women from Epworth who had been raped and beaten. One was too broken by her experience to talk. She lay silently in her bed, her eyes darting nervously around the room, the covers pulled up to her neck. But the other two victims, Liza Mwaramba and Yvonne Chipowera, were eager to tell their story. For Shona women, traditionally submissive, they were remarkably direct and open, and demonstrated an astonishing physical and emotional resilience.

'They came to my house on 8 June,' said Mwaramba. 'They said I was an MDC supporter. I was wearing my party t-shirt and I was about to go to a rally. They burned down my house and took all my things. I ran away and hid. But the next day they came back to rape me. I knew some of them as local ZANU-PF members. But some others were from another area. They put their penises in my mouth. They put sperm all over my face. They kicked my breasts, which are still badly swollen. They took me to a graveyard and raped me again. When I was trying to stop them, they took a hot wire and burned my hand. They looted my body like I was dead. They took my ID card and all my money.'

Chipowera's experience was similar, but her assault was more sustained. 'They came to my place at 8 p.m. on 9 June. I was with my baby. They told me to surrender all my MDC regalia and cards. They took me to their base. One guy raped me on the way. They poured cold water on me all night, so I was freezing. They beat me over and over again with rods. They beat my genitals, legs, back, buttocks and head. They called me names. They said I was a dog because I supported Tsvangirai.'

When I spoke to the women they were still in pain and coming to terms with new hardships. They returned to Epworth after being attacked to find their homes had been destroyed. They were also confronting the possibility of infection. A quarter of young men carry HIV, so the consequences of rape are potentially lethal. The women, who were all confident of their negative status prior to the attack, were dreading their test results. Chipowera was angry. 'I am stressed especially about the rape. I have contracted an STD from the rape and I must wait to know about HIV. I wish God would take them all. Mugabe is a pig. I wish he would die.' Mwaramba was more afraid: 'I am stressed because I have two children. They poisoned my husband and he is in the ground since 2006. Maybe I am HIV positive now because of these guys. Who will look after my children if I get AIDS? To be raped is like death.'

Amid so much horror, I was supposed to maintain some kind of objectivity and analytical scepticism. It was easy to believe that anything was possible. But exaggeration – always a problem in Zimbabwe, where hard information is so scarce – remained a possibility. Several contacts reported that ZANU-PF was amputating hands and arms in the style of Sierra Leone's barbaric rebels. In fact this story was untrue.

Another awkward issue to evaluate was the extent to which the MDC was also involved in violence. That MDC members did arm themselves for self-defence and retaliation is certain. It may well also be that some MDC hard men decided to get their retaliation in first. An MDC official in Masvingo told me, 'If they burn one in Masvingo, MDC will burn two.' Some cases of MDC violence were documented. On 10 June, men described as MDC-T thugs abducted and murdered two ZANU-PF supporters in the Cashel Valley near Chimanimani.

There is no way of knowing what the ratio of ZANU-PF to MDC violence was. Nor whether the MDC acted in every case in self-defence. My guess is that the MDC did strike the first blow in some cases and that overall there was perhaps one victim of MDC violence for every ten who suffered at the hands of ZANU-PF and the state. It seems unlikely that MDC militias were centrally organised or equipped. It is more likely that individual communities formed their own self-defence teams, a process often led by local MDC officials. One human rights

monitor believes that the large-scale deployment of the army in
May and June was a response to MDC militias, which could
fight on equal terms with ZANU youths carrying sticks and
axes, but not with soldiers bearing AK-47s.

What the creation of MDC militias shows is that both parties
have a culture of violence. In many parts of the country a generation of young men has been taught by experience that they
must choose a side, then fight with and damage the opposition.
It will take years, even decades, of patient conflict-resolution
work to persuade them to engage in non-violent methods of
solving problems. Even the beginning of such a process is a
long way off.

On 15 June I received a text message from a human rights
monitor in rural Masvingo: 'Bikita is now hell on earth beatings
killings and abductions at the hands of soldiers war veterans
and youth militia we are in hiding election already stolen.'
But despite such vivid warnings, I still felt personally secure –
ZANU's violence seemed remote, something I would only ever
witness after the event or at second hand. With hindsight, I was
terribly naive.

I was also naive about the endurance of the MDC. I had seen
for myself that ZANU-PF was using the most cruel and ruthless
violence against the MDC and that the police were complicit,
at the very least by covering up political murders and other
crimes. But I still wondered whether the MDC might be able
to cling on. Perhaps the rural violence was isolated? Perhaps the
tide of popular opinion had turned decisively? Perhaps Mugabe
could still be washed away? Indeed some victims and activists
continued to claim that the violence was only strengthening
their resolve to vote MDC. My bubble of confidence and wish-
ful thinking was about to be burst. My questions were about to
be answered. I travelled to Manicaland on the afternoon of 18
June for a two-day field trip.

The format for these trips was changing. Around the time of

the March elections, I used to travel with a driver, who would be a Zimbabwean working for the Embassy. Sometimes I would also have another colleague, perhaps a member of another Embassy, with me. So, for example, in March I had travelled to Masvingo with staff from the Canadian Embassy, and on election day, 29 March, with a Spanish diplomat, Eduardo Escribano. Travelling in multinational teams was useful as it became easier to secure international support for whatever conclusions we drew during our visits if these were supported by colleagues from other Embassies. The use of local drivers was reconsidered in early June after an American party making a field trip was detained for some hours at a roadblock. The Americans were ordered out of their vehicle, but refused to move. A window was broken, a tyre was slashed and, most worryingly, somebody hit the Americans' driver as he negotiated through an open window (as usual we had little idea if the attackers were police or ZANU-PF militias). The British Embassy decided that it could not put at risk Zimbabwean staff, such as drivers, who did not have whatever protection diplomatic status gives. We also decided that using British or American vehicles – which are easy to identify from the numbers on their diplomatic plates – was too provocative. So during the visit to Manicaland I found myself driving a Dutch vehicle. My passengers were Helen Richards of the UK's Department for International Development and Brechtje Klandermans, a Dutch diplomat.

The visit started quietly enough. We met an activist from Simba Makoni's campaign in the cosy bar of Mutare's Holiday Inn. He was reasonably impartial when it came to the run-off, so we put particular weight on his views. He felt that Tsvangirai could still win as he was solidly ahead in four of the ten provinces and competitive in three others. (Two of the battleground provinces were Masvingo and Manicaland, the places where I had been observing.) But new factors were changing the balance of power. The MDC was simply banned from campaigning in Manicaland. The police would break up any attempt to hold rallies. The party had no means of communicating with the electorate. ZANU was not exactly campaigning, but it was deploying army units to harass people and threatening a war against the MDC. ZANU was telling traditional leaders that they would be held responsible if their villages failed to vote ZANU-PF in numbers. Although Makoni was clearly out of the running, we heard that he still saw himself as a player. Our contact was disappointed that Makoni had unilaterally set aside the position he had agreed with his activists – that he would announce his support for Tsvangirai in the run-off. He had chosen to present himself as a neutral, apparently positioning himself as a conciliatory figure ready for high office in any government of national unity.

It was now mid-evening and we'd been trying to contact the MDC for a meeting. They suddenly called back and said they had assembled a high-level team of regional people and that we should come straight away. I drove to a smart house where eight men sat ready to meet us. (The women, as so often in Zimbabwean politics, were confined to making the tea.) A few weeks earlier they had been activists and candidates. But the MDC had far exceeded even its own expectations at the March elections, winning twenty of twenty-eight House of Assembly seats in the province and scoring similar success in the local and Senate elections. So we found ourselves talking to a mayor, a senator, two MPs and four councillors. But astonishingly, for people holding such senior office, the group felt that it was under siege from the state. We heard that the police had issued arrest warrants for five newly elected MPs in the province. Councillors were being beaten until they fled their wards. Polling agents, organising secretaries and other rank-and-file activists were named on lists that had been handed out to ZANU-PF militia units, which arrived at night banging their axes and clubs against their new Chinese pick-up trucks.

We were the only observers the Manicaland MDC had seen for some time and they vented the full force of their rage, fear and frustration. 'Do we have to wait for Zimbabwe to become

Burundi or Kenya?' asked the Senator. 'Do we need a large massacre before the international community does something? I am convinced that the people would vote for us in even larger numbers if they are allowed to vote freely. But we are a hundred and twenty per cent shut out. We cannot campaign at all. Rallies are forbidden. Anyone wearing our t-shirts is beaten. And they spread lies about us in the state media. This is not a contest between political parties. It is a government versus the majority of the people.'

The provincial party felt cut off from its national parent and much of its anger reflected the growing sense that the power which it had won the right to wield was being taken away by force. The MDC team berated us, as representatives of the wider world, for standing by and watching while the province wailed and burned. 'Our people are being shot dead,' said one of the newly elected MPs. 'We feel so abandoned. We need a rescue. We need UN peacekeepers here now to protect us. Or we need weapons to defend ourselves, but we don't have those resources. Why does the UN wait until we are all dead before it does anything? I honestly expect that I will be dead soon.'

We asked about displaced people and heard that the MDC had set up its own centres for people fleeing violence. This piqued our interest. We asked to visit one and were soon following an MDC vehicle through pitch-dark streets in Mutare's suburbs. The entire city was suffering a lengthy power cut. The only light as we arrived at the makeshift shelter was from the bonfires around which the refugees were huddling. There was no properly equipped camp, just a single building, perhaps a disused shop, where a dozen of the most vulnerable and badly injured were sheltering. The rest of the eighty displaced people had to sleep in the open. It doesn't rain in Zimbabwe in June, but it is bitterly cold. Mutare sits in a mountainous upland area and it's quite common for night-time temperatures to fall below zero. So the refugees were tightly gathered around the fire, several warming plaster casts and bandaged limbs.

We started collecting stories. Some people had hiked for two days, nursing fractures or internal injuries. Others could not talk, their eyes unfocused, due to a catatonic state caused by the horror of what they had seen and suffered. While we were speaking to the refugees, two men from Rusape arrived. They said that they had fled their homes following the murder of Farai Gamba, an MDC activist, by the army on 14 June. Other refugees were from Makoni, Nyanga, Buhera and other rural Manica areas. They were keen to show their injuries.

Many of the refugees' accounts were similar. ZANU-PF militias had come to their villages and ordered people to assemble. Men and women were separated and adolescent boys and girls were not spared. Some were beaten at once, first ordered to lie on the ground, sometimes naked, then beaten on the back, the buttocks, the head. A man with a broken arm said a ZANU militiaman had fractured it quite deliberately with a rock. What happened next varied. Some people said their homes were burned or knocked down. Others were told never to return to their villages. Several people said that the militias made a point of destroying personal papers which certified their right to vote, as well as seizing money and other possessions.

Others were taken to re-education camps where they suffered a long night of physical abuse and indoctrination. They were made to sit while ZANU-PF youths, often pumped up with marijuana, denounced their treachery. Each in turn had to stand and to beg forgiveness for voting MDC. A ZANU youth would then beat them. The beatings varied greatly in severity. Some escaped with a hammering on their back, legs or buttocks. Others were struck with axes, leaving ugly gaping wounds. The most unlucky were beaten on the head with rocks or iron bars. Some did not survive such beatings. We heard that a common form of assault was to destroy somebody's home, then to soak them in cold water. In the freezing conditions of winter in Manicaland, this could be enough to induce serious illness, particularly as Zimbabweans are generally under-nourished.

There were many more men than women at the camp. This may have been because men had received the worst of the collective punishment. But it seemed all too likely that women were just unable to travel because of their responsibilities of care for children, the sick or the elderly. Those women we did talk to were certainly not spared a savage beating. We did not hear any accounts of rape that night, but in Zimbabwe's culture it would have been hard for a woman to tell such a story so publicly. Despite the lack of facilities at the camp, these people were the lucky ones. They had made it to some kind of collective safety. The really unfortunate people from their areas were sleeping rough as militias searched their villages, or enduring sustained torture for days on end. Hearing the most gruesome stories of torture by fire, of gunfire in the forests around Nyanga, of army units going berserk, we realised that many people, categorised as missing, in fact had to be lying in unmarked graves.

The refugees said they had received no help from the UN, Red Cross or other agencies. The MDC helped them with food, but often did not have enough money. A local church had provided blankets. A low-level MDC activist, trying to rest on a freezing concrete slab under a single blanket, admitted his despair: 'The elections are not fair. There is too much intimidation now that they have guns. I now doubt that we can win, although we won overwhelmingly before.'

I reported after the visit that ZANU-PF's systematic violence was turning the tide in the election. Confirmed opposition supporters were being killed, hospitalised or driven from their homes. Rampant ZANU-PF militias, calling themselves war vets but actually made up of teenagers high on ideology, scuds of beer, amphetamines and marijuana, were effectively running the province. They were ordering ordinary voters to give their ballot-paper serial numbers to their village headmen. In turn, headmen were being told they were responsible for delivering a 100 per cent vote for Robert Mugabe, and that their efforts would be monitored. Some voters who confessed that they had supported the MDC on 29 March but promised to switch to Mugabe were being instructed to tell presiding officers that they were illiterate, so that the police could monitor their choices while pretending to be giving assistance.

Back at the Holiday Inn, we found a team of monitors from the Southern African Development Community in the bar. My impression was that the observers did a reasonable job in June. Human rights monitors confirmed that the SADC team was meeting victims and seeing militias in action threatening all-comers with axes and sticks. I told the monitors about what I had seen. They confirmed that they had seen similar things themselves and readily agreed that the election was a bloody shambles. At the time I was sceptical that SADC would publish a critical report on the elections, despite the findings of its observers, but I was wrong.

We slept more comfortably at the Holiday Inn than the refugees out in the cold. At breakfast, we found that a senior ZANU-PF delegation was also staying at the hotel. I tried to chat to the party but got a cold reaction until a jovial old man who held a position high up in the Manicaland party sparked on the fact that I was from the UK and reminisced with me about his time at the University of Sussex in the 1970s. He said that his team was travelling to a rally in Buhera. 'We're going to Morgan's home.'

During the morning in Mutare, we found more evidence of violence. A dozen people who had arrived overnight at a clinic were sitting outside waiting for medical treatment. Their cata-logue of brief accounts, obviously not comprehensive but told with indisputable sincerity, gave a vivid picture of the suffer-ing of ordinary people. A man from Nyanga North had been campaigning for the MDC. Men came to his shop on 16 June and took him to a base for two days. He was repeatedly assaulted, forced to sing ZANU-PF songs and soaked in cold water at night, leaving him with injuries to his limbs and a fever. I was particularly moved by the condition of a lady, tiny but still wiry, who had injuries to her breast and back. I asked her how old she was and she silently offered me her ID card, as if I would not believe what she said. She was seventy-five; her birthday was almost identical to my father's. Youths had broken down the door of her house in Nyanga on 13 June. They asked her why she supported the MDC and beat her. Shona culture celebrates the wisdom of age, so the abuse of such a lady by a gang of teenagers was particularly shocking.

A newly elected MDC councillor from Mutare was attending a party meeting on 17 June when he heard that people in his ward were being assaulted. He returned home to find his doors open and his family gone. He was sleeping elsewhere the same night when he was pulled from his bed by youths and beaten with sticks for thirty minutes and soaked with cold water. He had pains all over his body. He believed his family was safe, but had not seen them since the attack. A woman was at home in Nyanga on 17 June when a group of youths came to her home, demanded to speak to her and beat her because she was a member of the opposition. She had heavily bruised buttocks that she showed me with a mournful dignity. They were hugely swollen and coloured a deep purple. An older lady with a badly damaged foot in plaster said she had been beaten by ZANU-PF youths in Mutare North on 17 June.

We went on to meet civil society leaders who shared the frustration of the MDC that the world was standing by while such grisly violence was going on. Monitoring organisations were most concerned about Tinashe Pihri, a local monitor, who had been abducted on 14 June, five days earlier. Witnesses said he was given a punishment beating at a ZANU-PF rally in Rusape, then taken to the 32nd Brigade army base. The assumption was that he was dead, but his body had not yet been found, so some hope remained.

One civil society activist issued what he called a 'formal demand' that the European Union should take meaningful action by placing sanctions on South Africa to force Mbeki's hand, by introducing observers and peacekeepers, forcibly if necessary, and by clearly attributing the violence to ZANU-PF. The civic society people all thought that Mugabe would win the re-run comfortably. ZANU's most effective tactic was compelling traditional leaders to act as enforcers in each community. Several human rights monitors repeated the allegation that villagers were being ordered to give their ballot-paper numbers to their traditional leaders. All felt that this strategy of intimidation would work. One monitor concluded: 'People don't have the guts to defy the chiefs – it's going to be very different from 29 March.'

I left Mutare feeling utterly glum. What struck me hardest were not the strong words of Manicaland's leaders screaming to the world for help, but the sight of so many people injured – stoically going on or simply buckled under the weight of it all and waiting for fate to end their ordeal one way or another. I felt sure that for every one I had seen in Mutare, there were ten people – a hundred people? – too injured, too burdened or too mentally broken to flee. Nobody will ever know how many thousands of people were brutalised in Manicaland and elsewhere because the flimsy systems set up to monitor their pain were the first to be destroyed. There were very few monitors brave enough even to try to access rural areas. I certainly was not.

We had one stop left to make. An MDC lawyer, Eric Matinenga, had been arrested on a charge of high treason. He was being held in a remand prison in Rusape, halfway back to Harare. We wanted to stop and check on his welfare. I had always known Rusape to be a friendly, sleepy town. On the way back from one of my first trips to the Eastern Highlands, I had stopped here hoping to buy fuel. At the garage I was delighted to find not only diesel for the bargain price of $170,000 per litre, but also delicious fresh hot cross buns and honey. So I felt I knew the town and had little to fear. In line with my expectations, the prison seemed calm as I drove up a rough dirt track towards it and parked in a small area next to the perimeter fence. We spoke to the officer at the gate, who was decent and friendly, but rather as we expected would not let us see Matinenga. Apparently prisoners were entitled to only one visit per week and Matinenga had already seen his wife.

I spotted the pick-up truck pulling up next to my car a fraction too late. We had attracted the attention of a ZANU-PF team. Four of the five men in the pick-up wore yellow party t-shirts; the fifth was smartly dressed in a suit. We managed to get into my car and lock the doors. But I then spotted, several minutes too late, how stupidly I had parked the car. I had left it facing the perimeter fence when I should have taken the time to manoeuvre it around so that I could drive straight down the track away from the prison. It would not be safe to manoeuvre with the ZANU people around our vehicle. We would have to stay until they allowed us to leave.

In practice only two of the men engaged with me. The first, whom I shall always think of as 'Mr Nasty', was in his thirties with a thick, roughly trimmed beard. He wore his ZANU t-shirt with jeans. He demanded to know who I was, what I was doing. He demanded all my papers. At first I tried to be self-assured. I told Mr Nasty that I would happily give my documents to any uniformed officer, but that I did not know who he was and so I wouldn't give him my papers. He stared at me with an intense hatred: 'You are a very stupid boy. Now I need to get my gun.'

He moved off to his pick-up. I felt a sudden, teary panic that I managed to keep a lid on. Mr Nice appeared to argue with his colleague, then came over to see me. 'You have really upset my friend, which is not very clever. But let's try to start again. What is your name?' I said, 'Philip,' at which point he astonished me by giving me back my surname, the date I had arrived in Zimbabwe and a fair approximation of what I was doing at the Embassy. I first thought that this team must have been ready for me in Rusape, tipped off by the mandatory letter I'd sent to the Interior Ministry notifying the Government of my travel plans, but Mr Nice did not seem to know anything about my journey. I suppose they just saw a CD vehicle, followed it and acted when it stopped in their town. Had I been more alert, I might have noticed the pick-up when it began to follow me. Another mistake on my part. As to how and why Mr Nice knew so much about me, I still have no idea. Perhaps CIO men learn the details of foreign diplomats in Zimbabwe as a matter of course?

The classic interrogation routine worked perfectly. I was relieved to talk to a courteous, smart, soft-spoken man after Mr Nasty's threat. Although I had no idea who Mr Nice was I gave him my ID card and other documents. He asked me politely what I was doing. I told him I was election-monitoring. 'Let me check what we have to do on the radio,' and Mr Nice walked off, allowing Mr Nasty to come back at me. He probably spent no more than twenty minutes working on me, but it felt like hours.

Mr Nasty said he had spoken to the prison guards and found that I had come to see Matinenga. This was a serious abuse. Matinenga was responsible for murdering hundreds of ZANU-PF people. I was helping him. Zimbabwe was not my country, but I was interfering, acting like I ruled, trying to reverse the gains of the liberation war, trying to enslave Africans again, give land that was liberated back to whites. I hated blacks. I was a racist, an arrogant, colonial racist, and a very stupid boy. He suddenly stopped. His eyes shifted about as he considered what to do. 'You are not getting out of insulting our country like this. Give me your car keys.'

I was so scared now that my brain slowed down, moving like a reptile in the cold of Africa's morning. Obviously the allegation that Matinenga was a murderer was ludicrous, as was the accusation that I was helping him. But this was not a court of law. I tried to imagine what I would do if Mr Nasty did produce a gun. Would I give him my keys, get out of the car, abandon the illusion of safety the vehicle's metal skin gave me? But I had no idea what to do, no plan, no protocol to follow. I really wanted to cry, to say sorry, to beg these men just to let me leave. I stammered out that my Embassy had told me not to give my car keys away. Mr Nasty looked at me the way a predator looks at a sick animal. 'This time I really need to get my gun.'

I was so relieved when Mr Nice came back at that point that I had to work hard to hold back my tears. He said that I had broken the rules by stopping in Rusape and trying to see a criminal. That was not part of the work of an election monitor. He would try to protect me from the consequences of my actions, but could do so only if I gave him every possible detail of my trip – who I had spoken to, what they had said. We danced around for a few more minutes. I gave more and more names of ZANU-PF people, knowing both that I could not be criticised for making such calls and that the people I named would not face any repercussions. I pretended that I had spent two hours with the jovial old Sussex alumnus I had spoken to for a minute at breakfast. I said I had visited the Electoral Commission several times and tried to look round for polling stations that I could easily visit on polling day. I denied again and again that I had seen NGOs or MDC people. If I admitted it, I knew I would not be allowed to leave until I had given names and phone numbers. All the time, I could hear Mr Nasty talking loudly to his silent colleagues.

Finally Mr Nice said we could go. But it was his parting warning that chilled me most of all: 'You are just not safe here, particularly when you break the rules as you have done. We just cannot guarantee that you won't be shot. You should stay in your Embassy in Harare from now on.'

I drove off. I found it hard not to accelerate wildly down the dirt track leading from the prison. When I was back on the main road to Harare, I did drive much too fast for half an hour until I could persuade myself to slow down. I felt unmanned and useless, ashamed that I had been so scared, ashamed to be so precious as to make a fuss about the nothing that had happened to me, when so many people were suffering actual pain and misery.

I tried to rationalise it all. First of all, I was fine; everything was OK. Nothing had happened to me, not one slap. There had been the threat of a gun, but I hadn't seen one and, for all I knew, Mr Nasty didn't have one. Nor had there been any real threat to me. Both Messrs Nice and Nasty had been sober and in control of themselves. The Government liked to insult foreign Embassy staff and sometimes put irritating obstacles in their path, but no diplomat had ever been assaulted. Even in the midst of its violence against its own people, the regime acknowledged that there were rules, and that diplomats were basically untouchable. I knew all this, but I couldn't persuade my snivelling organism to accept it at a visceral level. In fact, I reasoned to myself, my safety had been guaranteed by the presence of Mr Nice. Perhaps if I'd run into a group of drunken ZANU youths without adult supervision I might have been in trouble, but Mr Nice was not going to allow the situation to get out of hand.

Indeed both of my questioners had had the same motivation and were surely just playing the classic good cop/bad cop roles. They wanted foreign diplomats to be cowed and intimidated – too scared to venture out of Harare and see what was happening. They had achieved that goal with me, as I was now reluctant to make any more field trips. I felt a deep shame at letting them bully me. I entertained a few violent fantasies of getting even. But I couldn't change the fact – a carload of bullies had successfully put the wind up me. Along with my fear I felt a powerful disgust at myself for being unable to handle infinitely less than thousands of others were enduring.

But I did feel my own tiny share of Zimbabwe's fear. Fear of the night coming and the militias driving in, banging their weapons against car doors. The fear of being dragged off to a re-education centre for a night of agony. The fear of not knowing whether friends and family were safe. I tried to multiply what I felt by a hundred. I could not, but I knew as I tried that Robert Mugabe was going to win his election. Nobody could face this terror down.

My companions Helen and Brechtje were less shaken by the incident in Rusape than me. Helen spoke mainly to Mr Nice, while I was dealing with Mr Nasty, and felt confident that the calm, smartly dressed man was in command and would not let verbal intimidation develop into physical violence. She worried for Mrs Matinenga, who was still at the prison after seeing her husband when we arrived and who was detained for questioning by the ZANU-PF unit when we left. Although we had checked with Matinenga's lawyers to ensure that a visit was a good idea, we all feared that we had brought trouble on the prisoner's family, which outweighed the benefit of our demonstration of concern for his welfare. Brechtje was haunted by this fear for some weeks and was greatly relieved when Matinenga himself called her after his release from prison to thank her for the visit. My Dutch colleague was almost unnaturally composed throughout the encounter, perhaps because it was not her most serious run-in with Mugabe's security personnel – she had been detained at gunpoint by aggressive guards around State House a few weeks previously. But her self-control came at some cost. She recalls now that she spent a family holiday soon after the bloody days of June 2008 behaving emotionally and erratically.

Even returning to Harare was an ordeal. The city was pitch-black, but I could see pick-up trucks unloading ZANU people in yellow t-shirts. Bonfires were dotted around any wasteland areas where these militias could make camp. It was the turn of Harare's MDC voters to be under attack. Over the next week supermarket car parks and school playing fields were transformed into twenty-four-hour ZANU-PF rallies which anyone found out on the street was required to attend. I could never look at Bon Marché in Chisipite without remembering those days.

Much was written in June and has been written since about

whether the MDC was still in a position to win the election as the violence reached its peak the weekend after I got back from Mutare. Was it possible for the party simply to be brave, stomach its casualties, tough it out and rely on the desire for change that had defeated Mugabe in March to defeat him again? And if it was possible, was it the right thing to do? Some made an argument for withdrawal from the elections on ethical grounds. After all, the MDC knew, even in early June, that its supporters were being assaulted and killed and that the entire population of large parts of the country was being subjected to collective violence – there were far too many reports of beatings of whole communities for this to be untrue. The MDC's leadership could predict with great confidence that continuing with a full-scale campaign would cost lives, though whether that would be a hundred lives or a thousand was harder to estimate. How could it be justified to maintain the pursuit of political office, knowing what the human cost would be?

To that argument, at least, there is surely a strong utilitarian answer. During each year of Mugabe's rule in Zimbabwe, the life expectancy of his people has fallen by one year. Zimbabweans, who used to expect a full working life followed by several years of retirement caring for grandchildren and dispensing wisdom to the young, now know they will be lucky to see their children enter secondary school. Premature death in Zimbabwe had cut short several million useful, rich lives. It had created over a million orphans. The causes of the HIV epidemic and poverty in Africa are complex, of course. But I was never in doubt about the cause of Zimbabwe's headlong fall from prosperity to poverty and the deaths that it caused. The ZANU-PF Government was not concerned about general prosperity or the sufferings of its people. Its only priority was its own survival under conditions that allowed it to accumulate wealth. The benefits of removing such a government, changing policy and saving thousands, ultimately millions, of lives would surely outweigh the costs of a bloody month.

But my trip to Manicaland convinced me that the MDC had absolutely no chance of winning the re-run. Persevering with this gruesome election would not deliver a change of government. Without hope of ultimately taking power it was hard to see how the MDC could decide to fight on. There were hardy souls who argued that the MDC should fight on despite expecting to lose. Some suggested that if Morgan Tsvangirai were to score, say, 40 per cent of the vote despite the campaign of violence, he would achieve an important moral victory and show that he would have won a fair, non-violent contest. That seems unsound to me. No opposition parties have come to power in Africa as a result of moral victories. Tsvangirai could justify fighting on if he thought he could win, but surely not just to make a point. The only issue the MDC had to consider was the pragmatic one: would it win? Despite the fear and the blood which deepened the redness of Masvingo's soil, would voters be ready to show their preference for Morgan's 'change you can believe in' over Bob's '100% empowerment'?

By 22 June it was surely apparent that they would not. Assuming that everyone who voted in March voted again in June, only one in twenty would need to switch sides to give Mugabe victory. By itself, the deep and plausible fear that opposition voters would be identified and punished would have delivered a greater switch to ZANU-PF than that. But it was impossible for tens of thousands of opposition supporters who had lost their homes or their identity cards to contemplate the effort, expense and courage required to return to their home areas and vote. The MDC, rendered impotent as a campaigning presence across much of rural Zimbabwe, would have been unable to encourage supporters. And always there was lingering doubt as to whether even electoral defeat would displace Mugabe. As he himself had said, how can the stroke of a pen on a ballot paper defeat a gun? His supporters put it another way: an MDC victory would lead not to a change of power, but to a war by the regime against its own rebellious citizens.

Morgan Tsvangirai's decision to withdraw from the election was surely, therefore, correct. He announced his withdrawal, condemning the election as a 'violent sham', but promising that victory would 'only be delayed'.

The remaining seven days of the campaign took on a surreal air. The state media called Tsvangirai's withdrawal illegal and insisted that a competitive election was still going on. The militias kept at it, though there were signs almost at once that Mugabe wanted to kennel his hell hounds, but did not know quite how to. Fearing a mass abstention, which would delegitimise Mugabe, the militias' message changed. They announced the launch of Operation Who Did You Vote For? Voters were told that they would be punished if their fingers were not stained indelibly purple, proving that they had voted. With a Mugabe victory certain, the goal of violence became a high turnout.

Polling day itself was quiet and orderly, but with none of the buzz of March. The streets were deserted of vehicles other than ZANU's fleet of Chinese pick-ups. Voters queued up well before 6 a.m., anxious to be seen prominently doing what they had been told. The determination which returning officers had shown in March to follow the electoral rules conscientiously was replaced by a desperate readiness to do anything required. Policemen, soldiers and ZANU-PF personnel of all types hung around the polling stations all day watching the shuffling processions of voters who, eyes downcast, were evidently terrified that even as they made their mandatory vote for Mugabe they would be humiliated or attacked again.

The pretence that this was a democratic exercise was maintained even as the hopelessly lopsided results were announced. Intellectually neutered pundits on ZBC's results programme commented on the impact that ZANU-PF's redesigned materials and recalibrated message had clearly made. They praised the party for rejuvenating itself and re-energising its campaign, an achievement they attributed to the re-elected President Mugabe. There was no mention of violence, of course, or of the fact that the only other candidate had withdrawn from the contest seven days before. It was a bizarre effort, even by Zimbabwean standards, as it is impossible to think of anybody watching who would have been fooled.

Miraculously, the result, which had taken more than a month to produce in April, was ready in little more than twenty-four hours. Mugabe had secured over 2.15 million votes, more than 85 per cent of all those cast, a million more than he had scored in the March election. There were flashes of popular defiance within the artificial landslide. Some 233,000 voters had marked their ballots for Tsvangirai despite the risk that they would suffer for doing so. Another 150,000 voters had spoiled their papers, some taking the chance to insult Mugabe expansively. For once even Africa acknowledged the electoral injustice which its observers had witnessed. Both the SADC and the African Union immediately accepted that the result was not a reflection of the people's will. This was the first time African institutions had ever given such a dismissive and immediate verdict on an election.

In the short term Mugabe was not bothered about any of that. Within an hour of the announcement of the result, he was sworn in as president. History will not remember the empty words he said to his pulverised, weeping people that day. Morgan Tsvangirai aptly called the inauguration 'a meaningless exercise in futility'.

7

CROCODILE TEARS

Whatever had held Zimbabwe together did so no longer. Communities, forced to divide along political lines and to damage themselves, would never be restored. The last pretence that ZANU-PF was fighting for a united people against foreign interference was abandoned. The basis and motive of Mugabe's rule was revealed to be the sustenance and survival at any cost of a handful of criminals. Even Southern African leaders, whose senses do not usually register little people in pain, noticed and denounced what Mugabe and his henchmen had done.

The ailing economy had been kept going until the end of June by the colossal volumes of Zimbabwean dollars injected into election preparations and the mobilisation of a large para-military force. But these increasingly hyperinflationary stimuli (inflation was now unmeasurable, but estimated to be well above one million per cent and climbing exponentially) could sustain economic life only for so long. The political battle won, Gideon Gono had to admit economic defeat. But that was a price worth paying. Who in ZANU-PF cared that the economy was in ruins, so long as the party had control of those ruins? The Zimbabwean dollar took to its deathbed and never got up again. Overnight, vendors began to refuse it, even in the kind of quantities usually attached to intergalactic distances.

The illusion of democracy, which tied some people into a hope for and belief in a national future, proved to be a ghost. People's faith – that they would ever see peaceful improvement – died. With it died the will to work and battle for reform or progress. It was clear that the dramatic change Zimbabwe had voted for would not come. A dispirited people realised that it had to accept whatever Mugabe wished to do. Anyone who could escape did so. Tens of thousands of people who had already fled their homes decided to keep on running. Flights and buses out were packed. The sight of white South African farmers rounding up on a vigilante basis desperate refugees, who had crossed the Limpopo illegally, was particularly ugly, as it brought back memories of the apartheid years.

I left the country too, for a holiday in Tanzania. I was crushed by what I had experienced. Everything I had done had been futile. What was the point of monitoring elections when they were grossly unfair, but the result still stood? What was the point of writing diplomatic reports and posting blogs about violent tyrants, when those words had no effect?

But, as an exercise in escapism, the holiday was pointless. I spent my time in the Serengeti thinking about Zimbabwe. I watched a three-metre crocodile dismembering a long-dead antelope, which was floating in a watering hole. With its jaws clamped round the carrion, the crocodile spun for a few seconds, then rested for a minute and spun again. It was going to take a while to rip a limb of festering meat away, but the crocodile was prepared to carry on for as long as it took. While I watched this amazing spectacle, I could think only of leading ZANU-PF power-broker Emmerson Mnangagwa, who is known as Ngwena, the crocodile. I pictured him slowly tearing chunks off the carcass of his own country, relentless, undying. Moses the guide whispered in my ear, 'The thing with crocs is you can't kill them. You can freeze them, boil them, starve them, shoot them, but they won't die. Even when their teeth are all gone and they're going to starve, they put themselves in suspended animation and last two more years.'

I was desperate for news of Zimbabwe, but when I got it, it came in the horrifying condition of Ben Freeth, a farmer from Chegutu. Ben was looking even worse than Bruce Rogers had in

May – heavily bruised, bandaged and braced, moving gingerly as if every step hurt. He was in hospital in South Africa. He had endured a sustained and brutal beating after going to help his elderly parents-in-law, whose neighbouring farm was under attack. Ben and Mr and Mrs Campbell, who were in their seventies, were held for several hours and beaten repeatedly by a large gang.

I liked and admired Ben. When I first arrived in Zimbabwe, he had invited me to visit his farm, Mount Carmel, in Chegutu. It was an astonishing experience. The farm was extraordinarily productive – field after field of vigorous mango and orange trees. I was also impressed by the ethics of the operation; Ben's family preferred to grow wholesome food rather than tobacco. The other remarkable thing about Ben was that he was posi-tive in his vision of Zimbabwe's future and – despite a number of frightening attacks on the house where he lived with his young family – committed to a non-violent, lawful way of life. But that physical pacifism was offset by a bone-shakingly direct delivery. 'Is the British Government doing *anything* to stop the genocide in Zimbabwe?' Ben would ask as I served myself a second helping of his excellent mangoes. Unlike those farmers who kept their heads down, Ben was always ready to brief the media about what he was going through. He once told CNN that farm invasions in Zimbabwe amounted to ethnic cleansing. He also inspired a groundbreaking legal action which his father-in-law Mike Campbell took against the Mugabe regime.

Ben had seen the potential of a new Human Rights Tribunal, established by SADC in 2007. The court was intended to serve a similar function to the European Court of Human Rights. Ben's argument was that Zimbabwe's farm-invasion programme was discriminatory in principle, as its targets were all white, and illegal in practice owing to the violence with which it was pursued. The court gave an initial judgment in December 2007 that it would need more time to consider the case, but that

Campbell should not be evicted until that final judgment. Despite this clear call for protection, the July torture squad ordered the Campbells at gunpoint to sign declarations that they were abandoning the case. The forced signatures obviously had no meaning to the court, other than as a demonstration that the Zimbabwean authorities treated its rulings with complete contempt. As usual, Mugabe was happy to denounce colonial farmers, while demonstrating that he had no respect for his many black African critics either.

Meeting white farmers in Zimbabwe produces conflicting feelings, the greatest of which is admiration for their courage. There are now perhaps 400 whites still farming their own land in Zimbabwe, compared with over 4,000 before farm invasions began. The 400 are the toughest of the tough. They have put up with beatings, theft and destruction of their property. But, more insidiously, they have endured a constant sense of dread and menace: big-wig visitors with entourages of lawyers and security guards demanding immediate ownership of the property, the hostile stares of squatters who have set up on their land, the drip-drip effect of threats, including threats of sexual assaults on wives and daughters, and the economic anxiety that a lifetime of work and investment could be taken away at any point. Mental strength in the face of appalling stress is the key to survival. A farmer's wife once recalled the misery of hearing her cattle – which besieging war vets would not allow her to tend – bellowing for food for days then falling silent as they starved to death.

In the context of a country that finds itself suddenly poor, unemployed and hungry, farmers also deserve great credit for creating jobs and growing food. Agriculture used to supply the infrastructure of rural Zimbabwean life. Farmers built houses, schools and clinics for their workers. They graded roads. They made dams and irrigation systems. They grew cash crops, which constituted the country's largest source of foreign-exchange exports. They contributed to the enormous maize harvests Zimbabwe used to produce – in 2000, Zimbabwe produced 50 per cent more maize than was needed for domestic consumption.

I found farming families extraordinarily friendly and hospitable. They invited me to visit – for lunch, for a weekend. They delighted in showing me their extraordinarily fertile fields, their sophisticated sorting and packing plants. They were proud of their advancement – the drop irrigation systems which ensured that precious water did not evaporate, the zero-tillage maize fields which grew tall each year, while harvests of conventionally grown maize – which leaches heavily from the soil – declined.

But there is an unpleasant side to white farming culture too. Most Zimbabwean farmers I have met have attitudes that would simply not be tolerable in modern Western society. I remember standing with a group of farmers outside court in Chegutu, waiting to see whether a magistrate wanted to prosecute them. As they got used to my presence, they started to joke about farm dogs chasing black labourers. In no time they were happily talking about niggers and kaffirs. With a change of accent, they would have fitted right into 1950s Mississippi.

I have also heard farmers argue that none of their labourers are capable of anything more than basic unskilled tasks. I once asked a farmer if he had thought of training any of his black staff for managerial work. He was astonished that I could imagine such a possibility. But I have seen in other areas of commerce in Zimbabwe that many black Zimbabweans are entrepreneurial and commercially imaginative – they have to be to stay alive in Zimbabwe's economic madhouse. The excellence of Zimbabwe's education system in the 1990s has created a cohort of skilled young people who could drive their country politically and economically, if they were only allowed to do so. But the farmers I have met operate a colour-coded working culture. Whites are farm owners and managers. Blacks are labourers.

There is also a downside to the social provision that most farmers make for their workforces. Yes, farmers give their workers houses (though sometimes this amounts to no more than the land and materials to build huts) and food. Farming communities – before they were depleted by invasions – used to assume collective responsibility for building primary schools and paying teachers to staff them. Farming families also take a real responsibility for the health of their workers' families, providing treatment and drugs even for the old and young who play no economic role. But these excellent conditions are not matched by decent wages. When I first arrived in 2006, most farm labourers were paid about $100,000 per month, which was at that time less than one US dollar. I asked a farmer about these wages once but got a robust reply: 'What would they need to spend money on? They have everything they need.'

One answer to the farmer's rhetorical question is education. While young farm labourers earn so little, they have no chance of progressing into secondary and tertiary education, perhaps to formalise their agricultural skills. Farmers create a workforce that is well looked after, grateful and loyal, but also dependent and unable to aspire higher than farm labouring.

This analysis may sound harsh. White farmers often tell me with great pride that their labourers are delighted to have their jobs and desperate not to lose them. Everything I have seen confirms that this is true. I was walking in Ben Freeth's field of spectacularly colourful citrus fruit in Chegutu when a labourer who'd heard I was from the British Embassy grabbed my arm and whispered urgently to me, 'Please tell Mr Blair – don't let the war vets take this farm. I will be homeless.'

My criticism of white farmers is not that they are evil men, because they are not. But I would fault white farmers for their Canute-like perseverance in managing their enterprises on such traditional lines. Had they educated and trained several thousand farm managers – a rural black middle class engaged in farming – it would have been much harder for ZANU-PF to argue that white agriculture had it in for the black man.

This links into the question – now sadly of no more than historical interest – of whether a peaceful and mutually agreed handover of land could have taken place some time before the violence started. The answer is, of course, yes. Mugabe could have implemented any of a dozen policies in the 1980s that would have secured a gradual transfer of land. There was plentiful donor funding to pay for land- and skills-transfer programmes, but much of it went unused. Mugabe could have given tax breaks to farmers who set up agricultural training programmes. He could have incentivised land sales to black purchasers. Rather more aggressively, he could have forbidden whites from acquiring new land if a black purchaser was available. He could have set quotas for land transfers each year and appointed an arbitration panel to impose fair prices on stubbornly unwilling sellers. But none of these gradualist, non-violent policies was interesting.

Land became a policy focus only when Mugabe began to run out of steam and saw the potential to link it to the politically explosive topics of race and colonial history. Land also became a useful, though quickly exhausted, medium for patronage. Mugabe took little interest in farming for his first twenty years in power. Indeed during the 1980s his Government issued over a thousand letters to immigrants into Zimbabwe – people without any association with the colonial era. The letters confirmed that the Government had no interest in the land the prospective farmers wished to buy. But the Mugabe Government has shown no regard for these commitments or any favour to the farmers who arrived post-independence. Most have been thrown off the land they purchased from Mugabe's own post-independence Government, which falsely labelled them colonial relics in the process. It is hard to think of a less justifiable and more plainly illegal act of misgovernance.

The most horrifying consequence of Mugabe's onslaught against agriculture is not what it did to whites – who nearly all escaped with their lives and most of whom now live a life of tolerable comfort – but what it did to black farm workers and

their families. Recent research by the farm labourers' union,
GAPWUZ, and the Justice for Agriculture Group, a human
rights NGO, has demonstrated that the sector employed
more than a quarter of a million people in 1998, supporting
1.5 million workers and dependants. While labourers had no
financial resources with which to enlarge the scope of their
lives, they were at least able to provide for their families shelter,
food, education and healthcare. In this they were – by African
standards – lucky. Since 1998, over a million of these people
have been made homeless and have lost their access to the need-
ful things of life. An estimated 40 per cent have died – several
hundreds of thousands of avoidable premature deaths. This toll
of around 400,000 deaths caused by malicious policy-making
is more than ten times greater than the number killed during
the massacres in Matabeleland during the 1980s. But the deaths
were silent and invisible – wheezing, malnourished, homeless
individuals dying from treatable diseases.

Incredibly, Mugabe has got away with this piece of brutal
social engineering. He has happily and with impunity caused
death on a massive scale and destroyed his economy's strongest
sector. His unworthy motives for this appalling damage were to
weaken the opposition, create terror and award so-called farms
– now vast untended grasslands turning into dustbowls – to
his supporters. During one of his most famous speeches, at the
UN's Earth Summit in 2002, Mugabe set out his attitude to
land: 'Land comes first before all else . . . This is the one asset
that not only defines the Zimbabwean personality and demar-
cates sovereignty, but also an asset that has a direct bearing on
the fortunes of the poor and prospects for their immediate
empowerment and sustainable development.' Mugabe's claim
to be working for the good of the poor was dented by some off-
the-cuff bombast at the end of that speech: 'So, Blair, keep your
England and let me keep my Zimbabwe.'

His supposed great achievement, land reform, is no
more than this: transferring land from a small, arrogant but

productive white elite to a small, arrogant and unproductive black elite. Four thousand of Mugabe's supporters have benefited, if ownership of a newly formed desert is a benefit. Ten million black Zimbabweans have gained nothing. But what did they expect? Zimbabwe is, as Mugabe declares, his, not theirs.

The attack in July 2008 on Ben Freeth, Zimbabwe's most prominent critic of agricultural policy, showed that Mugabe was taking advantage of his destruction of civic morale and popular resistance to punish anybody who dared to confront him. The next group to suffer this treatment was an inspiring and wholly apolitical group of women whose crime was to take to the streets and to march peacefully calling for bread and roses (symbolic of food and love). Women of Zimbabwe Arise! (WOZA) were the first people brave enough to demonstrate after Mugabe's empty Presidential victory. Sadly they suffered a quite disproportionate punishment.

I went to Rotten Row court for the WOZA trial on a Friday afternoon bright with wintry sun. It struck me as ironic that the people engaged there at the business end of repression were so well mannered. The police, prison officers, magistrates and others involved in arresting, abusing and detaining peaceful demonstrators did their immoral work with a cheery smile. I had an amiable chat about the weather with some cops with enormous assault rifles; a wave and a joke with a dozen prison officers, who had just transported the poor, benign WOZA women from one stinking overcrowded cell to another; and a friendly chat with the court clerk, who asked me (half seriously) for a visa to go to the UK, as she could not afford to live on her Government salary any longer.

After my usual aimless trek around the building, I found the hearing I was looking for in court six, where fifteen WOZA women were sitting, tensely waiting for the lawyers and magistrates to carve up their fate. They leaned over from the dock and told me that they had been locked up at Harare Central Police Station for two nights and were worried that their detention would be extended further. They were cold – Harare is at altitude and winter nights really are chilly. They were developing coughs. Three of them had been beaten, but shrugged the injuries off as 'not too bad'. They were trying to keep their spirits up, but were dreading a weekend, or more, in the grim and unsanitary cells. The women had not been found guilty of anything. Their offence was holding a peaceful demonstration without permission. Under the terms of Zimbabwe's Public Order and Security Act – remarkably similar to apartheid legislation – this was deemed a criminal act. A few women calling for no more than 'bread and roses' therefore experienced violent arrest and detention with no ready prospect of release.

After the usual long inexplicable delay, the magistrate came in. It was getting late in the afternoon and he clearly wanted to go home. He accepted the application from the women's lawyer that they be given bail, pending trial. Even the prosecutor could not dispute the argument that these were harmless, poor women with nowhere to run. But the Attorney General's man – a grinning little bastard, smug with the power of tyranny – had an ace up his sleeve. He immediately appealed against the magistrate's decision. Under Zimbabwe's legal code, which is always slanted towards the prosecution, he was given a week to prepare this appeal. The women were devastated as they realised the consequences. They would have to spend another week away from their families, in squalor, despite the triviality of the charges and despite not having been convicted of anything.

So, Zimbabwe in July – facing another five years of Mugabe Presidency – found itself blighted by continuing violence, economically collapsed, crushed by despair and divided right through the centre. The political parties, too, faced grave problems. The MDC's were obvious. It could not come to power no matter what it achieved at the ballot box. Its membership was depleted by murder, violence and disillusion. Was it humanly possible for the leadership to ask party members to hang tough, to reconstitute degraded organisations and networks, to wait another five years and then try again? Surely not. So then what? Give up? Go home?

Strangely, ZANU-PF faced problems too. It had activated its young people and worked them into a frenzy. Now the militias needed to be quietly shut down and disbanded, but there was no money to pay them off and, for many, no road back to normality. Some militias continued to roam, but now wholly feral, without political direction. Other youths tried to re-enter the communities they had attacked, only to find that the legacies of their violence endured. Without state-funded supplies of local beer – drunk in large volumes from scuds – and marijuana, blurry images of three months of beating and raping turned to clear memories of these crimes and then to fear.

Murderers found themselves haunted by their crimes. They visited the graves of their victims, adhering to a traditional belief that taking soil from them would assuage their murderers' guilt. Some, who had killed and dumped their victims in lakes, so that they could never be found, were driven mad that they could not use this means of atonement. ZANU's hard young grunts, stripped of their status and their stimulants, felt the vengeance of their victims rising from shallow graves, saw the hatred on the faces of their former friends and families and knew that they were going to pay some day for what they had done. They were right to be afraid. People may still smile, and thoughtful Zimbabweans now speak of truth and reconciliation, but most dream of vengeance.

ZANU's other key strategic problem was identifying a path forward when all the normal routes were blocked. The economy was dead and no donor or investor would now touch it. There would be no more business or naive aid projects to bleed. International friends were becoming very thin on the ground too. Official diplomacy after the election was predictable enough. Europe and the US denounced the poll and denied Mugabe's right to the Presidency, while UN Secretary General Ban Ki-moon called for a new vote under different conditions. Less predictably, African critics, particularly Kenya and Botswana, turned up the heat. They invoked SADC's extraordinarily critical report of the elections. The SADC observers had found that:

> The period leading up to the run-off election was characterized by politically motivated violence resulting in loss of life . . . On numerous occasions victims of politically motivated violence allege that the security forces did very little to stop the violence. This politically motivated violence led to the internal displacement of persons and impacted negatively on the full participation of citizens in the political process and freedom of association . . . Few rallies were held by the opposition party, and we observed with concern disruption of campaigning of the opposition party and the regrettable inaction of the law enforcement agencies.

The SADC observers also noted that there had been 'one-sided coverage on the part of the state media . . . no advertisements for the opposition party were carried' and 'numerous SADC observer teams reported being harassed in the course of their duties'. The observers' conclusions were obviously justified, but were surprisingly clearly expressed: 'the prevailing environment impinged on the credibility of the electoral process. The elections did not represent the will of the people of Zimbabwe.'

Despite the clear statement from his own region's observers that Mugabe's re-election was illegitimate, Mbeki tried to impede the build-up of anti-Mugabe momentum by saying that the old man was ready to hold a dialogue with the MDC. The fact that he was ready to stop killing for long enough to hold a conversation apparently amounted to a major concession. But despite its dubious moral basis, Mbeki's statement succeeded in deflecting the African Union from criticising Mugabe plainly at a summit on 1 July. The AU did, however, call for a government of national unity. While this was not a direct criticism of

Mugabe or his re-election, it amounted to a conspicuous failure to endorse him personally or to assert the legitimacy of his
claims to office.

After the AU's failure to condemn what Mugabe had done,
the UN Security Council represented the last chance to dignify
the victims of Zimbabwe's election with a meaningful international response. But the usual latterday Pontius Pilates – Russia,
China and South Africa – blocked even an acknowledgement
that many people had suffered and died at the hands of their
own Government.

The UK and US had some hopes that Russia would play
a more positive role than usual, after signing up to a G8
declaration a week after the election that '[The G8] will take
further financial and other measures against those individuals
responsible for violence in Zimbabwe.' Despite this apparent
commitment, however, Russia was prepared to block Security
Council action two days later. Its only concession – and its only
explanation for such duplicitous back-tracking – was to explain
that it had exercised its veto not to condone what Mugabe had
done, but to prevent the establishment of a precedent. Perish the
thought that the Council should ever be able to defend vulnerable people being attacked by their own rulers. What would that
mean in Chechnya or Tibet? Better that Zimbabweans should
– to use Mugabe's immortal phrase – go hang.

Politically, the bloody excesses of June had alienated all
Mugabe's supporters except possibly Mbeki. Perhaps even he
told his comrade, the ancient dictator, that some kind of change
was required. For Mugabe began, from very early in July, to say
that he would be prepared to negotiate some kind of unified
government – under his own Presidency, of course – with the
MDC.

So neither the MDC nor ZANU had options. Mugabe's only
remaining influential friend, Thabo Mbeki, was coming to the
end of his term of office – the ANC had already determined
that Jacob Zuma would replace him. Zimbabwe's economy was

finished and could not sustain the ZANU-PF patronage operation any longer. Mugabe could try to hold on to the bridge
of his sinking ship, but he knew he was going to drown. The
MDC's problems were different. It could win elections but
not take office. It could attract the verbal but insubstantial
support much of the international community will always give
a wronged loser, but that did not offer any means of improving
the party's situation.

In contemplating the decision whether to open talks leading
towards a unity government, both parties faced the same choice
– either to fade away or to turn towards a bitterly hated enemy.
Neither party had anything else to try. The MDC saw all too
clearly that no external power would or could push Mugabe
from office. Mugabe, happy to be pragmatic so long as he was
in office, understood that an accommodation with the MDC
would improve his appalling image and might attract new
resources into the bankrupt country.

Talks about talks began almost immediately. ZANU's
precondition for substantive negotiations was that the MDC
accept Mugabe's re-election. The MDC's red line (incompatible
with ZANU's) was that the March results should be the starting
point. Negotiators spent two weeks taking this round in circles,
before the MDC gave in and agreed to take negotiations up a
level, even though Mugabe remained president.

Tsvangirai met Mugabe on 22 July for the first time in a
decade. The MDC leader was struck by Mugabe's good manners
and ability to listen – qualities that others have noted during
tête-à-têtes with him. Tsvangirai was reportedly amazed when
Mugabe claimed not to have known about the violence in May
and June. What is really amazing – and a testament to Mugabe's
charisma and ability to be different things to different men – is
that Tsvangirai appeared to believe this claim.

Negotiations began in earnest on 25 July. Mbeki established
a facilitation team within his own office and invited ZANU-PF
and the two parts of the MDC to send delegations to a secluded

venue in South Africa. The only outcome of the first round of talks was that the Zimbabwean politicians were dissatisfied with their accommodation, which was no more than three-star, particularly when they found that the whisky served at the complimentary bar was not Scotch. The talks continued. The MDC did not really have a position at this stage on whether it could share power with Mugabe. The party was still adrift, traumatised by what it had suffered, and content to accept the momentum that others were putting into the talks. After all, Tsvangirai could always pull out later; there would be plenty of ZANU intransigence to provoke him into doing so.

One curious episode betrayed amateurism within the MDC's ranks, but also demonstrated the rapport that quickly developed between the lead negotiators: Tendai Biti and Justice Minister Patrick Chinamasa. The two men became convinced that somebody within the process was briefing the press on the latest developments. ZANU-PF suspected that the leak was coming from a junior member of the MDC's negotiating team: Theresa Makone, MP for Harare North. Makone was the woman I had seen in 2007 in such contrasting states of dress: in the dock of the Harare Magistrates' Court in a prison-issue sweater, then at the United States's 4 July reception in expensive clothes and statement jewellery. Chinamasa and Biti agreed to feed Makone a false rumour – that the ZANU team was going home for instructions. When the rumour quickly emerged in the media, Makone was exposed as the source of the leak and sacked from the MDC's team. The dismissal has not apparently harmed her long-term prospects, as she was made Minister of Public Works in 2009.

Theresa Makone's chummy relationship with the press was symptomatic of a cultural split within the MDC. The party is – like progressive entities around the world – a fusion of two elements. Much of its leadership is made up of educated, moneyed, urban liberals – lawyers, business people, journalists and so on. Theresa Makone is a rich retailer. Tendai Biti is a lawyer. Nelson Chamisa is a career politician, who moved straight from student activism into Parliament. In the cafés of Harare, senior MDC and ZANU-PF people chat and intrigue together, as politicians do. The MDC's elite is not immune from the violence to which the whole party is subjected – March 2007 demonstrated that – but it sees other sides to ZANU-PF too, and knows that there are people within the ruling party with whom it can do business.

But the people who constitute the muscles and guts of the party are different. They live, like most Zimbabweans, in small towns and villages. They are working people, often trade union-ists, and are suffering from the unemployment and poverty that have become normal for Zimbabweans – struggling in many cases for enough money to feed, shelter and educate their fami-lies. They suffered alone in 2008 when urban MDC activists at least had the support of large numbers of comrades close by. Their work for the party is largely voluntary. For most grass-roots MDC people, ZANU-PF is more than just a group of political rivals; it is a blood enemy.

Debate within the MDC about the possibility of a unity government reflected this division. The mood at grass-roots level was against a deal with Mugabe. How could Tsvangirai negotiate with the man who had sanctioned the killing of activ-ists just a month earlier? It was plain wrong – Mugabe should be in the dock of the International Criminal Court in The Hague, not rewarded with another five years in State House. And it was foolish – Mugabe could not be trusted. No deal with him would stick. However, many within the party leadership and the urban inner circle were positive about a deal. MPs liked the idea of power-sharing as it opened up the possibility of ministe-rial office. They knew people within ZANU-PF who said they were horrified by the killing and claimed not to be involved in violence. In any case, doing something positive was better than five more years sitting impotently in opposition while Mugabe completed his apparent project of creating Southern Africa's first fully failed state. Morgan Tsvangirai comes from the MDC's rural, working-class base but is now part of the urban elite. As he has made that transition, his advisers have changed too. People like Theresa Makone now have his ear. For this she is much resented within the party, but while she remains part of the inner circle she will retain office, despite mistakes like unauthorised press briefings.

Throughout the negotiation and thrashing out of power-sharing arrangements – a process which started in July 2008 and which in 2010 has still not finished – a sore point for the MDC has been Mugabe's habit of simply imposing arrangements which have not been agreed. Events inside Zimbabwe's plain, modest Parliament building in August 2008 showed Mugabe playing this game as usual, but being caught out. The MDC had insisted that Parliament should not reconvene until a power-sharing agreement was in place. Tendai Biti took this seriously, saying that 'Convening Parliament decapitates the dialogue'. So it was almost a matter of pride for Mugabe to defy Biti and announce that he would open the new Parliament on 18 August. There was little on the legislative programme – countries without functioning economies or proper legal systems need few new laws – but Mugabe perhaps wished to demonstrate that MDC Parliamentarians had to dance to his tune.

The MDC decided not to allow Mugabe to have things his own way. He could summon Parliament but he could no longer simply decide – as he used to – what happened inside the chamber. The party's status as the largest presence in Parliament had not been reversed by the June poll. If it ever wished to make a stand this was the time. The party needed to demonstrate that it could exploit its new large Parliamentary presence to make Mugabe's life difficult.

As Mugabe arrived to open Parliament, the MDC showed its will to defy him. The party's MPs refused to stand when he entered the chamber, booed him and jeered throughout his speech. 'You have killed, we won't forget,' they chanted. Mugabe, showing his age, looked more confused than angry. It was surely an indication of weakness that he did not walk out in anger, but rather read his absurd prepared text in its entirety, competing ineffectually with his detractors. His worthless words included a nonsensical forecast of economic development and an expression of regret for 'isolated' incidents of violence for which all parties were responsible. For once state television viewers heard this hypocritical rubbish with a proper accompaniment of abuse. Mugabe derided, to his face, live on national television – Zimbabwe had never seen anything like it.

Despite his rough reception and despite ZANU's minority status in Parliament, Mugabe sought to control the election of the House Speaker – a senior if ceremonial position in Zimbabwe, as in other parliamentary systems. He pledged the support of his MPs for Paul Themba-Nyathi of MDC-M against Tsvangirai's candidate, Lovemore Moyo. Mugabe had been exploiting Arthur Mutambara's ample ego for some time before this incident. When staring at his handsome reflection in the mirror, Mutambara had started to see a statesman staring back – a man who held the balance of power, who could make peace between Mugabe and Tsvangirai by pointing out the faults on both sides. Tsvangirai's squeamishness about forming a unity government was merely delaying the inevitable. Obviously Mugabe was not going to retire, so it would be better for the opposition to assume as many executive positions as it could. Mutambara was attracted by the idea that an MP from his faction could become speaker, as a first step towards such an assumption of authority.

But Mutambara's MPs rebelled, preferring to vote against their own colleague than to vote for Mugabe's choice. Lovemore Moyo won by 110 votes to 98. The absurdity of Mutambara's pretensions to peace-making and his lack of visceral connection with the opposition's loathing of Mugabe were cruelly exposed. Team Tsvangirai was elated. Finally, after a decade of trying, they had secured one of the offices of state and had made a fool of Mugabe in the process.

As Moyo emerged from Parliament, the streets were transformed. The secret policemen, who had been hanging round Parliament hoping to arrest a significant number of MDC MPs on synthetic charges to prevent them from voting, had gone. Instead a crowd had gathered, excited by Moyo's victory. The new Speaker himself was elated. He announced that his election marked the start of a new era for Parliament, when the executive would have to negotiate with the legislature rather than impose its will. Some part of the MDC's mechanics clicked into a new position. The party had humiliated Mugabe twice in two days – barracking him, then defeating his preferred candidate. These were hardly the type of great victories that would alter the fate of the nation, but after the gut-churning disappointments and miseries of June, even symbolic triumphs were welcome.

The party's successes cast a new light on how a government of national unity might work. To date, a power-sharing agreement had seemed to be no more than a means of validating Mugabe's illegal rule. But now the MDC started to wonder if a unity government would be more like a game of poker – plenty of risk, bluff and luck, but a chance to secure a few wins. In that case, for want of anything better, it might be worth taking a seat at the table and dealing the cards.

8

Shaking Hands and Touching Elbows

Lifted a little by the pleasure of harassing and outsmarting Mugabe at the opening of Parliament, the MDC decided to continue to negotiate a power-sharing arrangement with ZANU-PF. Both parties needed a deal. The MDC, despite its symbolic triumph in the contest for the Parliamentary Speakership, had no other means of gaining even a share of power. True, Mugabe's re-election had been widely condemned; most countries had refused to acknowledge him as a legitimate president. But the killing had stopped, meaning that the Zimbabwe problem was dropping out of the news and consequently falling down the political agenda. Any MDC belief that international disgust at the bloody manner of Mugabe's victory would force him from office was clearly unfounded. Mugabe claimed that he had been re-elected for another five years. He would not be president of much – no economy, no foreign friends, an unhelpful Parliament, a dwindling population – but it was not clear who could deny him the pleasure of ruling his ruined country. So the MDC had no choice. It had to negotiate or wither into the irrelevance of permanent opposition.

Despite its corrupt election victory, ZANU-PF needed a deal too. Since the turn of the millennium – the beginning of the long downhill slide for Zimbabwe – the party had survived by appropriation (which often looked very much like robbery and looting) and patronage. Awkward constituencies, like the war veterans, could be placated by gifts of stolen farms. These properties soon ceased to be going concerns, becoming instead rambling country estates. Useful people like traditional leaders and judges could be influenced and ultimately bought with gifts of Chinese-made electronics. Fifty thousand televisions – one for each headman – do not come cheap, but great leaders know when to prioritise the important business of securing influence rather than lesser matters such as education or health.

However, patronage was drying up, because the country was effectively bankrupt. At a micro level, individual businesses were facing difficult decisions. Nobody was making any money and the short-term prospects for the economy were bleak, so that even fundamentally sound companies were not saleable. Entrepreneurs despairing of Zimbabwe's economic lunacy faced an unpleasant choice: abandon their businesses and leave the country with nothing, or hibernate and hope for something better. For many the second half of 2008, once Mugabe had demonstrated his continuing brutality and insatiable hunger for power, was the right time to leave.

At a macro level, exports were close to zero, and the revenue of the entire public sector had fallen below US$100 million per year – less than the budget of a London borough. That amounted to about US$10 per person per year to provide a complete range of public services. But of course not even that tiny amount was available for spending on the needs of the people. The Government had more important things to do with what little money it was able to take in.

Gideon Gono, Zimbabwe's central banker, was a prisoner of his own actions. Under pressure from the ruthless hard cases within the JOC, he had printed colossal quantities of money to fund the June onslaught, inevitably causing hyperinflation. From that point on he could wring further purchasing power out of the currency only by upping the volume of money he printed by a factor of ten or more each week, accelerating inflation correspondingly. As prices leaped up exponentially, the currency's credibility and value plunged towards zero, a point it was to reach within six months.

Zimbabwe's enthralment to inflation had begun a decade earlier, when the central bank printed several hundred million dollars to fund payments to disgruntled war veterans. Ever since then, central bankers had been unable to drain inflation from the economy and were constantly tempted to fund a little more public spending by powering up the printing presses, rather than through the normal methods of taxation or borrowing.

When I first arrived in the country, new banknotes in higher denominations came along every few months. The largest note at the start of 2006 was $20,000. I needed several bundles of one hundred of those to pay for dinner – we used to call a plastic carrier bag a Zimbabwean wallet – so it was a relief when Gono produced a $50,000 note a few months later. Crazy notes followed each other. Gono held out against a $1 million note for several weeks as he thought it would make him look stupid. But he looked stupid in any case when he produced a $750,000 note to maintain his pretence a little longer. Queues formed as shoppers took time to work out how many $750,000 notes they needed to hand over to pay a bill of, say, $19 million. But the million-dollar note came soon enough, followed rapidly by those for 5, 10, 25, 50, 100 million. In mid-2006, Gono had announced that he was going to replace Zimbabwe's debased old currency with a new mega-dollar. Three zeros were removed from the old currency, which was withdrawn in favour of a new set of notes. Many people, particularly those out of touch in rural areas, had little idea this was happening. Around a quarter of old notes were never redeemed for the new currency, effectively robbing many of their savings. Gono was to repeat this zero-abolishing trick twice more, but failed to stop printing the new money which was the true cause of inflation.

At that stage, inflation was a nuisance, but it did not make life for me intolerable. What did hurt was the Government's insistence that international money exchanges should be made at an official rate which was typically 5–10 per cent of the figure obtainable on the black (known as 'parallel') market.

Most residents with hard currency exchanged money with parallel-market traders. But I – like some other diplomats – was unwilling to risk engaging in these technically illegal trades. So I bought Zimbabwean dollars at the punitively low official rate.

This hurt in two ways. Morally, I knew that I was helping the regime by paying much too much valuable sterling for my Zimbabwean dollars. And practically, the artificially low rate of exchange made everything expensive. I remember standing in agonised indecision in my local supermarket, wondering if I could really bring myself to pay £10 for a small packet of ineffectual washing powder that should have cost 50p. The alternative plan was wearing increasingly smelly clothes for another couple of weeks until I could make the trip to a plentifully stocked mall in South Africa.

Ordinary Zimbabweans were in a much worse position, both because of their poverty and because they earned and held only Zimbabwean dollars. As I was paid in sterling, my money was safe from rapid erosion by inflation until the moment I changed it. But a Zimbabwean teacher, for example, faced multiple frustrations every month. Public-sector salaries were raised only periodically. Immediately after a pay rise, the teacher's salary might stretch to the components of a basic diet – a sack of maize meal, a bag of the small fish known as kapenta, which make an excellent sauce for sadza, greens and cooking oil – but a month later the same amount would buy nothing worth while. This left teachers with poor alternatives – to work for nothing or to give up what little security a job offered. Amazingly, about half of them continued to go to work, believing that it was important for their long-term prospects to cling on to employment.

But those nominally in work felt little obligation to perform their duties, particularly as they could make more money than their salaries by playing the parallel currency markets, which resulted from controls on the availability of cash. Rationing banknotes was Gono's cruellest trick. When he printed new money he wanted to use it himself to buy foreign exchange, not to hand it out to the public. So he imposed limits on the amounts which bank account holders could withdraw. The consequent shortage of cash made it a more valuable commodity than the notional money represented by a cheque or money transfer. Parallel market foreign currency traders therefore set one rate for cash and a second for cheques.

At one point in 2007, Gono's daily limit on cash withdrawals was Z$20 million, which was worth US$10 on the black market, whereas purchasing US$10 by means of a cheque cost ten times more – Z$200 Million. Clever people – like public sector workers away from their desks – would join the remarkably orderly bank queues which stretched the length of Samora Machel Avenue and, a few hours later, withdraw the maximum Z$20 Million, which they immediately sold on the street for US$10. Then, moving through Zimbabwe's monetary looking glass, they would buy a *cheque* for Z$60 Million at a cost of US$3 and deposit it into their bank account. By the end of this chain of transactions – which could be repeated daily - quick-witted speculators would have US$7 in their pocket and Z$40 million more in their account.

It was a sad day when the manager of my favourite supermarket in Rolfe Valley told me that she could no longer afford to accept cheques, as they lost their value in the three days it took for the funds to clear. I had to make a furtive US-dollar payment, which became the norm from then on. Those with savings saw their value collapse. They worried about the future, but what could they do? Planning for tomorrow was impossible. The only rational strategy was to spend money the moment one had it. The poorest Zimbabweans in rural areas stopped using money at all, reverting to subsistence and barter.

By late 2007, Gono's new currency was just as much a joke as the old. How could he satisfy the regime's spending plans without printing ever more cash? He fell back on a favoured tactic of central command economies everywhere – rigid price control. Gono simply banned retailers from increasing their prices. This policy was popular in the short term. Retailers faced the choice of breaking the law or of sticking to official prices for goods that were worth a great deal more. Gono demonstrated his ruthlessness by establishing a price-control task force – another manifestation of the usual hybrid teams of party thugs and law-enforcement personnel. These teams toured shops, identified overpriced goods and arrested the management. Other shop staff were then compelled to sell the entire contents of the shop at whatever rock-bottom prices were dictated to them.

Corruption was rife, of course. I watched a price-enforcement team raiding a large central Harare supermarket on Leopold Takawira Street in late 2007. As police cars, trucks of riot police and soldiers arrived, a huge crowd formed outside, ready for the giveaway. Police arrested the shop's managers for overcharging and carried them off for questioning. Military and police units then took their pick. They blatantly and publicly loaded their trucks with maize meal and other groceries, while shop staff and what was by now a waiting riot of would-be looters looked on. Once the security forces had left with the best of the pickings, the public was let in to strip the shop of its entire contents within minutes. Staff allowed people to take what they wanted without payment, keen to avoid the fate of their bosses.

So it was little surprise that Gono's price-control regime was popular. Free food is always a vote winner. Basking in the short-lived glow of popularity, the regime turned up the rhetorical heat on retailers – the state media carried a string of stories about profiteers caught charging too much for their goods. The frenzy came to an end after two weeks. Having sold their entire stock for a pittance, retailers were unable to afford fresh supplies. In any case, the managers who took such decisions were in jail or had fled the country. Supermarkets closed. Gono denounced this wrecking behaviour too and ordered that they remain open. So they did, despite the fact that they were empty. I wandered through the enormous Bon Marché in Chisipite in September 2007, watched by a dozen staff with nothing to do, unable to decide which of its three available offerings – peach jelly powder, putrefied butternut squash or cheap Chinese-made patio furniture – appealed to me least.

Once satisfied that price control had squeezed every drop of loot out of the retail system, Gono tacitly relaxed his policy and let newly criminalised business people out of jail. Business confidence of course took a serious knock. It did not recover – and shops were not properly restocked – until the Zimbabwean dollar was officially pronounced dead more than a year later.

By 2008, everybody was wise to the Reserve Bank's relentless money-printing. The currency was deflating so quickly that prices needed to be changed every week, then every day. If contractors agreed to price services in local currency, they would give quotes valid for one hour, payable in full on commission. Many stopped accepting Zimbabwean dollars at all. At the pharmacy, where stocks of what little was available were kept well hidden, I would be given a bill in 'units' and invited to go to the offices at the back of the shop, where I would drop my US dollars into a drawer, which was quickly slammed shut. Companies adopted a fictional bookkeeping system, maintaining nominal accounts in Zimbabwean dollars, complete with bogus invoices and records of payments never made. The real business was not written down – Zimbabweans became used to unwritten transactions of foreign currency conducted furtively. Businessmen operating in this shadow fashion were vulnerable to stings and shake-downs. Unscrupulous restaurant diners ate their meals, knowing full well that they were expected to pay in US dollars, but then insisted on a bill in worthless local currency. If the amount of that bill proved to be too high, they would threaten the restaurateur with a visit from one of Gono's anti-profiteering teams.

By late 2008, the diverting silliness of high prices which went up every week or so had accelerated into a manic chain reaction and ceased to be a joke. Prices just moved too fast to note, let alone convert into a grown-up currency. But Gono pressed on. Without any sustainable source of revenue, as there were no viable businesses to tax, he could secure foreign currency only by printing money in ever greater quantities. It is one of the many hypocrisies of the Mugabe regime that it exploited currency traders to fund its operations, while at the same time denouncing the parallel market as criminal and the cause of Zimbabwe's monetary problems.

With the currency's final demise in sight, Gono twice made colossal devaluations – withdrawing everything from circulation and issuing new notes, poorly printed on cheap paper without all those awkward zeros. In late 2008, Gono struck ten zeros off his currency, transforming a trillion dollars into one. But within weeks the new currency was debased too. There was no holding back its gallop towards stratospheric face values. But there soon came a day when nobody was ready to swap even the smallest foreign currency note for any number of Zimbabwean dollars.

Gono tried the same trick one last time in February 2009, this time removing thirteen zeros – a wholly pointless and wasteful exercise as the local dollar had been abandoned by all meaningful economic players by that time. The 100 trillion dollar bill ($100,000,000,000,000) was his final desperate attempt to wring more foreign currency from increasingly unwilling traders. I bought some of the $100,000,000,000,000 notes as souvenirs. I only had to pay a couple of greenbacks for a dozen. Zimbabwe's currency – which stood at parity with the pound in 1980 – was finally dead and worth nothing more than its amusement value.

So, in late 2008, staring straight at a point in the very near future where money-printing would cease to be an available proxy for raising public revenue sustainably, the regime needed a deal. Taking the MDC into government might bring some funds into the country, if Tsvangirai could persuade foreign donors and businesses to invest. ZANU-PF was confident that it could capture its usual large slice of any new money. Doing a deal would be politically expedient too, as it would please

SADC and confer legitimacy on Mugabe's shabby mandate to rule.

Talks reconvened. The negotiating teams met frequently in South Africa and Mbeki called the principals together too, judging correctly that neither Mugabe nor Tsvangirai gave his team much flexibility to negotiate. Chinamasa and Biti could not go far without referring back to their masters. It was often more effective to bring the party leaders together and work with them directly.

The deal that took shape – grandly termed a Global Political Agreement (GPA) – offered the MDC a substantial amount on paper, in return for one huge concession – an acceptance that Mugabe would remain as executive president, the most powerful office in the country. This was of course the only prize Mugabe really cared about. Ever pragmatic, he was ready to give the appearance of conceding a good deal so long as he could hold on to the top job. He was confident that his cunning, his network and his ultimate willingness to be more ruthless than the other guy would ensure that he kept a grip on all the power that really mattered.

The GPA is a curious document, which fuses the MDC's rhetoric of democracy, human rights and the rule of law with ZANU-PF's language of respect for the values of the liberation struggle, meaning the defence of independence and the primacy of the land question in Zimbabwe's politics. Even at a conceptual level there are obvious tensions between these agendas. The liberation struggle was a violent reaction to the tyranny of apartheid-style government, but also led to the imposition of a one-party African nationalist system. It is hard to see how such an ideology is compatible with a plural post-colonial society, in which the struggle against occupation and its legacy are no longer paramount and various parties can contest for power peacefully, offering different visions of the future. Human rights are supposed to be colour-blind, yet Mugabe's nationalism was explicitly anti-white and his mode of government marginalised those outside his own ethnic group.

The MDC made other concessions concerning the language of the GPA document. During the election campaign, the party had argued that ZANU-PF had caused the economic crisis. But Tsvangirai – perhaps intoxicated by the spirit of unity – was prepared to brush this allegation under the carpet. The GPA blamed the country's economic distress on 'international isolation [which has] created a negative international perception of Zimbabwe'. From my perspective, this stood reality on its head. Was it not the bloodshed during Zimbabwe's recent elections that had created the negative international perception, which in turned caused isolation?

Just as generously, the MDC signed up to a commitment to work for the repeal of the travel ban against the leading members of ZANU-PF. This was a strange undertaking for several reasons. The only people to suffer from restrictions were the senior ZANU-PF men involved in violence against Tsvangirai and his supporters. Permitting Grace Mugabe, derisively known as Zimbabwe's First Shopper, to resume her publicly funded retail pilgrimages to Milan and Paris would not do much to assist the economy. Nor was it wise to offer to deliver what was not in the MDC's power – the party has been unable to persuade the EU, US and others to lift travel bans, allowing ZANU-PF to accuse the party of reneging on its pledges.

The GPA also noted that 'compulsory acquisition and redistribution of land has taken place under a land reform programme undertaken since 2000' and that these acquisitions were 'irreversible'. Generous with the money of those not involved in the negotiations, the parties agreed 'to call upon the United Kingdom government to accept the primary responsibility to pay compensation for land acquired from former landowners for resettlement'. I thought of the black farming people put out of their homes by the land invasions. Nobody thought to mention them in the agreement or provide for any compensation to them despite the life-rending nature of their losses.

The MDC secured commitments in the GPA to non-violence,

political freedoms and processes that might heal national rifts and develop a new constitution, and to restore the independence of the media, the civil service and traditional leaders. All these words look fine on paper and may even be transformed into new realities one day.

At the business end of the deal, power was ostensibly neatly divided in two. Mugabe would be president and would appoint two ZANU-PF vice-presidents. Tsvangirai would be prime minister and would appoint two deputy prime ministers, one of whom would be Mutambara. Fifteen ministers within a cabinet of thirty-one would be appointed by Mugabe, thirteen by Tsvangirai and three by Mutambara. Both Mugabe and Tsvangirai would exercise 'executive authority'. Mugabe would chair the cabinet; Tsvangirai would lead a new Council of Ministers.

The million (US) dollar question was of course how all this would work. It looked very much as if the agreement set up two structures of government – one led by Mugabe, the other by Tsvangirai. Which committee would consider which issues? Or would both duplicate the same responsibilities? If the latter, what would happen if the two cabinet-like bodies wanted to go in different directions? Would ZANU-PF Ministers be ready to attend the Council of Ministers chaired by Tsvangirai? Would the MDC's Ministers attend the cabinet chaired by Mugabe?

The deal was signed with great flourish on 15 September at the Rainbow Towers Hotel – a tired building at the west end of Harare's city centre. The leaders made equally tired speeches about the new dawn the agreement represented. Mutambara smirked idiotically at his inclusion on his nation's top table. Mugabe and Tsvangirai did not look much like men who had made an exciting win-win deal. Rather, they had each seen no alternative to signing a deal which pleased neither. While shaking hands, Mugabe tried to raise Tsvangirai's triumphantly above his head, in the same way that he had celebrated the merger of ZANU and ZAPU with Joshua Nkomo a quarter of a century earlier. The MDC leader resisted this symbolic gesture, no doubt recalling that Nkomo had capitulated only after the massacre of his fellow tribesmen and died a few years later, by which time it was plain that unity with ZANU meant the subordination of the Ndebele to the Shona. Tsvangirai no doubt feared ending up in the same state.

What limited optimism there was in Harare on the day the deal was signed evaporated almost at once as the agreement unwound. Extraordinarily, Tendai Biti alleged that Chinamasa had made unilateral last-minute changes and had inserted his redraft under the leaders' pens. But, more substantially, it soon became plain that crucial aspects of the division of power had not been agreed. The most important unresolved issue was who would control which Ministries. Both sides agreed that the MDC should control the various economic and development portfolios – the idea behind the agreement was, after all, that Tsvangirai would be able to restart the economy by appealing to foreign donors hostile to Mugabe. Mugabe insisted that he had to control the Ministry of Defence. But both parties wanted the Home Affairs Ministry, which offered the prospect of control over the police.

So lengthy negotiations about the text of the Global Political Agreement were followed by lengthy negotiations about what that text meant and the gaps within it. More undiscussed issues emerged – the MDC wanted to appoint some provincial governors, permanent secretaries and ambassadors. Mugabe responded by making unilateral appointments to all these senior posts. Formal politics remained deadlocked. Parliament did not sit, as there was no draft legislation emerging from the executive. Government drifted. The economy crawled along the bottom. The currency gave its death rattle.

Nothing demonstrated Zimbabwe's precipitate collapse and flight from civilised norms more than the 2008–9 cholera epidemic. The initial outbreak was both widely anticipated and wholly preventable. Zimbabwe's water-treatment infrastructure used to be of a first-world standard. Tap water was drinkable and domestic drainage exemplary. Water-borne diseases had not been a problem for decades. That changed – along with so much else that was good – as the Government starved public services of investment and pared their running costs not just to the bone, but to the marrow. Pipes began to leak and were not repaired, leaving homes without supply. Water-treatment plants ran out of chemicals. Their septic tanks filled and overflowed, mingling with water being pumped out for drinking. Public standards of hygiene inevitably suffered, as people could no longer wash or flush away their waste. Those left homeless by Murambatsvina had for some years had no alternative to using shallow pits as latrines, but other town dwellers began to do the same. Sewage first appeared in ditches, then in the streets. Urban areas began to smell. Civil society groups had been warning of an impending problem for months. Zimbabwe's towns – formally models of high-quality social provision – became breeding grounds for bacteria.

The epidemic exploded at the beginning of the wet season in November. Zimbabwe's rains are not showers, but tropical monsoons, biblical deluges. The rain can fall so hard that visibility is cut to fifty metres or less. It is unlucky to be caught on the open road in such conditions – the dilemma is whether to continue despite not being able to see the road ahead or to stop and risk being hit by the driver behind. Twenty centimetres of rainfall per year is the norm for many parts of the UK, but that amount falls each week at the height of the rainy season in Zimbabwe.

The large quantities of human waste, filth and contamination lying in pits and on waste ground in November 2008 were washed down Harare's streets, where children played, flooded over the vegetables being cultivated in urban back gardens and flowed into drains where they soon entered circulation: the failed water-treatment system was no longer able to remove bacterial contaminants from wastewater, so whatever infections were washed down Harare's drains soon emerged from its taps. The number of new cases of cholera leaped rapidly from dozens to thousands per week. People started to die. The epidemic was most heavily reported in Harare, but it was probably most devastating on a per-capita basis in smaller urban areas – Kwekwe and Gweru were hit early and suffered particularly badly.

Of course water treatment was not the only service to have been starved of funds. Healthcare was in utter disarray. Doctors' salaries were equivalent to less than US$80 per month and nurses earned less than US$10. Their unions called a series of pay strikes, but it was hard to know if these had any impact, as most health workers had just stopped coming to work anyway, calculating that the cost of commuting exceeded their pay. Nominally state-funded hospitals effectively became private. Arriving patients were asked for several hundred US dollars before a doctor would even assess them. Medical insurance schemes became worthless as medics refused to work for the theoretical promise of Zimbabwean dollars.

This added a frightening new dimension to life in Harare. Nobody could assume that care would be provided in an emergency. I wondered what would happen if I was injured and taken to hospital. Would I lie untreated until somebody thought to call the Embassy and a colleague arrived with some cash? And even if I were assessed, would the hospital have the staff, equipment and supplies to treat me? Stories abounded of hospital workers selling stolen drugs to make ends meet. Rumours circulated of pregnant women and trauma victims dying for want of a length of plastic tube or a pint of blood.

Victims of cholera collided with this failed healthcare system. The cholera bacterium should not cause death. It is nasty – it infects the gut, causing severe diarrhoea and vomiting for about three days. But if the patient can survive that long, the bug dies and the symptoms pass. All that is required to sustain life through those three awful days is relentless hydration. Patients need to drink litre upon litre of fluids to replace what the body is expelling. Those weakened by old age or other sickness may find the strain of this regimen too much, though many of these can be saved by a basic saline drip. In poor but organised countries the death rate from cholera is below 1 per cent. By contrast, more than 4 per cent of those infected in Zimbabwe died: a grim confirmation of the extent of the collapse of medical care as well as water supply.

The authorities set up isolation centres for the infected, but it quickly became clear that these centres were intended to isolate news of the epidemic from the outside world rather than to provide any medically worthwhile quarantine. I visited a cholera ward in Mbare, a densely populated suburb of Harare, with a brave and brilliant young civil society activist. We dressed smartly, parked at some distance from the hospital and entered through a hole in the fence, avoiding the security guards at the main gate. We headed straight for the cholera ward, only to find that all the beds in the hospital had been dedicated to victims of the disease. The nurse looked at me suspiciously and told us that no observers were allowed, but we tried a bold bluff, saying that we were both related to one of the patients. Perhaps it was the effect of our smart dress or our confident manner, but she accepted this patently untrue story and we made our way on to the ward.

Row upon row of patients lay on beds or crouched uncomfortably near buckets. Some were unnaturally still, some groaned and clutched their bellies. Porters and nurses, masked and wrapped in plastic, moved through, removing buckets of waste and mopping vomit off the floor. My activist friend stopped by one of the beds on which a man was sitting, looking relatively healthy. The patient was ready to tell his story. He had felt ill that morning and had been lucky because his family had brought him straight to the clinic. Many sufferers in his area were too sick to travel by the time they realised what disease they had. Suddenly the man sat up alertly, looking shocked. My friend pulled me backwards just as the eruption of watery vomit struck the floor where I had been standing.

By now I could hear raised voices outside the ward – administrators, nurses and security guards were arguing about whether we should have been allowed on the ward and how we should be removed. It was not going to be long before the police arrived. We quickly took some photographs, left through the far end of the ward and hurried back to the car. As we drove away we saw dozens of people waiting patiently on the street, despite the persistent rain. My friend told me they were waiting to collect relatives' corpses.

I drove home, trying not to get my hands anywhere near my face. I had no running water or electricity at home, but – unlike the large majority of Harare residents – I had a bore-hole in my back garden and a generator in my garage, so I was able to jump straight into the shower and wash thoroughly in water that was probably uncontaminated. I felt the usual combination of relief and guilt that I was so privileged.

The epidemic powered its way right through the rainy season. All urban areas were affected: Marondera, Chinoyi, Masvingo, Mutare, even Victoria Falls, which the authorities usually try hard to isolate from the rest of the country's problems, to avoid scaring away the last of the tourists. Life felt dirty. Harare was now stinking. Zimbabweans are justly proud of their good manners and of the friendly welcome they give each other. I was equally proud to be included in this collective warmth and had become semi-proficient in the three-part handshake, with which men greeted each other: first a standard handshake, then a movement of both hands upwards into a more macho clenched grip, then back again. With friends and close colleagues I learned to linger in this final position for a minute or two, standing close – definitely within what British people would consider each other's personal space – during which it was somehow possible to speak with more candour and directness than usual. But this charming ritual became risky during the cholera outbreak. Washing hands was difficult when the water supply was so patchy and probably infected anyway. The traditional handshake was replaced with a cautious touch of elbow to elbow.

Even the Embassy lost its water supply. During my time in Harare the British institutions – Embassy, DFID, British Council – were on the top floors of a decrepit office block in central Harare. We were just about the only country whose offices were still in such a location. Central Harare used to swing in the 1980s – a trendy Zimbabwean friend recalls shopping for clothes in beautiful air-conditioned malls, then spending Saturday night working along the happy, multiracial nightclubs on First Street. She felt entirely safe whatever she was wearing, at whatever time of night. During the 1990s and into the new century the makeup of the town centre slowly changed. As businesses began to contract or fail, shops closed or moved downmarket. The town centre became less attractive and well-to-do people began to move out into the northern suburbs. Embassies soon started to drift away too into attractive suburban houses, converted for business use.

The British got left behind somehow, perhaps because scarce resources were needed for unsafe buildings in other countries facing a greater terrorist threat. But by late 2008 it was clear that we had stayed in our office block far too long. With no running water, the building became foul smelling. Harare's water laced with the deadly *Vibrio cholera* bacterium was obviously no use for drinking, but it was still helpful for flushing toilets and I certainly missed it. My toiletry routine took on a semi-African form. I filled a bucket from a butt and carried it down the corridor, spilling a little to present a banana-skin walkway to my colleagues. We'll skip the next part of the story; suffice to say that I emptied my bucket. I tried to wash my hands using 'water-free purification liquid', which smelled like something a mortician would use, and succeeded only in making me feel like a dirty person with clean hands.

The Embassy did not suffer from a lack only of water. By late 2008, Zimbabwe's electricity-generating system – based on hydroelectric power from the colossal Kariba dam and dirty coal from the Hwange mines – was supplying no more than half of what the country needed. Neighbouring countries no longer exported their own power, as Zimbabwe could not pay for it. Power cuts were daily occurrences. Indeed most Zimbabweans grew used to life without power – one friend experienced a three-week outage. Electricity supply to the central business district was supposed to be safeguarded, but the Embassy seemed to lose power at least once a day. Staff got a little relief from cursing vigorously as their computers crashed and they lost whatever lengthy draft emails they were composing for London. It was not clear if we were cut off deliberately, as an act of harassment, or whether we were just unable to escape Zimbabwe's general failure. Either way, the situation had gone beyond a joke, even allowing for British toilet humour. The Embassy has now finally moved to an out-of-town site, where it can at least install its own generators and bore-holes.

ZANU-PF offered commentaries on the cholera outbreak that were bizarre even by its strange standards. In November, ZANU-PF officials blamed the outbreak on 'biological warfare' waged by Britain. A spokesman clarified this suggestion by accusing the Rhodesian army, defeated during the liberation war, of having laced the soil with a latent cholera infection, activated some years later. Just as curiously, Mugabe himself, in a rambling speech on 11 December 2008, said, 'I am happy to say our doctors have been assisted by others . . . so now that there is no cholera.' This insane remark worried even Mugabe's handlers. George Charamba, his spokesman, attempted to explain away his master's folly, claiming both that Mugabe had been speaking sarcastically and that he had been misquoted by Zimbabwe's enemies. He did not trouble to explain why the President should use irony while addressing a health crisis that was affecting every family in the country, nor how he could be misquoted when his remarks were made during a televised address to the nation.

Despite Mugabe's deluded belief that his wasted health service was addressing the epidemic, the numbers of cases and of deaths continued to climb steadily. Rural areas began to be affected, which was curious, as many had never had the benefit of piped water. The most likely cause of rural infections was the traditional practice of touching the dead brought back from the cities to their ancestral homes for burial. Many people died in the country far from any medical intervention or even certification of death. The World Health Organisation's final report on the epidemic, published in June 2009, is therefore certain to be an understatement of the true death toll: '98 424 suspected cases, including 4 276 deaths, have been reported . . . since August 2008. Fifty-five out of 62 districts in all 10 provinces have been affected.'[3]

The event that brought the cholera epidemic to a halt was no human intervention but the end of the rains. None of the causes of cholera have been addressed since the outbreak died down, so the infection will flare up again at the start of each rainy season until Zimbabwe's water-supply system, which now lies in ruins, is rebuilt. An annual epidemic of preventable disease is just one more element of Mugabe's legacy to his people.

Mugabe – fully recovered from his dip in confidence in the weeks after his electoral defeat – returned to top form at ZANU-PF's party congress on 19 December. A few days beforehand, he had given assurances to SADC that he was ready to take his place at the head of a government of unity with his rivals, ready to heal and rebuild the nation, but he struck a different note at the congress: 'I will never, never sell my country. I will never, never, never, never surrender.' He also promised to complete the removal of whites from Zimbabwean agriculture. The contrast between the defiant Mugabe of ZANU-PF party rallies and the humble man who appeared so flexible at SADC summits was striking. Even for him, it was bizarre to pretend to be ready to share power one day while screaming intransigence and unending racial war the next.

During his speech to his party congress, Mugabe also erected the straw man of African military action against him, only to dismiss that remote prospect: 'I don't know of an African country that is brave enough.' Nonetheless ZANU-PF began to allege that Botswana, which had emerged as Mugabe's greatest critic within SADC, was plotting invasion. Anyone familiar with Botswana's modest military capability would understand how absurd this idea was.

Mugabe's brutal words coincided chillingly with a frightening ZANU-PF onslaught that dragged the country suddenly and shockingly back into the fear of six months before.

I had met Jestina Mukoko, from the Zimbabwe Peace Project human rights group, several times during the year. She had accurately advised me where political violence was most likely to occur and had blown the whistle on the fact that ZANU-PF was diverting United Nations food distributions funded by DFID for its own purposes. I admired her courage and intelligence and liked her directness. Although we met only professionally, I felt that we had a rapport and considered Jestina a friend as well as a valuable contact.

So I felt a personal horror, not just the concern a diplomat might express, when I heard that she had been kidnapped from her house in Norton, north of Harare, on 3 December. According to her son and a niece that she cares for, seven men and one woman forced their way into her house in the middle of the night. The intruders were not in uniform, although one of the men claimed to be a police officer. They refused to let her change out of her nightdress, find her glasses or pick up drugs that she needs to take regularly. These details terrified me, as they suggested that the kidnappers did not intend to keep her.

Nobody knew who the kidnappers were, but colourful rumours spread fast, as usual. Three other members of Jestina's Zimbabwe Peace Project were also arrested for legitimate human rights monitoring activities such as photographing uncollected refuse, bank queues and cholera victims, but were released after three days when the police conceded that they could not sustain any charges.

Mukoko was not a party-political figure, but she was certainly a critic of Mugabe and was therefore assumed by the regime to be an MDC fellow traveller. To reinforce that alleged connection, seven MDC activists were also lifted from their homes in Gokwe, Makoni and Gutu between 10 and 17 December, bringing the total member of political prisoners being held without trial to thirty. I looked hard at the name of the activist from Gutu South taken on 13 December – Peter Munyanyi. I couldn't place him, but I wondered if I'd met him during my several trips to Gutu during the year.

Everyone – diplomats, human rights workers, MDC leaders – was pessimistic about the fate of those abducted. It was all too likely that this situation was going to end up as it had done for Tonderai Ndira, who had been murdered almost immediately after being kidnapped back in June. The non-uniformed men who took away Mukoko and the latest seven MDC people were presumably ZANU militiamen working under the party's direction or a group of thugs hired for the occasion by an individual. Either way, the abductees were in great danger and as their detention turned from hours to days to a week and more, the danger grew.

Nobody knew where the missing people were or who was holding them. Human rights workers trawled around police stations, all of which denied having the detainees. The abduction shocked Harare greatly, partly because Jestina was so well known. She had been a newsreader before joining the NGO sector. There was also a sense among human rights activists that if Jestina could be 'disappeared', then nobody was safe. Lawyers immediately made an application for her release, though it did not seem likely that she was being held within the formal law-enforcement system. Shamefully, the High Court stalled for five days before hearing the application. It was not until 9 December that a judge, Anne-Marie Gorowa, ordered the police 'to dispatch a team . . . to search for Jestina Mukoko'. The authorities simply ignored the ruling. Police said they had no jurisdiction to search military or intelligence premises, implying that they believed that she had been taken by one of the state security agencies.

The abductions and presumed murders surely marked the end of the road for the political process. Clearly, Tsvangirai could not deal with Mugabe while his supporters continued to be abducted, mistreated and (presumably) killed. Many gossips thought that this was the real point – the hardliners in the JOC wanted power-sharing to fail, so they had decided to carry out another batch of murders to drive Tsvangirai away.

Also at the end of the road was Mbeki's role and reputation as an impartial mediator. In late November, he had written a stinging letter to Tsvangirai apparently in response to Tendai Biti's dismissive reaction to the latest SADC commandment that Tsvangirai should agree to join a unity government despite the MDC's discontent with the proposed arrangements for power-sharing. The state media gleefully reproduced Mbeki's rebuke:

> Such manner of proceeding might earn you prominent media headlines. However, I assure you that it will do nothing to solve the problems of Zimbabwe . . . Realistically, Zimbabwe will never share the same neighbourhood with the countries of Western Europe and North America, and therefore secure its success on the basis of friendship with these, and contempt for the decisions of its immediate African neighbours.

Mbeki saw no irony in instructing Tsvangirai to conform to decisions made after debates from which the MDC leader was (in a truly contemptuous style) excluded. Another striking feature of Mbeki's letter was his use of the ZANU-PF propaganda line that Tsvangirai cared only for the opinion of the West: 'It may

be that, for whatever reason, you consider our region and continent as being of little consequence to the future of Zimbabwe,
believing that others further away, in Western Europe and
North America, are of greater importance.' Mugabe himself
could have drafted much of the letter. Mbeki appeared not to
have asked himself why Tsvangirai would want to place confidence in SADC, after watching that organisation exclude him
from its discussions throughout 2008 while including the man
who had presided over the murder of MDC party members.

Mbeki continued to press reality into his own peculiar mould,
when he claimed that South Africa had welcomed Zimbabwean
refugees 'in a spirit of solidarity'. Four months earlier, as
Zimbabwe burned, the United Nations High Commission
for Refugees had reported that South Africa was deporting
17,000 people per month back into danger. Speaking unusually
plainly, the UNHCR's spokeswoman expressed 'concern that
these refugees who are fleeing political violence and upheaval
in Zimbabwe could be at risk of being sent back to danger if
they are caught up in this large-scale deportation'.[4] The UN's
criticism of South Africa's deportation standards was actually
rather muted. Human Rights Watch had reported in 2007 that
Zimbabwean refugees in South Africa were unlawfully detained,
mistreated and robbed of their possessions before being handcuffed inside trains which took them back over the border.[5]
South Africa routinely deported unaccompanied children
throughout Zimbabwe's year of misery. So much for Mbeki's
solidarity, which, as usual, extended only to Zimbabwe's dictator, not to its rightfully elected leader or its people.

Extraordinarily, Mbeki prefaced his scolding letter to
Tsvangirai with the words, 'I say this humbly.' It is hard to
think of a less humble act than writing a patronising and offensive letter to the man who had won the Presidential election
of a neighbouring state. Indeed Mbeki's letter revealed plainly
the extent of his contempt for Tsvangirai. For a decade during
which Zimbabweans had been murdered and starved and

the economy painstakingly vandalised, Mbeki had declined publicly to criticise his comrade Mugabe. Yet he was happy to break his 'quiet diplomacy' rule and slap Tsvangirai in a letter that was quickly leaked to the press, for no greater offence than speaking in a manner Mbeki disliked.

So, all things considered, the pre-Christmas season was cheerless even by Zimbabwe's doleful standards. Jestina Mukoko's ghost sat at the Embassy party daring us to have fun. Having another beer seemed like a safer bet than a glass of possibly infected water, which was fine up to a point, but led to some grisly hangovers. The prospects of even a half-baked political settlement seemed to have disappeared, along with the credibility of the mediator. Mugabe was eating his turkey at State House and seemed set to do so for another five years, even if the country became a bankrupt desert during that time.

To cheer us up, I wrote some silly satirical lyrics for a Christmas revue. But it was no good. The jokes fell flat. Even such a worthy and quintessentially Zimbabwean act as mocking Gono didn't make me feel any better. I thought I knew what Mugabe's Christmas present to Zimbabwe was going to be – Jestina's dead body.

9

Faint Hope

But Jestina was alive. I heard the amazing news that she had been found just before Christmas. It was a marvel that she was alive, but she was not yet safe. She had been held by the gang which kidnapped her for a week and had suffered an agonising torture known as falanga – a prolonged beating on the soles of the feet similar to the bastinado – that left her unable to walk properly for several months. After that she was dumped at a police station, then transferred to the grim and unhealthy surroundings of Chikurubi prison. She was sick and needed medical attention which the authorities were denying her. For some days she was not allowed to see even human rights lawyers or her family.

But she was alive. I had been asking myself the grimmest questions – whether her body would ever be found, whether her family would be able to bury her. I had been remembering the empty hope I had felt during the days before Tonderai Ndira's body was found. I wondered now how pain and the closeness of death would have changed Jestina. Would she still be confident and brilliant, boldly denouncing the regime to its face? Or would they have managed to break her mind or her spirit? But whatever Jestina's mental and physical condition, her reappearance in the living world gave a boost to many and reignited the seasonally appropriate glowing sentiment of optimism. Maybe the apparently phoney power-sharing agreement was in fact real. Maybe the violence and killing of 2008 had ended. Maybe there was some tiny hope for Zimbabwe's future.

There was more unexpected good news. The thirty MDC abductees were also alive. They too were now in Chikurubi. All had faced frightening and painful ordeals at the hands of the irregular squads of thugs who had detained them. But they were now somehow inside the formal criminal justice system. The state never even attempted to explain the legalities of how people kidnapped and tortured by a party militia could be transferred into the court and prison system. But the detainees were at least alive and visible, albeit in prison and facing the usual absurd charges of terrorism.

It seemed that Jestina's story was going to end well, but she faced a gruelling ordeal before she was finally released. Despite her untreated long-term illness and despite the obvious illegality of her abduction and detention, she was detained for another three months, for most of which time she received no medical care.

Like the thirty members of the MDC arrested between October and December 2008, Jestina was said to be a terrorist and was charged with training guerrillas in Botswana and plotting an armed rebellion. The charges had a familiar ring to them. ZANU-PF had charged MDC prisoners with terrorism in 2007. On that occasion the supposed plot involved training camps in South Africa. The location of these fictional facilities was now switched to Botswana to assist Mugabe's efforts to portray that country as a threatening and hostile nation.

Mugabe had become infuriated by the directness and strength of Botswana's criticisms of his leadership. For example, Botswanan Foreign Minister Phandu Skelemani said in January 2009, 'Clearly what Mugabe is doing is wrong. He can't pretend to act as if he won an election because he didn't . . . if you starve people to death deliberately because you are putting in place programmes which don't work, or you are doing nothing to prevent people from dying unnecessarily, I think some people would describe it as genocide. But you know it's genocide against all Zimbabweans.' Skelemani was equally critical of

SADC: 'SADC have failed the people of Zimbabwe. We have simply failed to tell the leadership . . . that what they are doing is wrong . . . SADC has virtually achieved nothing in respect of Zimbabwe . . . Too many of the leadership in SADC feel some kind of obligation towards Mugabe.'[6]

Such plain speaking is rare in African politics and shows how frustrated the Botswanan Government had become with the situation on its eastern border, not only because of its immorality, but also because of the flow of refugees into Francistown and Gaborone, which swamped the modest resources of what is a lightly populated country. Mugabe responded sharply, alleging that Botswana was now acting as a proxy for Western interests in Southern Africa and was planning to launch a UK-backed invasion. Jestina Mukoko and the other prisoners were supposedly a part of this project, training foreign fighters to invade their homeland. It is significant that Mugabe's circle of supporters was shrinking rapidly. Back in 2005, he had been able to count on strong support from all his SADC neighbours in endorsing a bloody election process. But by 2009 not only had his SADC neighbours condemned the manner of his election, but some of the organisation's members even felt moved to lay into Mugabe publicly.

There was so little substance to the allegations against Jestina that magistrates and judges regularly ordered her release. But her detention dragged on. It was heartbreaking to see such a benign and peaceable woman so badly mistreated. When she appeared in court on 16 January 2009, she cried as she recalled her pain: 'The experience I have gone through is really frightening and I do not wish that on anyone.' But the Attorney General, Johannes Tomana, declared Jestina to be a threat to security and determined that she should remain in jail. It took more than two months before she was allowed to go to hospital. Even then an absurdly excessive team of six riot police, who cruelly handcuffed her to the bed, guarded her. It was another week before she was released.

I went to see her at the clinic where she was recovering. I could tell at once from her composed and dignified manner that she had not been broken, but she was somehow smaller in her skin. I saw little of her wonderful, gappy smile. Jestina told me about the agony of being hung upside down and beaten on the soles of her feet. She still could not walk without pain. But more painful had been the loss of hope: she thought she would never see her family again. She had been sure that her kidnappers were going to kill her.

Compounding her treatment's cruelty, the charges against Jestina were revived several times over the coming months; once she was even taken back into detention for a night. But rather than flee, she bravely took the issue of her mistreatment to the Supreme Court, seeking to use the proper processes to curb the regime's contempt for the constitutional rule of law.

The news that the detainees had not been killed generated a tiny amount of trust and goodwill between the parties. Only in Zimbabwe could violent abduction, illegal detention and torture be seen as restraint, a positive outcome. But, certainly, had the MDC detainees been killed, the idea of power-sharing would have been dead too. As it was, they were still alive, so the talking could go on.

But Tsvangirai faced growing disillusion and anger within his party. Many in the MDC woke up on 1 January 2009 feeling just as pessimistic as they had a year before. The unity accord had always been a flawed idea. But after three months of circular negotiations about the precise borders of the MDC's executive power, it now looked thoroughly bad. The regime was showing its true colours again – intransigent in negotiations and heartless in its unlawful detention of activists. The promise of early 2008 and the feelgood times at the signing of the Global Political Agreement were gone. ZANU-PF had shown cunning as well as ruthlessness in holding on to power. The world had allowed Mugabe to cling on to the office he had secured by cheating and violence, and now SADC called Tsvangirai the deal-breaker for refusing to enter an enfeebled government in which he would be a junior partner.

SADC leaders were fed up with talking about Zimbabwe. For much of 2008 their irritation had been mainly directed at Mugabe. Why could he not just retire or die, as all the other liberation-era leaders had done? What had been the point in holding bloody and farcical unopposed elections in June? That method might have worked in the 1980s, but this was the twenty-first century. Mugabe did not appear to realise that he had destroyed what little credibility he still possessed when he demonstrated that he could win only by terrifying his people.

But since the signing of the Global Political Agreement in September, the SADC leaders' annoyance had shifted towards Tsvangirai. They had persuaded Mugabe to accept the MDC into government. Morgan had signed the deal too, but was refusing to deliver what he had agreed by taking up his designated role as prime minister. A short period of negotiation was fine, but Tsvangirai had now been holding out for four months. What more than the office of prime minister did he expect? Why was he delaying the point at which Zimbabwe could start to normalise politically and recover economically?

In this impatient mood, Southern Africa's political elite met again to discuss Zimbabwe on 27 January in Sandton, South Africa. Sandton is Johannesburg's Mayfair – a district of five-star hotels and boutique shops, sealed off from the city's problems and bad reputation. Zimbabwean negotiators had found previous South African accommodation insufficiently luxurious. There were no complaints about Sandton.

As before, SADC leaders discussed Zimbabwe with Mugabe while Tsvangirai sat outside the room – a humiliating demonstration of the inequality of the power-sharing dynamic. Mugabe did his usual numero on his SADC brothers. He was ready to share power. He had been ready for four months. He had set up an office for Tsvangirai, purchased cars for his nominated Ministers. He had humbly submitted to what SADC had asked him to do – surrendering a part of his power despite winning an overwhelming mandate at the ballot box. The problem was Tsvangirai, who was constantly seeking to reopen the agreed deal; after all he was a puppet figure, directed by the West.

SADC ganged up on Tsvangirai. An uncharitable observer from Mutambara's faction said that Tsvangirai was almost pinned to the wall and that he caved in quickly to SADC's demands that he join the Unity Government, supposedly like a falling house of cards. This was unfair as well as unkind. Ultimately Morgan did bow to the pressure of SADC's great and good, but he won some last-minute concessions, principally the right to appoint the governors of five provinces. He also demonstrated plainly to the world that he was not power-hungry and was entering the Government reluctantly. He did not consider the mechanisms of power-sharing to be practical and was becoming prime minister only because there was nothing better that he could do.

But it was true to say that Tsvangirai had been planning to hang tough at Sandton. Most of his party members considered the power-sharing arrangements to be grotesquely lopsided and unjust. The agreed position ahead of the SADC summit was that the MDC should hold out as long as possible, so as to obtain every possible concession from Mugabe. So it was a retreat of a sort to agree to SADC's demands.

Confusion and division crippled the MDC for a week. The party issued press releases denying that any deal had been done, even though SADC was emphatically saying the opposite. The party's publicity operation, under the control of Nelson Chamisa, failed to grasp or acknowledge what Tsvangirai had done at Sandton. Tendai Biti was dismayed by Tsvangirai's sudden collapse of resolve. He told friends that he would stand with Morgan until the new Government was in place, but would have no part in it afterwards.

Tsvangirai slowly got a grip. He spread the word that he had agreed to join the Government. He appeared in Harare with his key deputies, including a dignified but subdued Biti, to confirm that he was to become prime minister. He called a meeting of his party's National Council and explained his decision. He had extracted key concessions from Mugabe. The MDC would be able to appoint its people to the important positions of governors of those provinces where it had won the popular vote. It would have more control in the appointment of ambassadors, permanent secretaries and the heads of key state agencies such as the central bank. The National Council endorsed his action. What else could it do?

Tsvangirai had one last mental hurdle to cross – the humiliating and infuriating fact that he was set to become prime minister while some of his comrades remained in jail. The thought of leaving Mukoko and the MDC Thirty in Zimbabwe's prisons was even harder to bear because the vile conditions in those prisons were coming under close examination. NGOs trying to monitor the criminal justice system had been making grim reports for several years. Prisoners just did not get enough to eat and were dying at a horrifying rate. By early 2009, the budget allocated for the prison system had fallen so low that Zimbabwe's prisoners began to starve to death. Some prison officers – who, in my experience, were decent people doing an impossible job – could bear it no longer and told journalists what was going on. Out of a population of 1,300 at Chikurubi prison, 721 had died in the previous nine months. Five per cent of prisoners were dying each month. A two-year sentence for a modest offence was effectively one of death, as the human body could not endure substantial malnutrition for that long.

Prisoners received one meal of sadza with a little oily cabbage on good days. Sometimes they got nothing. Many of the dead were certified to have succumbed to pellagra – a lack of protein and vitamins. Others, in their weakened state, were taken by tuberculosis and HIV-related infections. Cholera was rampant too, as prisons received the same inadequately treated water as the rest of the country. Prisons were overcrowded and prisoners had no proper clothing, which further aided the rapid spread of disease.

Death marked the end of prisoners' suffering but not of the indignity of their dying. The Chikurubi prison officers admitted that their mortuary system had failed. Of course there was no electricity, so corpses rotted quickly, added to which families could no longer afford to collect and bury relatives. At one point in early 2009, over a hundred bodies were piled in a makeshift mortuary. Rats and flies were feeding on the remains. Eventually the officers were ordered to bury bodies themselves in mass graves inside the prison. They objected to the filthiness and the health risks of this task but had to comply in the end.

An undercover South African documentary captured some of this horror. Pictures of half-dead stick men wearing only rags horrified viewers. Prompted by these images more than by the reports that had been coming in for several years, the International Red Cross began a feeding programme for prisoners later in 2009 – an intervention which has saved lives, but which came far too late for many.

Paradzai Zimondi, head of Zimbabwe's prisons and a member of the JOC, made no comment on the bestial state of his system and showed no sign that he cared. He had, after all, spent a year propping up Mugabe by directing a terror campaign against the MDC. He could hardly pretend now that he was concerned about human life or about the fate of political prisoners he incarcerated without trial.

Tsvangirai understood well enough that Zimondi's JOC – the hardliners running the security services – were trying to provoke him and make it impossible for him to join the Government. The JOC had been in its comfort zone for the last four months – with Mugabe, the magnanimous deal-maker, in State House and Tsvangirai, the ranting deal-breaker, outside of the Government. The JOC does not like change and never relished the idea of a 'Western stooge' like Tsvangirai joining the regime; pushing him to the point where he broke off the power-sharing process was a perfect strategy.

Tsvangirai recognised that he was being baited. The detention of his comrades was cynically designed to prevent him from joining the Government. But he decided to make an effort to free them and to address the angry rumblings within the MDC. The rank and file were not pleased that Tsvangirai was going to gratify Mugabe by joining the same Government that was holding thirty party activists as political prisoners. Tsvangirai humbled himself and went to see Mugabe to ask for the prisoners' release. He found the great leader personable and apparently ready to help. Mugabe said that the MDC prisoners would be released. With that hurdle apparently crossed, the two men discussed the ceremony to swear Tsvangirai into office, which could take place on 11 February.

Of course it was not that simple. Zimondi simply refused to release the MDC prisoners. Perhaps Mugabe was party to this double-cross, playing Tsvangirai for a fool. Perhaps Zimondi and the JOC were just more powerful than the old man now and could ignore his instructions. Either way, ZANU-PF had induced Tsvangirai to set a date for the formation of a joint government, then had reneged on the promises it had made to secure his participation. So Tsvangirai had one last decision to make, yet another dose of bitter humiliation to gulp down. He correctly surmised that he would never have an opportunity to join the Government without enduring some engineered indignity. He concluded that he could refuse to enter government only if he was content always to do so. So he decided to swallow his pain and his pride and stick to his decision to join.

Tsvangirai's swearing-in by Mugabe on 11 February was an uncomfortable occasion. Neither man was entirely happy with the development. They stood together ill at ease, unwilling to make small talk, unsure of the protocol, neither wanting to look weak, before gabbling through the oaths of office.

From the creaky formality of State House, Tsvangirai moved on to Glamis Stadium in the high-density area of southern Harare, where a euphoric crowd made him feel much more at home. The MDC's speechwriters had been working hard to produce words of enduring resonance that might signal a change of political culture. Tsvangirai was happy to place himself in great company; during his speech he compared himself with Nelson Mandela and echoed Martin Luther King:

> For too long, Zimbabwe has endured violent political polarisation. This must end today.
>
> For too long, our people's hopes for a bright and prosperous future have been betrayed. Instead of hope, their days have been filled with starvation, disease and fear. A culture of entitlement and impunity has brought our nation to the brink of a dark abyss. This must end today.
>
> Economic collapse has forced millions of our most able to flee the country seeking menial jobs, for which they are often overqualified but underpaid. This must end today.
>
> I have a vision for our country that will guide me as prime minister. I will work to create a society where our values are stronger than the threat of violence, where our children's future and happiness is more important than present political goals and where a person is free to express an opinion, loudly, openly and publicly without fear of reprisal or repression. A country where jobs are available for those who wish to work, food is available for those that are hungry and where we are united by our respect for the rights and dignity of our fellow citizens. This is the Zimbabwe that I am working towards.

ZANU-PF's decision to retain the political prisoners continued to have the desired effect – it gave Tsvangirai a problem as he spoke to the tens of thousands of supporters gathered to hear him. He had to break off from his purple prose to acknowledge that MDC activists were in prison. This did not go down well with the crowd, nor did the studiously legalistic line that Tsvangirai took: that the process of the courts needed to be respected and allowed to run its course. MDC activists knew what that meant. ZANU-PF would continue to interfere with the legal process, detaining opponents at will, whereas Tsvangirai was declaring himself unwilling or, more likely, unable to intervene on behalf of those wrongly detained.

To recapture the crowd's approval, Tsvangirai made an unrehearsed pledge: 'I make this commitment that, as from the end of this month, our professionals in the civil service, every health worker, teacher, soldier and policeman will receive their pay in foreign currency.' This populist promise went down well. Many in Tsvangirai's audience were public workers, tired of receiving worthless salaries. The thought of receiving a wage that could actually secure goods in Harare's well-stocked US-dollar shops was thrilling. And everyone in the crowd was suffering the effects of failing health and education services. If the public sector were to return to work, the Unity Government would certainly have achieved a major early success. Tsvangirai had no reserve of foreign currency to meet his extravagant pledge, but that problem could wait for another day. Basking in the acclaim which his promise brought, he was able to move past the awkward issue of the MDC detainees and towards his big finish: 'People of Zimbabwe, we face many challenges but we are brave and resourceful. By uniting as a nation and a people we can succeed. If you match our efforts with your own, we will succeed, if you match our desires with your own, we will succeed, if you match our dreams for Zimbabwe with your own, we will succeed.'

I was impressed by Tsvangirai's words, but moved more by the way his supporters received him. Despite the tarnished nature of his accession to a limited sort of power, MDC activists were in the end overjoyed that he had become prime minister. Thousands cheered at the stadium and thousands more danced and sang in front of the party's town-centre HQ. Nobody could say Tsvangirai was undeserving. He had nearly died twice, been charged with treason and endured a decade of pain and disappointment. He must have known as he spoke as prime minister for the first time that he would soon suffer more. There was singing and dancing everywhere – in the stadium, in the streets, in the villages around Zaka. Despite the ordeal of 2008 and the long delay in securing the consequences of election victory, the MDC was still ready to celebrate.

But, for all Morgan's blazing rhetoric, I did not feel that I was present at a defining, transitional moment in history. Maybe it is always like that for those too close to events. But I could not share in the celebrations whole-heartedly. I was just not convinced that important things were going to change. Like most Western observers I was sceptical of the power-sharing Government. I saw all the negatives – Mugabe retained the real power, while Tsvangirai had been co-opted into a lesser position than he deserved. Mugabe would retain control of the security forces, while Tsvangirai would be passed the responsibility of reviving a looted, bankrupt economy. There would be no justice for the victims of violence, no definitive point of transition to a new society of the kind Tsvangirai had described on the day of his inauguration.

But in the days after the inauguration, my scepticism was shaken, firstly by the degree of confidence and hope which ordinary people placed in the new Government. The professional moaners within civil society – drawing on their long and deep experience of betrayal and disappointment – were largely critical, but the man on the Chitungwiza combi was upbeat. From day one, people told me about things getting better – more goods in the shops, cross-border trade liberalisation, expats coming home and more tolerance. I couldn't quite see these things myself, but maybe I was looking through grey-tinted glasses.

Whether or not any of the realities of life truly changed on inauguration day, I could not deny the change in popular mood. The response from ordinary people to power-sharing was that the country needed change – any change – and that the Unity Government was just that: something new, behind which the country should rally. I used to talk regularly to a team of security guards who, for as long as I had known them, had shrugged their shoulders hopelessly about the fate of their country and bemoaned Mugabe's longevity in office. From the first day of the Unity Government, their attitude changed: 'The Government is a good thing. After all, we are all Zimbabweans and need to work together now.'

I was also surprised by the readiness and mental brightness with which the MDC took power and the concerted determination with which the party's new Ministers declined to react to the behaviour of ZANU-PF, which continued to be insufferable. I was astonished that they were prepared to put up with so much and realised that power-sharing could go on for some time, maybe even years, if the MDC was truly ready to be so pliant.

The MDC made it clear in the days immediately after coming into office that many things in Zimbabwe were unsatisfactory. A particular irritation was that Gideon Gono and Attorney General Johannes Tomana remained in their positions, contrary to the MDC's demands. The continued detention of the MDC Thirty was also a constant goad to Tsvangirai, although he stuck to a starchy official line on this, arguing that they could be released only once the legal process had gone its way. More humiliation was to follow. Roy Bennett was a ZANU-PF hate-figure – a white farmer, but a man popular among black Zimbabweans because of his folksy manner and fluent Shona. Bennett had – like many white farmers – supported the MDC and was elected MP for Chimanimani in 2000. The presence of a man like Bennett in Zimbabwe's Parliament infuriated Mugabe. Bennett was finally stripped of his position and served eight months in prison for supposedly assaulting Patrick Chinamasa in Parliament in 2004. So when

Tsvangirai nominated Bennett – who fled to South Africa on his release – to be Deputy Agriculture Minister in the Unity Government, he must have expected a ZANU-PF reaction. There was, and an immediate one: Bennett was arrested on his return on the usual charges of threatening national security, and imprisoned in Mutare. He was released after a week, for part of which he shared his cell with a corpse, but has still not been sworn into his office.

Despite these substantial grievances, Tsvangirai and his party were positive about the new Government. For the umpteenth time, I realised that I did not understand everything about Zimbabwe. I could see that an emotionally based hope was a happier foundation for living than a rational pessimism. I could see that some restoration of trust between countrymen was good. I could see that a surge in economic confidence could only help this lovely but broken and impoverished country. But I could not be happy, because I just could not see a way for these things to be possible. All I could perceive was that Mugabe retained ultimate power. When I looked at his face, I saw a murderer, albeit a clever murderer, who could charm and persuade people to see him otherwise. I am still afraid that Mugabe is ready to kill again.

But with these negative feelings, out of kilter with the mood of the country, came a clear sense that my time in Zimbabwe was up. In any case my tour was over, so I had to go. But more than that, the negative lessons I had learned were preventing me from believing in this new Government with my mind as much as I wanted it to succeed in my heart. Perhaps that made me sensible, but it certainly put me out of alignment with the prevailing mood on Harare's streets. I hope I am wrong, as I was so often during my years in Zimbabwe.

10

Moving on

Since the formation of the Unity Government, Zimbabwe has enjoyed a year of stability – with important exceptions – but has not taken any meaningful steps towards solving its problems. The country may be embarking on slow and modest reform in some areas, but being in government is dragging the MDC down towards ZANU-PF's level. It is hard to tell sometimes whether the MDC is changing the nature of the state, or whether the ZANU–state continuum is slowly absorbing its most potent critic.

The two main achievements of the administration have been results of inertia rather than activism. The central bank has abandoned its hopeless money-printing operations, thereby allowing the nation's currency to die, and has accepted that the US dollar, the rand and the pound are legal means of payment.

This solved the inflationary crisis. Businesses were suddenly free to trade in foreign currencies, which spared them the burdens of having to handle a currency that was devaluing 50 per cent in the time it took to carry it to a bank. Legalised dollarisation also relieves the pressure of having to conceal trades in foreign currencies. As producers and retailers became used to trading in FOREX and imports flowed, Zimbabwe experienced the phenomenon of prices *falling* in US-dollar terms by up to 50 per cent in the first part of 2009. Until Gideon Gono finds a printer capable of producing US dollars, inflation is dead.

But dollarisation is hardly a long-term solution. In its lack of a functioning currency Zimbabwe joins a select list of the most failed states – lawless places like Somalia, where the Government struggles to control even its capital city. However, the restoration of the Zimbabwean dollar can wait at least until some kind of rational monetary policy-making body has been established. A precondition for that is the removal of Gideon Gono, one of the most incompetent central bankers in world history. A possible step towards currency relaunch might be the introduction into the Reserve Bank of hard-nosed advisers from Frankfurt or New York intent on preventing whoever comes after Gono from using the printing presses as a means of generating Government funds. But such a prospect continues to look remote – a sign of the lack of real reform under the Unity Government.

The second substantial achievement of power-sharing has been a year without the nationwide violence I witnessed in 2008. This again has little to do with the Government, which has failed to launch any conflict resolution or truth and reconciliation activities, similar to those in South Africa after apartheid. ZANU-PF does not need to use force while there is no threat to its substantial share of power. The threat posed by the MDC is neutralised while that party is in government and while elections are several years off. The apparatus and culture of violence are still in place, but for a time, while the Unity Government holds together, Zimbabweans can try to forget them.

Other achievements which some claim to see are more questionable. There is a little evidence of greater tolerance and judicial independence. For example, the women of WOZA were allowed to march in Bulawayo in May 2009 without being assaulted. Unfortunately when they marched again in June, the police attacked the modest group of chanting women, arresting several. Disgracefully, four of the women were badly beaten while in custody, a grotesque demonstration that torture of the innocent and peaceable remains a reality. Such brutality was not what many expected once the MDC was in power, but illustrates the importance of democratic control over Zimbabwe's thuggish cops.

Judges seem to be more willing to rule against the state. In May, Bulawayo magistrate Moses Murendo dismissed charges against members of an earlier WOZA demonstration and even praised the women for their spirit. Barack Obama echoed this praise when giving WOZA the Robert Kennedy Human Rights Award in November 2009. But WOZA's representatives highlighted the contrast between their glittering evening at the White House and the ordinary lot of Zimbabwean activists. Magodonga Mahlangu reflected that she and her sisters had to return to their homeland to face prosecution for the supposedly subversive claim that Zimbabweans needed food aid. 'We are facing five years in prison,' Mahlungu told the President. Jeni Williams recalled the final ordeal of an elderly activist, Maria Moyo: 'She was abducted from her sickbed by police and interrogated in the bush for hours. Maria died days later, never recovering from the trauma of her torture.'

Judges also threw out idiotic charges against a human rights lawyer, Alec Muchadehama, and – best of all – ruled in September 2009 that Jestina Mukoko should never face trial on concocted terrorism charges, as the torture she had suffered had contaminated the legal process. A series of judicial rulings in 2009 and 2010 undermined ZANU-PF's continuing attempts to prosecute MDC Senator Roy Bennett* on the usual fantasy charges of terrorism and banditry.

The Unity Government's failures are the absence of change in the management of the economy and the lack of any serious effort to reform the authoritarian conduct of government or to introduce respect for human rights. The domestic media remain restricted, although the BBC has, with some fanfare, returned. Zimbabwean activists were greatly encouraged by Victoria Derbyshire's live broadcast from Harare in December 2009, while pointing out that the kind of debate she facilitated

---

* Following his prison term and a period of exile in South Africa, Bennett was appointed a non-constituency Senator by Morgan Tsvangirai in 2009.

between the MDC and ZANU-PF was still wholly absent from Zimbabwe's own domestic broadcast media.

Basic freedoms to meet, form associations, demonstrate and criticise the Government are still denied. The security services remain politically partisan, thuggish and deaf to the cries of the ordinary victim. The performance of schools and hospitals has improved a little, as some teachers (disgracefully not those belonging to ZIMTA, a pro-Mugabe association) have been willing to work for their US$100 per month, but overall stand-ards are still poor. Nothing has been done to curb the lethal effects of HIV and of cholera. The latter will kill people around Christmas each year for the foreseeable future.

Most of these imperfections are sins of omission – the Government simply lacks the cohesion, moral rigour, strategy and, to a lesser degree, resources to make changes. But when it comes to the treatment of the last few hundred commercial farmers, the Government has gone beyond mere impotence or incompetence, by ignoring murder, arson, cruel persecution and the continuing wilful destruction of the country's failing food-production system. Ben Freeth, whose Chegutu farm was so splendid when I first saw it in 2006, has borne the brunt of this cruelty and of the Government's indifference. In September 2009 thugs burned down the beautiful thatched farmhouse, where I ate home-grown mangoes with a delicious whisky cream. Ben and his family could do nothing but watch as their home and possessions were destroyed; his farm workers wailed fearfully, knowing that the hardships of eviction, homelessness and unemployment were looming ever closer. Since the forma-tion of the Unity Government, Ben has also been arrested, assaulted and insulted and has put up with soldiers tramping around his farm trying to discover arms caches to justify yet more fanciful terrorism charges.

Despite his own serious problems, Ben has kept in touch with a number of other farmers in Chegutu who have also come under attack. He recorded in November 2009 his frantic phone conversations with a neighbour, who said, 'Last night from midnight, the drums were beating constantly outside the house. The invaders lit a fire on the porch under the thatch, flames rearing dangerously close to the tinder-dry grass.' Ben heard the farmer say, 'They are breaking in,' then banging noises before the phone abruptly went dead. Government Ministers, MDC and ZANU-PF alike, have done nothing to help. Ben has written repeatedly to the Prime Minister asking for protection and has now lost confidence in the Unity Government. 'Tsvangirai could at least be calling for action. He doesn't seem interested in doing anything to get the rule of law respected.'

Relations between the governing parties have been fraught. Mugabe has been on his best behaviour when on the international stage, reassuring CNN and potential investors that all Zimbabweans are now pulling together in the nation's best interests. But when speaking to his own supporters his rhetoric has not changed. Days before an exploratory visit by EU Development Ministers in September 2009, Mugabe told the youth wing of his party, 'We have not invited these bloody whites. They want to poke their nose into our own affairs.'

Morgan Tsvangirai has taken to accentuating the positive. His life has been just as hard since he became Prime Minister as it was when he was being beaten half to death in Harare Central Police Station in 2007. Susan, his wife for thirty-one years, died in a car crash in March 2009. They were a close and traditional couple and had six children. Many suspected – and indeed remain convinced – that the crash was an assassination attempt by the JOC. I do not believe that, as the degrees of conspiracy and technical difficulty involved in killing by that method seem too great to make a murder plot credible. Curiously Mrs Tsvangirai's death may even have improved relations between Zimbabwe's two chief executives, as Tsvangirai appeared to be touched that Mugabe attended the funeral and spoke feelingly.

But, inches beneath the surface pleasantries, fundamental disputes have blighted any possibility of real co-operation. The parties disagree about key appointments – particularly Gono and Tomana – and the process of drawing up a new constitution. The MDC also remains infuriated by what it sees as a campaign to harass, prosecute and disqualify its MPs and debar its Ministers.

While the MDC's desire to dismiss Gono and Tomana has been the main fault line between the parties, Mugabe has exploited the substantial powers of his office to antagonise Tsvangirai further. He has continued to appoint ambassadors, permanent secretaries and provincial governors unilaterally. The MDC has had to use up much of its energy obtaining influence over such decisions, but has at least succeeded in securing a handful of senior posts for itself.

ZANU-PF has devised grievances of its own to rebut the argument that all the faults are on its side. Mugabe's Ministers, who used to blame 'illegal sanctions' for the country's problems, now berate the MDC for failing to honour its commitments. The new narrative is that the MDC's part of the power-sharing bargain was to deliver the lifting of sanctions and the ending of 'pirate' radio broadcasts into the country. ZANU-PF is relentless in its media messaging and has, by constant repetition, succeeded in giving these alleged omissions some substance to counter-balance the MDC's grievances. ZANU-PF's allegations also put Tsvangirai in an awkward position. It is not in his power to lift travel bans imposed by the EU, US, Australia and others, nor can he close radio stations operating in foreign countries. Nor can it be pleasant or easy for him to lobby Western governments on behalf of the regime which has hurt him so grievously.

Watching Mugabe chatting with Christiane Amanpour during General Assembly week in New York in late 2009, it seemed strange that he was so happy with life. But he had – and continues to have – reason to be cheerful. He has come through seemingly impossible challenges and remains exactly where he wants to be – in State House. His domestic opponents now answer to him. The world has moved on and forgotten

his crimes. Grace Mugabe, the First Shopper, can continue
to spend scarce resources in the world's boutiques and to act
with impunity, even escaping prosecution in Hong Kong when
she punched a *Sunday Times* photographer who was recording
her profligacy. Tactically, endless debates about Gono and the
constitution suit Mugabe perfectly. While those rows continue,
nobody is having the real argument – should the old man still
be in charge in Zimbabwe?

Ideologically, Zimbabwe remains a colonised state. The dogmas
of British and independent white rule may be fading from
memory, but the country still has an ideological hangover
from the Chinese and Soviet doctrines pumped into its current
leadership during the Cold War. ZANU-PF was formed spir-
itually in the jungles of Mozambique and Zambia, as a military
organisation. It fought a grisly guerrilla war for a decade, learn-
ing lessons of racial hatred and the efficacy of brutality. Robert
Mugabe's forces were trained by Chinese advisers who preached
the supremacy of the party, the need for control of the peas-
antry and the fallibility of bourgeois democracy, as well as the
correct use of an assault rifle.

Mugabe's rule and his methods of retaining power channel
Mao and Pol Pot. He understands that control of a semi-feudal
agrarian society means controlling the rural poor. He understands that the rural poor can be cowed – by violence, by
restricting the food supply, by monopolising information and
by subordinating traditional leadership structures to the party –
and is ready to take the necessary measures, no matter what the
human and financial cost. The entire leadership of the nation
has been trained to believe that the transfer of power is a defeat
for the party and for the nation as a whole. Of course ZANU-
PF's *chefs* want to retain power for low personal reasons – to
protect themselves from prosecution and to pile up fortunes.
But somewhere in their corrupted hearts remains a deep-seated
belief formed in the 1970s – that they are the instruments of

national liberation and that if the people do not want them, then the people are wrong and must be shown their error.

The old guard in Zimbabwe will never willingly give up their places at the top. They will die, they will lose their faculties or they might conceivably be forced out. But they will never surrender power willingly because of something so impotent as an electoral defeat. Mugabe said it himself after the March election – how can a ballot box defeat a gun? He and the hard men around him don't know how to give up and are scared of life without their fearsome uniforms. In 2009, Mugabe refused the resignation of Vice President Msika, a sick and exhausted old man, making it clear that he should hold his post until he died, which he soon did. That refusal indicates Mugabe's intentions for himself.

Africans recognise this trait in Mugabe more clearly than Westerners, who are inclined to hope that elections will provide the change Zimbabwe needs. Leaders in other African countries have shown the same stubborn desire to overextend their terms of office. That is why Mugabe's peers have been so ready to play things long, to opt for unjust stability, rather than the unpredictable dynamic of backing a weak MDC government while the Establishment remains solidly ZANU-PF. They know that there is little they can do to force the old-timers out, other than waiting for time to catch up with them. Until then, better that bloodshed is minimised; there is after all no point in stirring popular expectations of democracy that cannot be met.

But Western ideologies and pretensions have failed in Zimbabwe too. The most cataclysmic failures were those of the global government system – the United Nations, which, twenty years on from Srebrenica, continues to pretend that it can help those who cannot defend themselves. Despite its much-vaunted Duty to Protect, the UN did nothing except wring its hands while Zimbabwe bled. Much of the blame lies with the institutions, like the Security Council, which proceed at the pace of the slowest. When it came to the heart-rending violence in Zimbabwe in 2008, it did not proceed at all. The Russians and Chinese chose to render the Council ineffectual even though doing so cost lives; they were only African lives after all.

It would be uplifting to believe that the UN's staff stood for something, even if global political leadership is lacking. But so often its agencies aspire to nothing more than pragmatism. It has been shocking to see sympathisers of ZANU-PF being recruited to the UN staff in Zimbabwe, then adopting ZANU-PF positions or collaborating with the Government, in the face of powerful evidence of its corruption and bias. Different agencies follow different agendas. All seem too focused on unfeasible development projects or on delivering humanitarian aid, even if it is being looted by the regime.

My own role in Zimbabwe was questionable too. The regime certainly accused British diplomats of unjustified interference. ZANU-PF believes firmly that diplomats should be mute and impartial observers, watching events disinterestedly. Foreign governments are not supposed to interfere in other countries' elections. But the idea of the diplomat as someone who files bland reports of massacres, which governments can then ignore, has changed. Sir Martin Ewans, Britain's Ambassador to Zimbabwe during the Matabeleland massacres, gave a good example of the old-fashioned approach to the killing of 20,000 or more Ndebele people. 'It wasn't pleasant and people were being killed but . . . I don't think anything was to be gained by protesting to Mugabe about it . . . I think the advice [from London] was to steer clear of it in the interests of doing our best positively to help Zimbabwe build itself up as a nation.'[7] The quotation sounds complacent, even callous. But Ewans should not be demonised for openly explaining what used to be a standard foreign policy approach: that the UK acted only when its own interests were in play. Throughout the 1980s, the UK took little official interest in horrendous goings-on in countries like

South Africa, even unilaterally preventing the Commonwealth from placing sanctions on apartheid South Africa – facts that Mbeki remembered clearly when he heard Westerners urging him to act in Zimbabwe.

The British approach changed explicitly in 1997, when the Foreign Secretary at the time, Robin Cook, spoke of an ethical dimension to foreign policy, and the Foreign and Commonwealth Office began to treat human rights, as well as national interest, as a reason for taking action. Some of the muscular foreign policy successes of the early New Labour years – such as the deployment of a battalion into Sierra Leone to defeat Sankoh's rebels – could not be justified by the UK's national interests alone and would not have taken place without the new willingness to consider also the human rights of suffering people abroad.

But the appetite in the first New Labour Government for humanitarian intervention, fuelled by the success of military action in Sierra Leone and the former Yugoslavia, came to an abrupt end after 9/11 and the embroilment of British forces in lengthy wars in Iraq and Afghanistan. By 2008, Ministers were ready to condemn Mugabe's abuses roundly, but there was no question of the British response extending beyond diplomacy.

Can Zimbabwe's new arrangements keep working? Given the MDC's attitude to power-sharing, it seems that they can, and for some time. The state media continue to describe the MDC as criminal, disloyal and subordinate to ZANU-PF within the Unity Government. Journalists mocked Tsvangirai's 2009 tour of Western capitals and urged Mugabe to 'recall' him, as if the President had the power to control the movements of the Prime Minister.

Yet, in the face of these provocations, clearly intended to induce Tsvangirai to walk away from power-sharing in disgust, the MDC has not only remained in the Government, but has defended its record. Tsvangirai told President Obama in June 2009 that Mugabe was part of the solution to Zimbabwe's problems. He has also compared Mugabe's approach to post-colonial reconciliation to that of Nelson Mandela. He told David Frost during an Al Jazeera interview while in London in June 2009 that the country 'is coming out of a political conflict and economic collapse. The new political dispensation we have crafted is an attempt to arrest this decay.' One might almost imagine from these words that Tsvangirai prefers a junior position to the Presidency to which he is entitled.

The MDC has gone further, enraging sympathisers within civil society groups by minimising ZANU-PF's transgressions. Tsvangirai himself infuriated commercial farmers by claiming in May 2009 that 'so-called farm invasions' were 'isolated incidents' which had been 'blown out of proportion'. Even more bizarrely, a junior MDC minister, Murisi Zwizwai, told a Kimberley Process* conference in Namibia in June 2009: 'Contrary to allegations in the media, nobody was killed by security forces during an operation at Marange.' Zwizwai was referring to a brutal military clearance of diamond prospectors from a remote area near Mutare. Human Rights Watch interviewed over a hundred victims of that 2008 operation and concluded that 'Soldiers indiscriminately fired AK-47 assault rifles, without giving any warning. In the panic and ensuing stampede, some miners were trapped and died in tunnels. Over three weeks, the military assault resulted in the brutal deaths of more than 200 people. Soldiers forced miners to dig mass graves for many of the dead.'[8] Zwizwai's remarks were in line with the MDC's general approach, which is to gloss over Zimbabwe's problems, but were so far from reality that the party had to issue a partial retraction.

The MDC has two motives for absolving its Government partner of its sins. It wishes to get on with the job of reviving the economy by persuading the world – particularly donors

---

*The Kimberley Process is an international body attempting to prevent the trade in 'blood diamonds'.

and investors – that the bad days are over. Zwizwai was trying to persuade the mining companies, who have mothballed their Zimbabwean operations since Mugabe began to talk of 'indigenising' them, to reinvest. During his world tour, Tsvangirai was attempting to convince donors that violence on the farms is over. Unfortunately, the MDC will find its efforts to attract money into the country thwarted by Mugabe's reputation for corruption. Even more unfortunately, the MDC's efforts at spin ignore the truth so crudely that they instead call into question the party's judgement and grasp of reality.

The MDC is also talking up Zimbabwe's status so as to convince ZANU-PF that it is a reliable partner. Sadly this effort too is misguided. ZANU-PF calculates on the basis of strength, not merit. The more MDC Ministers flatter their ZANU-PF partners, the more they will be seen as weaklings. ZANU-PF is likely to respond not by trusting the MDC – that will never happen – but rather by bullying and harassing it even more. The MDC's best tactic would actually be the opposite of its current approach. Staying in government but plainly criticising what is wrong with ZANU-PF's approach would put Mugabe more on the defensive. The MDC is playing the unity game as if a win-win outcome were possible. ZANU-PF knows only zero-sum games and always plays to win them absolutely.

Journalists from tame Government-sponsored publications have taken to commenting, since the formation of the Unity Government, that it represents the African way – that a sharing of power is the continent's wise alternative to the brutal switches of personnel and direction that cripple Western countries every few years. This of course ignores the fact that some African governments become all-inclusive clubs not because African politicians like to co-operate and share power, but because there are too many who are ready to kill until they are bought off with a piece of power and too few effective mechanisms of continental policing.

But, that said, in dealing with Zimbabwe's great challenges

a Unity Government may not be the worst arrangement. The country is politically polarised, meaning that half of it would be alienated from a government drawn only from one of the two major parties. Even at a time of near-total collapse in March 2008, ZANU-PF was able to secure more than 40 per cent of the nationwide vote and a position of political dominance in most of Mashonaland. A million Zimbabwean voters clearly retain a loyalty to, or at least a fearful respect for, the party. Indeed it is doubtful that any Zimbabweans want to forget their liberation from the apartheid-style system of the British and then of Ian Smith. Nor would many want to forget the military heroism and sacrifice that made that liberation possible.

The two men who form Zimbabwe's new duumvirate share to a degree the goal of economic recovery. Mugabe may be the architect of his country's collapse, but that was a by-product of a succession of short-termist measures, not a policy objective. Mugabe has nothing against economic success; after all, a booming economy offers more scope for plunder. He would be happy to see the economy begin to recover, provided he is not required to make sacrifices to achieve that goal.

The key question is how long Tsvangirai can swallow his pride and stay in such a government. A related issue is what is best for Zimbabwe. The period of the Unity Government is likely to be a hiatus for the country as a whole, in both bad and good ways. Donors and investors will remain wary while Mugabe is in charge, so the economy will recover only slowly, if at all. But the unity period may offer a respite from the violence and terror of 2008. It may give ordinary people a chance partially to remake their lives. Public services will not bounce back to their excellence of a decade ago, but there may be some slow improvement on their current dreadfulness. The main risk for Tsvangirai is that he spends too much time defending Mugabe and presiding over stasis, thereby losing support within his party. There will be times over the next couple of years when the MDC rank and file mutiny against the party's continued role within a government that will be able to do very little to improve living standards.

Some purists within civil society are arguing that more elections at an early date are the only way to deliver a government of real legitimacy able to make effective changes. I fear that Zimbabwe is just not ready for fresh elections. People are terrified that the horrors of June 2008 will be repeated. A period of real peace and greater pluralism is needed to restore confidence. Even elections in 2010, perhaps under a new constitution, will be too early. ZANU-PF's urge to bludgeon its way to victory will not have been tamed as early as that.

The most productive thing Tsvangirai can do with the Unity Government period is to tease the instruments of state power out of ZANU-PF's hands. Long-term success, for both the MDC and Zimbabwe, depends upon the gradual dismantling of ZANU-PF's merger of party with state and ending the culture of violence and intolerance. For now, the only means of achieving this – given that external influence is so ineffectual – is to work from within. The MDC's Ministers are inexperienced, but they have an energy and freshness which Mugabe's ailing cronies lack. Their hope must be that they can use their limited share of government to dismantle parts of the one-party structure. After a few years of joint working, by when mortality will have thinned the numbers of the old guard most resistant to change, it may be that the country will not revert to violence.

My own guess is that the arrangement will last and that neither party will see much benefit in early elections. Offered the right price, I would take a bet on this Parliament running its full course until 2012, by which time Zimbabwe will still be in the doldrums, but may possibly be a calmer and more tolerant place.

The attitude of foreign donors will be key. Tsvangirai hopes that South Africa will cover his bold pledge to pay public-sector salaries. But it is hard to see Pretoria underwriting an entire country for long, given the financial pressures of the 2010 World Cup and the aggressive demands of those South Africans who continue to enjoy no more than third-world lifestyles. Western donors are to date refusing to answer Tsvangirai's plea for large amounts to restore services and restart the economy. One reason for their reluctance is obvious: Mugabe. While he remains the real power, there is little confidence that donor funds will be put to good use. The regime's leading personalities are adept at channelling international money into rainy-day funds abroad. Even transferring money directly to MDC-run Ministries is problematic while Gideon Gono – the man who stole funds from the Global Fund to Fight Aids, Tuberculosis and Malaria – remains in overall charge of much economic policy.

The less palatable and less publicly discussed cause of donors' hesitation to pile into Zimbabwe is doubt about the MDC. The sight of MDC Ministers clamouring for imported new cars to glorify them in their new offices was nauseating. It would have been a spectacular positive gesture if the incoming Ministers had en masse refused such unaffordable luxuries. But, with the odd honourable exception, they did not.

Eric Matinenga, the man I had been trying to visit in jail in June 2008 when I ran into a ZANU-PF militia, is now Minister of Constitutional and Parliamentary Affairs. He took delivery of a large new ministerial Mercedes, saying, 'I know it's not a good excuse, but will I make a difference if I turn this down?' It would of course have made all the difference, demonstrating that the MDC's new team cared more for the plight of ordinary people than for dipping their snouts into a trough that the country could simply not afford to fill.

The MDC remains largely untested in government, with inexperienced Ministers, some of whom seem obsessed with no higher goal than enjoying the trappings of office, which they have so long been denied. The party also shows worrying tendencies towards autocracy. Its Ministers often refuse media interviews, as they dislike the indignity of answering probing questions. The party would rather push out triumphalist press releases than submit to Q&A. Journalists recall that this was exactly how Mugabe behaved in the early 1980s, arguing that liberty had been hard won and that intrusive media would undermine the country's new freedom.

Ultimately the Unity Government cannot opt out of its own responsibilities. If it does not act, it cannot expect donors, the diaspora or international business to fill the void. If by some miracle Mugabe and Tsvangirai find the energy and sincerity to grapple with even one key challenge, they could make a dramatic difference overnight. The crucial first steps, on which so much else depends, are restoration of a culture of legality and justice and the prosecution of offenders, including human rights abusers. Orderly life in Zimbabwe has been undermined by a legal system that has sold itself to the ruling party. Until there is justice, there will be no lasting peace, and until there are property rights, business will not revive.

As I have moved from Zimbabwe to Turkey, where I am what the Foreign Office tactfully terms a 'trailing spouse', I have seen obvious differences. Having again such everyday things as water, electricity and a telephone, let alone a supermarket and broadband, is welcome. I just have to get out of the habit of buying things in huge quantities on the assumption that they won't be around tomorrow. But I have also come to realise how much tension and unhappiness I absorbed while in Zimbabwe. It is wonderful to be around people who have no fear, who say what they think and who are planning for long lives. I look back on so many happy Zimbabwe memories, but begin to understand that I ingested the country's sadness too. My feelings turn out to be a set of paradoxes:

Zimbabwe feels safe, though there is no respect for the rule of law.

It is a peaceful country, but when violence breaks out it is
   savage and ruthless.
It is a beautiful place, with areas of hideous ugliness.
Zimbabweans are so brave, but can be such cowards too.
There's incredible freedom in Zimbabwe, but civil liberties
   are denied.
The land is rich and the rainfall is heavy, but nobody gets
   enough to eat.
It is a society of the highest standards, but so many have
   slipped.
People are highly educated, but schools are failing.
It has been a great country, but so much that was good has
   passed away.
I love Zimbabwe, but hate it too.

Above all my reaction to living in Zimbabwe is emotional. I
remember walking under big skies – whether in Harare among
its sweet, friendly people or in Hwange surrounded by the
world's largest elephants – feeling safer and freer than I have
ever felt. As I remember those good feelings, a light bubble of
sentimentality and regret for what I have lost rises up my chest
and settles just under my tear ducts.

I don't see Mr Nasty's face any more when I try to sleep, as
I did for a while. I've stopped imagining what it was like to be
tied up in that office in Zaka, doused with fuel, waiting for
the match to strike; I'm not haunted by the dead, as I hope
their murderers still are. But I can still feel the destabilising
fear which drives out hope and reason, the mortal dread of the
pounding knobkerrie, the helplessness in the face of tyranny
wielding superior force. And I still find myself raging too easily
and quickly.

There is a difference between what Zimbabwe deserves and
what it will get. It is the most beautiful, the most fertile, the
most spiritual and the most blessed country. Zimbabweans who
have been driven away by the grisliness of life under Mugabe

never become used to other countries' lack of sunlight, want of good manners or low crowded sky. Zimbabwe deserves a government that gets out of the way of its good people and allows them to enjoy the good life – a life that is becoming a memory but could be a reality again.

The MDC, for the first time in charge of its destiny, has a choice about what it aims for and what it settles for. Given the options open to him, nobody can blame Tsvangirai for taking a small share of power and working to dismantle a system which has so nearly killed him. But in doing so he may be tempted to compromise on some values that are fundamental, thereby becoming a part of the system himself. He is a constructive and positive man, whose consequent hesitation about criticising his new and improbable colleagues may mean that he is absorbed into what he set out to demolish. Of course he should try to co-operate, but he should know and say when he is being wilfully obstructed. Of course he should hope for the best for his country, but he should not deny that it is living through the worst. Of course he should try to rebuild the economy, but he should acknowledge that there is a limit to what he can do while in tandem with the man who destroyed it.

In a couple of years, somebody – an election observer, a diplomat or a journalist – will publish another book or series of newspaper reports about Zimbabwe, documenting the horrors and injustices of the 2011 election. The author will record that in the months beforehand, Robert Mugabe's ZANU-PF party made intimidating statements and warned both the people and the opposition that it would not relinquish power under any circumstances. The book will contain harrowing accounts of the terrifying but carefully calibrated violence which ZANU-PF militias employed to ensure that rural voters ticked the correct box, without generating more than a few hundred corpses – a number of dead black Africans which ZANU-PF knows to be insufficient to trigger international outrage or meaningful action. In the aftermath of the election, Southern African Governments will promise to mediate between Zimbabwe's parties. The United Nations Security Council will discuss the situation but be unable to agree on any resolution. Zimbabwe's history tells us this is all certain and that there is one certainty above all others: Robert Mugabe – or, if mortality has finally caught up with him, a member of his cabal – will still be the President.

I hope, of course, that I am entirely wrong about all of this, but I believe I am not. ZANU-PF has learned the lessons of history, including the 2008 election which I observed. The party cannot win fairly, so appalling is its record of economic regression and inflicting wholesale human misery. But Mugabe's clique has discovered that they can beat and cheat their way to victory. Given the absolute imperative of remaining in office, which the party has publicly stated, using violence to retain power is the obvious and logical choice.

The predictability of a bloody election in 2011 has been identified by Zimbabwe's human rights groups, the people who will have to count the bodies and tend the injuries of those attacked. A collective statement by these groups in October 2010 argued that political interaction is volatile and polarised, that repressive legislation has not been repealed, that violent militias remain active and that the administration and oversight of the electoral process will be partisan and inadequate.

The dread which the prospect of early elections causes is exacerbated by the improvements in day-to-day life which Zimbabweans have enjoyed for the last two years. Since the formation of the ZANU-PF/MDC unity government, the country has enjoyed a modest economic recovery. The IMF estimates that Zimbabwe's economy grew 5.9% in 2010. Ordinary people have felt some benefit; a friend in Harare recently commented that 'Zimbabwe has been slowly moving in the right direction in certain respects. It is definitely easier to manage with a proper currency and food in the shops.'

There are three elements to Zimbabwe's current feel-good interlude. The halt to wholesale political violence since July 2008 has given families and communities a time to repair, if not to heal. The legalisation of foreign currency as a means of exchange has allowed retail businesses and cross-border trade to operate reasonably normally. Shoppers with Rands or US dollars can now buy what they want – certainly what they need – in Zimbabwe. And money is coming into the country, by means of remittances from expats and refugees, which now amount to more than one billion pounds per year, and aid projects which have quadrupled in value since 2008.

The extent of economic recovery should not be exaggerated. There will be no sustained growth until the rule of law is restored. The two hundred or so farms still operational in Zimbabwe continue to be threatened by looters, against whom the police will not act. Ben Freeth, who was viciously beaten in 2008 and burned out of his home in 2009, was finally forced to abandon his operations in 2010. The attitude even of the MDC to farm invasions was questioned by Catherine Jouineau-Meredith, whose Twyford Farm was burned and looted in September 2010 despite the supposed protections of a High Court ruling in her favour and an Investment Protection Agreement between France and Zimbabwe. Jouineau-Meredith wrote to Morgan Tsvangirai, 'All the promises given to me personally by you and your office have stood empty and no action has ever been undertaken to rectify all the illegalities that have taken place.' Nor has ZANU-PF been willing to leave in peace those former farming areas which have been trashed over the last decade – its malicious assaults on rural populations continue. The International Organisation for Migration has verified that squatters on former farms in at least three districts have been burned out of their homes by the authorities. Multinationals have been targeted too. Nestlé came under attack when it stopped buying milk from Gushongo Dairies, a farm under the control of Robert Mugabe's wife, Grace. Affronted by Nestlé's reluctance to deal with Mugabe, the ZANU-PF Indigenisation Minister Saviour Kasukuwere stated that, 'Nestlé is a prime candidate for indigenisation', by which he meant the mandatory transfer of a majority of the company's shares to a member of the ruling clique. Similarly, a German delegation cancelled a visit to Zimbabwe in March 2010, saying Zimbabwe had become a 'no-go area' for foreign investors.

The relative calm on Zimbabwe's streets and in its villages can be overstated as well. ZANU-PF no longer has everything its own way, as it must go through the motions of working with the MDC; but the party is still in control and so has no need to use large-scale violence. One Zimbabwean characterized the mood during the unity Government period as a temporary absence of violence rather than the advent of peace. It remains true that wherever two or three people gather to discuss the prospect of a better society, violent wreckers will soon be in their midst. ZANU-PF units have attempted to take control of a series of public meetings intended to inform the drafting of a new constitution. Observers at these consultations report apparently scripted demands that any new constitution should include a provision that Mugabe be made President for life. More perniciously, militias have attacked participants at meetings expressing dissenting views. In Mbare in September 2010, Crispen Mandizvidza died as a result of such an attack. The constitutional consultation process has deteriorated into a bad joke – it has not offered ordinary people a chance to speak freely, but paying its many participants handsome *per diems* while they tour the country has soaked up huge quantities of international aid. The time it has taken to roll out the pointless process is time during which Robert Mugabe has been relaxing in State House, still enjoying its gilded surroundings as he moves well into his fourth decade of residence.

Morgan Tsvangirai, Prime Minister of Zimbabwe, has spent the two years since his inauguration juggling conscientiously the difficulties of simultaneously fulfilling his duties and speaking the truth – the challenges of holding office but not power. Determined to relaunch his country, he has presented its best possible face to the world, telling an *Economist* conference in October 2010, 'I was prepared to work with Mr Mugabe to allow him to address the mistakes of the past, and to help him to rebuild his legacy. This is why, despite the challenges that I have faced in working with him, I have repeatedly said that whilst our relationship was not perfect, it was workable.' It is impressive that Tsvangirai has been willing to put co-operation ahead of a desire for revenge that would be natural. But his claim that his relationship with Mugabe was workable is hardly credible. Mugabe has continued to use the substantial powers of the Presidency, without meaningful restriction by the MDC's ministerial team or a parliament which is largely unfriendly. He has unilaterally appointed ambassadors, provincial governors, senior judges and a new police commissioner. Tsvangirai's extraordinary patience may be running out – or he may be thinking ahead to the prospect of an election where he will need to differentiate himself from the man with whom he has shared office. At the end of 2010, Tsvangirai took the extraordinary step of advising some foreign governments that Zimbabwean ambassadors in their countries were not properly selected and told his supporters that, 'All Zimbabweans know that Mr Mugabe and his colleagues brought the restrictive measures on themselves through the flagrant abuses of human rights and the economic disaster which they inflicted on this country. You can count on me to ensure that you will be able to participate in a free and fair election to choose who should lead your country.' As usual one admires Tsvangirai's courage more than his judgement in making a promise which he does not have the means to keep.

Elections in 2011 are frightening to anticipate. MDC MP Eddie Cross reported remarks made by Khaya Moyo to a ZANU-PF meeting in Mutare, 'We are a revolutionary party and any other party which thinks it will rule this country is day dreaming. We will not relinquish power.' It is difficult – despite the richness of Zimbabwe's resources and the talents of its people – to see a positive scenario for the future. Many hope that Mugabe's death will trigger a positive transition to a non-violent politics, the restoration of property rights, and the start of a national rebirth. Sadly, even that happy event may actually make Zimbabwe's short-term plight worse. Mugabe's leadership has suppressed and managed rivalries within his own group which might deteriorate into power struggles. The people below him – Mujuru, Mnangagwa and the rest – have all of his ruthlessness but less of his intellect and charisma. If the great leader goes they may grapple for power causing a greater collapse.

ZANU-PF is more energetic and better resourced in the run-up to 2011 than it was in 2008. Its new strength stems from its control of the substantial diamond deposits in Manicaland. The army first seized the Chiadzwa field from independent prospectors in late 2008, killing more than 200 of them. Zimbabwe desperately needs the resources that transparent and lawful exploitation of such a valuable resource would bring, but the proceeds of diamond sales have been captured not by the Finance Ministry but by ZANU-PF and a disreputable band of smugglers, able to trade Zimbabwe's bloody gemstones in the corrupt and murky international market. As a Zimbabwean analyst told me, 'The party has consolidated its monopolistic grasp. Diamonds have proved to be a curse rather than a blessing for Zimbabwe as no trickle-down effect has been felt. We hear India is vying for a big chunk of our diamonds while Chinese and South African magnates have sunk their teeth into Chiadzwa's glitter without regret.'

There is a question for the wider world here. Readers of this book often ask me what they can do to help Zimbabwe, to which my usual answer is 'little or nothing'. But by purchasing Zimbabwean diamonds, the Western world sustains the cruel regime of Robert Mugabe. The Kimberly Process offers consumers the illusion of an ethical trade, but in practice – given the frailties of certification and the great incentives to ingenious and well resourced black-market traders – it is impossible to buy a diamond and be confident that nobody died as a result of its extraction.

When I left Zimbabwe at Easter 2009, there was a limited optimism that the Mugabe-Tsvangirai unity Government might not only preside over a period of stability and non-violence, but might – as it promised to do – also lead an economic recovery and a restoration of rights and freedoms for Zimbabweans. Taking those promises at face value, Bulawayo artist Owen Maseko displayed a collection of his paintings exploring the Matebeleland massacres at the National Gallery in March 2010. He was arrested the next day and – once the authorities had cast around for an offence he might have committed – charged with insulting the person of Robert Mugabe, which carries a maximum sentence of ten years. While Zimbabweans remain unable to discuss the events of thirty years ago, the prospects of an election which allows them freely to debate and decide their future must remain poor.

Philip Barclay
November 2010

Notes

1 Media Monitoring Project of Zimbabwe, Statement 31 March 2008.
2 Trymore Macvivo, *The Zim Daily*, 28 May 2008.
3 World Health Organisation, *Cholera in Zimbabwe*, Update Four, June 2009.
4 UNHCR spokeswoman Jennifer Pagonis quoted on UN Radio, 11 July 2008.
5 Human Rights Watch, *Keep Your Head Down*, 27 February 2007.
6 In an interview with Violet Gonda, Short Wave Radio Africa, 23 January 2009.
7 In an interview with Fergal Keane in March 2002, as quoted in a letter to *The Times*, 10 December 2007.
8 Human Rights Watch, *Diamonds in the Rough: Human Rights Abuses in the Marange Diamond Fields of Zimbabwe*, 26 June 2009.

Acknowledgements

It would have been impossible to write this book without support, advice and information generously given by hundreds of people during my time in Zimbabwe.

The British Embassy team housed, fed and tolerated me through times when all of those tasks seemed impossible. I am not supposed to name individual colleagues, but without the work of the entire Embassy staff, I would not have been able to live and work in Zimbabwe. I am particularly grateful to the management section, which, against all odds, consistently secured fuel and food; and to the members of my Community Partnership Programme team (you know who you are) for their work. I will break the 'no names' rule for three people. I am grateful for the guidance of the Ambassador, Andrew Pocock, who encouraged me to write, suggested pithy one-liners for which I was happy to take authorial credit and reminded me when necessary, which was too often, to get back in my box. I will also name the UK's Defence Attaché through the nightmare days of 2008, the late Lieutenant Colonel John Kane. John was the ideal of a modern British soldier – decent and dynamic in pursuit of a progressive agenda. His savage humour and robust good sense helped me through many a bad day. I miss him.

I also want to thank by name my wife Emma, who served as the Embassy's Human Rights Officer through four grim and bloody years when those rights were in short supply. It often seemed that whenever a detainee was on trial or a few committed demonstrators began their short march towards police truncheons, Emma would be there, recording and reporting, so at least somebody, somewhere knew that Zimbabweans were defying their cruel leaders. She was the oracle within the diplomatic community and willingly shared her reports of abuse with colleagues of all nations, even if they took the credit for them in their own capitals. I remember her spending many evenings repeatedly dialling the unreliable mobile phones of lawyers in remote areas, trying to find out whether individual prisoners had been released. She, like other colleagues, is not named in the book, but readers should be aware how much of its content derives from Emma's work.

The international community circled its wagons in Harare; certainly relations with other Embassies were much warmer than I have found elsewhere. I enjoyed the friendship and co-operation of aid workers and diplomats from many countries and from colleagues in other parts of the British set-up, particularly the DFID women's team (you too know who you are). My picture of goings-on in Zimbabwe would have been incomplete without the benefit of this network of information sharing and discussion.

I am particularly grateful to my agent, Anne-Marie Doulton, whose idea this book was. She used a fine combination of persuasion and bullying to extract the words from me and curbed my regrettable tendencies to florid prose and literary quotation.

The team at Bloomsbury – Michael Fishwick, Anna Simpson and Alexa von Hirschberg – have been wonderfully supportive and tolerated all the follies of a first-time writer. I am grateful to Bloomsbury also for finding in Peter James a knowledgeable and thorough copy editor who greatly improved my text.

Helmut K Watson and Mark W Adams (who both have dramatic middle names) have kindly allowed me to use their photos on the beautiful jacket around this book.

Without my family's support it would have been hard to keep going. Emma – a wife as well as a fellow diplomat – was more than a loving companion, an anchorage on stormy days or a source of strength – though she was all of those things. She was muse and enabler combined – she made this book happen. She urged me to write, made me believe that I could and then supported me emotionally and materially when I did so.

My mother Janet and father Leslie gave me the best upbringing I could wish for and have been a lifelong inspiration to get my act together and write. In the Zimbabwean style I define my family broadly; certainly within it fall my domestic staff in Zimbabwe, Philip and Savemore, whose labours saved mine, and the greatest of friends: Antonio, Carolyn, Dyane, Mark, Mark and Ruth.

I am grateful to the following for corrections to the original text of this book and for other helpful comments on the new edition: Claire Freeth, Leif-Erik Stabell, Judith Todd, Trevor Grundy, Clifford Chitupa Mashiri, Her Excellency Trudy Stevenson, Mark and Ruth Walkup and Derek Ingram.

Finally and most importantly, I must acknowledge the input I have received from the battered but unbowed members of Zimbabwe's civil society. I have no idea how it is possible to operate as a human rights lawyer, to treat torture victims, to campaign for human rights or to work for the improvement of communities and public services, when such work carries the constant threat and frequent reality of abuse, beating, detention, torture, imprisonment and death. I will not name individuals, as doing so would place them at risk. In any case there are many thousands of people in Zimbabwe, trying to help their country discreetly in the type of areas where thugs carry out their attacks. I would not like to name any, if I can't name all of these courageous people who confront every day a fear that I found quite crippling.

Despite the pressures of their work, members of Zimbabwe's civil society groups were unstinting in their help, work, friendship and supply of information. Without this generosity this book would have been impossible to write.

Friends in civil society often say that the fears and horrors they face are more bearable knowing that somebody overseas cares about their struggles for a better country. It was a great privilege to be posted in Zimbabwe so that I could demonstrate that the world did care and a greater privilege still to record my friends' continuing struggles in this book.

INDEX